THE IRAQ
OF KU

RELIGION, IDENTITY AND OTHERNESS IN THE ANALYSIS OF WAR AND CONFLICT

HAMDI A. HASSAN

Pluto Press

LONDON • STERLING, VIRGINIA

First published 1999 by Pluto Press
345 Archway Road, London N6 5AA
and 22883 Quicksilver Drive,
Sterling, VA 20166–2012, USA

British Library Cataloguing in Publication Data
A catalogue record for this book is available from
the British Library

ISBN 0 7453 1416 3 hbk

Library of Congress Cataloging in Publication Data
Hassan, Hamdi A.
  The Iraqi invasion of Kuwait : religion, identity, and otherness
in the analysis of war and conflict / Hamdi A. Hassan.
    p.   cm.
Includes bibliographical references.
ISBN 0–7453–1416–3 (hc.)
  1. Persian Gulf War, 1991. 2. Persian Gulf Region—Politics
and government. 3. Panarabism. I. Title.
DS79.72H425   1999
956.7044'2—dc21   99–40502
                                                CIP

Designed and produced for Pluto Press by
Chase Production Services, Chadlington, OX7 3LN
Typeset from disk by Stanford DTP Services, Northampton
Printed in the EC by TJ International, Padstow

CONTENTS

ACKNOWLEDGEMENTS

Working on this book has been invigorating, maddening and wonderful. It would have been impossible without the meticulous support of three individuals: Dr Azza M. Karam, Professor Ziauddin Sardar, the editors of this series, and Roger van Zwanenberg, Pluto press' publisher. I would like to thank Azza and Zia for the rare gifts of good counsel and continuing faith. They both sustained me throughout, but especially when crossing dark and barren terrain. Azza was not only a sharp, discerning and untiring reader of several versions of the manuscript but also an unfailing source of encouragement and wisdom. She helped me to refine the book's sentences and notions with astute and penetrating comments. I am more moved than I can say by the great amount of time Azza spent on my work, generously sharing her wide knowledge with me.

Roger van Zwanenberg is not only a talented publisher, but also a committed intellectual whose prompt and considerate feedback helped me to clarify my thinking and yielded suggestions that significantly strengthened the manuscript. Roger's quick eye for what does and does not work moved things swiftly along. He delivered me, as promised, 'a personal and professional service'. In this context I am deeply grateful to Anne Beech and Robert Webb who (together with Roger) made my experience with Pluto a fruitful and enjoyable one. Thanks also to Helen Skelton who meticulously copy-edited the book and vastly improved the quality of the text.

A number of people through the years have helped in different ways while working with this book. I would like to express my gratitude to my colleagues Kjell Engelbrekt, Jacob Westberg, Kristina Boréus, Eric Stern and Welat Songür who read and thoroughly commented on earlier drafts of the manuscript. Parts of Chapter three have been presented at the Nordic Society for Middle East Studies' conference (June 1995) in Joensuu, Finland, where Professor Saad Eddin Ibrahim of the American University in Cairo and Dr Jørgen Bæck Simonsen of the University of Cobenhagen (among many others) gave insightful comments on the similarities and differences between Arabism and European nationalism. Part of Chapter four was presented at the conference on The Peace Process and Future Vision of the Middle East (September 1997) at Lund University, Sweden. Many people gave valuable comments on the significance of the contrasted collective identities of Islam/Arabism and Zionism to Middle Eastern politics. I am particularly grateful to Professor Jan Hjärpe and Khaled Bayomi of Lund University; Professor Osama al-Ghazali Harb of Al-Ahram Foundation; Professor Raymond Cohen and Dr Paul Rivlin of the Hebrew University; and Dr. Helena Lindholm Schultz of Gutenberg University.

Dr Essmat Abdul al-Maguid, The Arab League's Secretary General and Egypt's Foregin Minister 1987–91, was very generous in granting me time on several occasions to interview him and discuss the events that took place before the invasion of Kuwait. In this context, I would like to thank Egypt's ambassador to Sweden, my friend Hamdi Nada, and before him ambassador Ibrahim Alaam, who helped to facilitate my contacts with Arab officials. Mr Abdullah Jasem al-Sane, Under-secretary for Scholarship and Cultural Relations in the Kuwaiti Ministry of Education, showed a great interest in my research. Besides sending me much valuable material pertaining to the Iraqi-Kuwaiti dispute before the crisis, Mr. al-Sane has helped to grant me a six month scholarship in 1993 from the Amir Sabah al-Salem Foundation, which helped to facilitate my travel around the Middle East to collect much-needed material and documents. My friend Zaid al-Sherida, the Kuwaiti ambassador to Sweden, was an invaluable source of moral support and encouragement, who during our frequent discussions enriched my knowledge of Kuwaiti and inter-Arab politics. In addition, I would like to express my deep gratitude to Mr. al-Sane, the Amir Sabah al-Salem Foundation and to Ambassador al-Sherida.

Many people have offered very different kinds of help. My close friends Dr Ibrahim Gouda, (Golfpro) Sayed Cherif, Samir al-Rafie, Taha Mowafi, Dr Gail Ramsay and Dr Ali Yaklef have shared their vision of the world with me. Their generous support was decisive in times of near-despair. In this context, I would like to express my gratitude to Lise-Lott Åhman, Omar Sheikhmous, Donald Levery and Alan Dixon. Despite the intensity of the daily focus on the rehabilitation of people with multiple handicaps, my current workplace, Arbetsmarknadsinstitutet-Haninge, has provided an atmosphere most conducive to finishing this book. In particular, I would like to thank Ann-Kristin von Euler for her kind consideration.

My partner in life, Kristin Hammer, and my two daughters, Rosa-Linn and Camilia, have always provided me with a warm emotional base upon which such extensive an intellectual undertaking is profoundly dependent. Their spirit is my essential nourishment and I am privileged to have them around me. I have the extraordinary good fortune to have Camilia, P.L. de Silva, Rosa-Linn, Azza and Kristin, whose individual and collective friendships always keep me so firmly rooted in the things that really matter.

For Edward W. Said
and
Nasr H. Abu Zaid

My foremost exemplars of intellectual integrity
and brilliant scholarship

1 UNDERSTANDING THE IRAQI INVASION OF KUWAIT

INTRODUCTION

At the time of writing, the latest figures indicate that since 1991 4,500 children have died in Iraq every month as a result of UN sanctions.[1] Each time yet another debacle between the UNSCOM team, led by Richard Butler, and the Iraqi regime (primarily portrayed as Saddam Hussein) takes place, we all hold our breath in trepidation. The US and the UK carry out air bombing missions almost every day and, in the Western world, the media reports the 'safety' of the American and British pilots and the 'minimum casualties' suffered by Iraqi civilians. This news has become so commonplace that we do not even pause to think it through. Even other Arab regimes, who once stood divided over the 1991 Gulf War, seem now to distance themselves from events in the Gulf, preferring instead to focus either on their borders or pledge consistent support for 'the other' Middle East (Israeli) peace process. But in many respects, what is taking place in the Middle East today is simply a replay of the complex web of events that unfolded prior to and in the immediate aftermath of the Iraqi invasion of Kuwait in August 1990.

The unprecedented Arab support for Iraq and for the leadership of Saddam Hussein during the 1990–91 Gulf crisis should be viewed within the framework of Middle Eastern political discourse and the regional state of affairs during June and July 1990. At that time all the agitated and volatile forces of discontent throughout the Arab world waited for a leader to deliver. The Middle East was in turmoil, immersed in a *status quo* of economic misery and frustration with the political stalemate – the 'seamless web of significance'[2] was so thick that something dramatic had to happen. The situation was further

1

aggravated by the growing prominence of Israel following the huge
Soviet-Jewish immigration. The indignation of Arab intellectuals and
activists at the United States, Zionism and the Gulf rulers, also
manifested in grass-roots demonstrations on the streets of Arab cities,
should be understood within the context of the unique discursive
formation of Arabism. This discursive formation, involving a holistic
self-image on the one hand and prejudice and bias about 'others' on
the other, can be seen as setting the context for the decisive moments
that led to the invasion of Kuwait, the crisis that followed and the
devastating outcome for the Iraqi people and state. The political
manoeuvrability of the Iraqi regime became very limited as a
consequence of its decision to invade Kuwait. The Iraqi state's infrastructure was extinguished. It was likened by a United Nations report
to conditions in premodern societies. Even worse, since 1991 the Iraqi
people have objected to the severe punishment received both from
their own regime and as a result of the United States and other Western
powers' over-militarization in the Gulf region. The public discourse
about Iraq in the West sees it as 'thirsty for wars against lesser,
dehumanized enemies'.[3] The media coverage is so obsessed with the
homo Arabicus, Saddam Hussein, that one gets the impression that
Saddam is the only inhabitant of Iraq. The terrorized women and
children of Iraq all appear as 'blank spaces'[4] characterized by ontological
emptiness (see the Appendix).

The aim of this book is to *discuss and understand the Iraqi invasion of
Kuwait*. The point of departure is that: in order to account fully for
the invasion of Kuwait, it is of fundamental importance not only to
discuss the motivations of Iraq, but also to understand the conditions
that accelerated and facilitated this decision, namely the Arabic political
discourse. The focus will be on the events that brought about this
decision, as well as on the *discourse* (Foucault, 1972: 7, 21–30) through
which the actors involved understood their world and acted
accordingly.

During the spring and summer of 1990, so it seemed, Saddam
Hussein understood that in order to realize his aim of reviving a
charismatic pan-Arab role for himself he had to concentrate, primarily,
on demonizing Zionism and the American attitude of indifference
towards the Arabs. The language used by Saddam was carefully chosen,
seeming to convey metaphoric pan–Arab and Islamic sentiments. The
target in focus was the West, and in particular the United States and

Zionism which had been blamed for a long and abominable history with disastrous implications for the Arabs. By the same token, Kuwait, the main target of dispute and conflict, was almost invisible. This always resonates with the mainstream Arabs who held the view that the United States was being manipulated by international Zionism, partly in favour of Israel and definitely against Arab interests. There is also a firm belief that United States' policy in the Middle East is influenced by the biased pro-Israeli lobby and, therefore, completely manipulated by Israel. Indeed, US officials and policy-makers throughout the history of American involvement in the region have never missed the opportunity to confirm this widely held perception.[5] The situation was aggravated by the Israeli election in June 1990, which resulted in the first, most extreme right-wing coalition in the history of the Jewish state, headed by Prime Minister Shamir.[6] Moreover, on 4 February 1990, the Israeli cabinet accepted as a new member of the government Rehavi Zeevi, leader of the right-wing Moledet Party which advocates the mass expulsion of Palestinians from the occupied territories. For the first time, the Palestinians were depicted by Israeli government officials as animals devoid of any human traits. Israeli polls in 1990 found that 52 per cent of Jewish citizens of Israel supported the expulsion of Palestinians from the occupied territories in order to preserve the Jewishness and democratic character of the state after the annexation of the occupied territories (Mattar, 1994: 39). Moreover, three years of *Intifada* (uprising against political oppression) and almost two years of intensive diplomatic efforts by the Palestine Liberation Organization (PLO) were to no avail, despite the PLO's recognition of Israel, its acceptance of UN Resolution 424,[7] and its renunciation of terrorism. It was the Iraqi president who could offer them hope, however illusive, by using stern and self-confident language that could intimidate Israel, and by promising to challenge and destroy Israeli hegemony (Muslih, 1992). It is in this sense that the invasion of Kuwait is more closely, and indeed vividly, linked, on the one hand, to the United States' indifference toward the Arabs and its staunch support for Israel and, on the other, to the Jewish state's existence and behaviour in the region as such.

The Iraqi invasion of Kuwait on 2 August 1990 unleashed the Gulf crisis, in which the Middle East witnessed an unprecedented projection of power by the United States. What was considered as a purely internal 'Arab affair' became a global concern involving the United

Nations, almost all the major world powers and world public opinion, in a rare moment of Western consensus. The Iraqi leadership seriously underrated this fundamental transformation of the international system, which was to prove a major miscalculation. It was not, however, the fatal one.[8] Judging by the analysis of how the Iraqi leadership reasoned when it decided to invade Kuwait, the American response was thus far the most significant development. First, the US was able to rally the United Nations and world opinion against Iraq. Second, against all odds and against the history of repeated failures by US policy-makers to comprehend inter-Arab politics, the United States persuaded Saudi Arabia to allow a massive American-Western army onto its territory, something the Iraqi leadership failed to foresee (Viorst, 1991; Al-Gosaibi, 1992). By this shrewd strategic move, which proved decisive in ejecting Iraq from Kuwait, the US breached a covenant in Arab politics (Brown, 1992; Telhami, 1994). It was widely believed that such an action would be impossible and would trigger and provoke a powerful anti-Western reaction in the Arab and Muslim world. It was feared, too, that such an action would be seen as an intervention by Western forces in the Holy land of Islam. As such, it would unify the Arabs and Muslims against the West and in particular the United States. Saddam Hussein did in fact attempt to exploit this situation, but to no avail.

The Iraqi strategy to keep the crisis 'an Arab affair' totally failed. Thus, Iraq was exposed to world opinion and to the military might of the most powerful nations in history. Iraq, it seemed, had never considered that the Saudi government or any other Arab state would collaborate with the United States and the West.[9] Whereas it took a few weeks in September 1980 for the Iraqi leadership to discover that the 'Blitzkrieg' it was waging against Iran had turned into a devastating and prolonged 'Sietzkrieg', it took only few days for them to find out that the invasion of Kuwait was a major miscalculation, and that the situation was much more complicated than they had assumed it would be. To be sure, all these developments are landmarks in modern Middle Eastern history, and even more in the way world politics had been hitherto conceived by analysts and practitioners alike.

The personality of the Iraqi president Saddam Hussein has attracted much attention, generating an impressive amount of media coverage as well as academic research (see the Appendix). The assumption of several analysts that his enigmatic personality and leadership style is, among many other considerations, essential for understanding the crisis in the Gulf has certain grounds and appeal. However, it would be inadequate to treat the initiation of crises and waging war as if it were the making of 'isolated utility maximizers'. Rather, decision-makers are part and parcel of their society, and when dealing with foreign states they actually reflect their societal culture and values (Robinson, 1994: 417).

Having said that, the economic problems that faced Iraq after the war with Iran, the territorial disputes with Kuwait and even the Iraqi claims on the whole or part of Kuwait,[10] and the conflict over oil quotas with OPEC and Iraq's accusation and Kuwait's counter-accusation over exploiting the Rumaillah oil field, all are critical factors in the crisis. Similarly, the endemic instability of the Iraqi state and its intensive culture of violence, as well as the regime's alienation from society and its lack of political and social legitimacy, are factors of definite relevance to the analysis. These features, however, are common traits to most authoritarian states and governments, and have to be put within the Arabic political discourse in order to comprehend Iraq's decision. The political and cultural identification of Saddam Hussein and the Iraqi polity, and the way it is manifested, are far more appealing to our analysis. Arab leaders usually do seek backing for their policies and legitimize their state-centred actions by invoking transstate factors (i.e. Arabism). Moreover, political actions are designed to satisfy the expectations of the far-flung pan–Arab audience.

The Gulf crisis stemmed to a great extent from the internal dynamics of the Arab world. It was linked to state formation, the imperative of nation-building as well as the establishment of the state as a sovereign territorial unit, the regime's political legitimacy, and the lack of coherent sociopolitical institutions. The invasion of Kuwait and the crisis that ensued have asserted anew the centrality of Islam as a constructed cultural domain entwined with Arabism (the way Arabs collectively conceive of who they are) and, by implication, the societal and political crisis in the Arab world. There was unprecedented sympathy, even enthusiasm, from many Arabs – politicians, the grass roots, intellectual and Muslim activists – from Morocco to the Gulf, in support of Iraq's illegal (in any possible sense of the term) occupation of the state of Kuwait. This Arabism was manifest in people throughout the region expressing their rejection of the boundaries between states in the Arab world as artificial colonial arrangements. For many Arabs, the division of the Arab world into several political units is the exception not the rule. Moreover, there are social and economic divisions that separate the 'haves' of the Gulf royal families and their wealth from the 'have-nots' of the rest of the Arab world, and these divisions are the most unpopular of all. The entire course of the Gulf crisis should be seen within the context of Arab linguistic unity, political discourse, collective identity and the psychological union of sympathy – variables which mark the discursive formation of Arabs, and thus render their consideration significant. Using this approach, the book is organized into three different yet related perspectives: the realist, the institutional and the reflective. Each perspective is situated analytically and explained empirically. In fact, each one constitutes a different pair of lenses for the glasses through which one can perceive the Iraqi invasion of Kuwait.

THE REALIST PERSPECTIVE

The motivations behind Iraq's invasion of Kuwait could be analysed in the following manner. First, the relationship between Iraq and Kuwait could fit perfectly into a power preponderance framework, in the sense that Kuwait, as a much weaker and a vastly richer neighbour, seemed at one point to be attractive booty for its resentful, egoistic, power-maximizing neighbour. Thus, for the Iraqi leadership harsh economic problems are on the way towards being solved; a geostrategic outlet to the deep water of the Persian Gulf, and the achievement of the much-longed-for political hegemony in the Gulf region and the Arab world, seemed to be imminent and forthcoming.

At this juncture, let me discuss the issue of the role of the individual decision-maker. The individual as an actor having active or leading roles in the policy process (e.g. the rational actor model) has always been a problematic enterprise in explaining the outcome of decision-making. Allison (1971: 166) in rather assertive and tautological terms, wrote that:

[t]he hardcore of the bureaucratic politics mix is personality. How each man manages to stand the heat in *his* kitchen, each player's basic operating style, and the complementarity or contradiction among personalities and styles in the inner circle are irreducible pieces of policy blend.

The question for our purposes in explaining the Iraqi invasion of Kuwait concerns the freedom of choice that individuals are assumed to have in forming decisions and executing policies. Are individuals (i.e. Saddam Hussein) essentially products of their environment and historical context? Or do decision-makers control the circumstances in reference to which they formulate and execute decisions? As far as this book is concerned, the superstructural factor, i.e. the identity of Arabism emanating from Islam, is assumed to be a major theme, in the sense that Islam and Arabism engendered and facilitated the conditions and gave focus to the frame of reference that triggered the invasion of Kuwait and the crisis that followed. The support at grass-roots level all over the Arab world for the Arab leaders' foreign policy decisions has always been instrumental in the motivations and outcomes of these decisions. One could say that certain types of claims and counter-claims, agitations, activities and events took place that render the theme of Islam/Arabism topical and meaningful in explaining and comprehending the political processes in the Arab world, as well as the particular Iraqi decision to invade Kuwait. Thus, the history and the political development of the personality of the Iraqi president are to be put in the wider framework of the Iraqi state and polity; and the environment with which they clearly identify themselves is Arabism. This is in line with the fact that political and military decisions, like other human actions, are common traits of the decision-makers and their external social, cultural and political conditions (Mathews, 1993: 4–5, 51).

THE INSTITUTIONAL PERSPECTIVE

In this chapter both the link between the Iraqi polity and its institutional impact, and the invasion of Kuwait will be accounted for by examining the implication of normative and material power. The link between domestic political conditions and the state's international behaviour – where authoritarian regimes usually exploit foreign adventure and aggression to divert attention away from home or simply to tighten their control of the internal political fronts – is a classical theme (Regan, 1994; Workman, 1994; Ayoob, 1995). Iraq is a case in point and provides qualified evidence for such an assumption as all the political and social ingredients have always been in place. Being politically illegitimate the regime has always been virtually isolated from the majority of the population. Ethnic and civil strife against the central government in the north with the Kurdish uprisings since the early 1960s, and in the south with the pro-Iranian Shi'ite fundamentalist groups, had grown more intense. Such endemic political instability generates economic hardship that becomes more severe for an overstretched state with an obligation to meet its population's basic needs for day-to-day living. In fact, the invasion of Kuwait (like the assault on Iran ten years earlier) must be seen against the background of the political and social turmoil of modern Iraqi society and the unusual atmosphere of political violence that the Ba'ath regime created.

However, the interweaving of Iraqi polity with Arabism is considered not only to explore various dimensions in this canvass, but also to highlight the paradoxical nature of its intimate affinity with Arabism. In this vein, an attempt is made to explain the peculiarity of inter-Arab politics and the role of institutions, not only as the embodiment of the political processes (mechanisms of state policies), but also as a concrete manifestation of sociocultural realities. In other words, the articulation of Arabism as a collective identity is manifested in how individuals understand their role within institutions and the world around them (Goldstein and Keohane, 1993). The entire Iraqi polity can only be approached, and therefore understood, within the way it relates, identifies and manifests itself, namely, in the framework of Arabism and its discourse. Social scientists familiar with the region have contended that 'Middle Eastern political processes defy observation, discourage generalization, and resist explanation' (Bill, 1996: 503). Otherwise, it would be like any classical authoritarian state that engages in foreign adventures to divert attention away from home, and would, thus, ignore an important dimension of the Gulf crisis.

THE REFLECTIVE PERSPECTIVE

The overriding objective of this chapter is to integrate the questions of identity of Arabism (with Islam as its core variable and the language as its clear manifestation) to Iraq's action against Kuwait. The point of departure here is that modern Arab leaders have always been eager to seek pan-Arab support for their policies, and the ultimate arbiter for their policy objective is that it should satisfy the expectations of all Arabs. Arab leaders are always eager to present to the Arab peoples their political objectives (which are in essence immersed in egoism and the pursuit of personal power) under the guise of serving the common good of Arabism and Islam. Ironically, there are sets of historical experience, sociocultural realities, and the political make-up of the states and regimes that enhance this political behaviour. The connection between on the one hand the Arabic political discourse and on the other the Iraqi leadership's world view and the invasion of Kuwait will be presented and established within the following framework. Since the Iraqi leadership is seen to identify itself with the Arab nation, then Iraqi foreign policy-making and its outcome are to be seen as legitimate by all Arabs. They were, by the same token, motivated by purely *realpolitik* objectives. The Iraqi leadership, as it were, put their case within a pan-Arab framework which turned out to be their most effective weapon. The unprecedented support the grass-roots Arabs gave to Iraq (to an extent that had not happened during the war with Iran), came about after the Iraqi leadership introduced itself as a viable champion of the cause of the Arab Nation, opposed to the United States and Israel.

The basis of the reflective approach to the Iraqi invasion of Kuwait suggested here is an understanding of Islam's connection with the identity of the Arabs. In this vein, the Islamic variable is suggested in so far as it is expressed in the arresting self-image of being who they are (i.e., pan-Arab identity), so that Iraq's political rationale and role enactment (or rather conflict) in invading Kuwait can be fully comprehended. The outbreak of wars and violent conflicts are the outcome, direct or indirect and intended or unintended, of actions taken by an array of factors, forces and individuals. Explaining or understanding such events requires not only the analysis of the immediate realities that generate conflicts and wars, or the mechanisms and procedures where the decisions (that lead to wars) are shaped and executed, but also the historical, societal, and political circumstances and their superstructural framework. In this book it is assumed that this framework consisted of the discursive formation of Arabism, and that this discursive formation was the instrumental variable (Stake, 1995) that engendered and facilitated the conditions for the invasion of Kuwait and the crisis that followed.

As is usually the case, crises and wars are the combined outcome of immediate or accidental societal, cultural and historical factors (i.e.

structural factors). These factors shape and influence what and how political actions are likely to be taken at any one time (Mathews, 1993: 51). They also determine the course of the crises and wars. While accidental circumstances determine which options are chosen in an immediate sense, it is the societal, historical and cultural factors that set the context within which crises arise, the pace at which wars are fought and, moreover, make up the outer context of choices that decision-makers face. There is, presumably, an interactive correspondence of relationships between the different variables. The modern experience of wars in the Middle East with non-Arab actors exhibits marked manifestations of the prevailing sentiments, feeling of solidarity (organic and psychological) with other Arabs who engage in conflicts with outside non-Arab powers. The Libyan war with Italy in 1911, the Arab–Israeli conflict with its many poignant episodes, and finally the Gulf crisis of 1990–91, are cases in point.

In short, what has to be emphasized is that inter-Arab politics has always been designed to underline Arabhood for the simple reason that 'the Arab world still paradoxically constitutes a single area of psychological, emotional and intellectual resonance transcending state frontiers' (Khalidi, 1991: 7). For Arabs, as we shall argue below, the conception of Arabism is the one single visible source that embodies their identity and unifies them irrespective of their sometimes striking differences in religious (here including ethnicity), regional, and social backgrounds. Moreover, for many Arabs, Arabism is synonymous with Islam. It is the fount of the culture. Arabism is not merely a modern political ideology articulated and pursued by modern and urbanized middle classes seeking to take over the state.[11] Pan-Arabism, like Islam, is part and parcel of being an Arab. This approach differs essentially from the discourse of Orientalism in the way Islam is related in the framework of this study; it is a genuine attempt to consciously understand Islam's role and meaning in modern society.

The social meaning of the 'hidden layers' and 'concealed motion' of religion are significant to understanding socioeconomic and political developments and evolution[12] through the main efforts of the urban and commercial classes, which are the most active constellations of civil society. Hence the social transformation has to be assessed within the scope of the changing forms and substances in the meaning of Islam as a religion in so far as the middle class in Arab societies is concerned; the diversified forms and configurations of the religious experience that are deliberately located over a broad spectrum of social transformation and politicoeconomic processes that have, through natural evolution or forceful integration, incorporated Arab societies into the modern global capitalist system.[13] The picture that surfaces is rich, multifaceted and delicate. Viewed in this way, Islam is connected with the sociopolitical domain by virtue of its significance to these social groups and their collective self-image. Therefore it has to be integrated into the analysis of the political processes in the Arab world, and into the way states and political elites always identify themselves with Islam, by using its symbols and idioms, especially when they are in conflict with outsiders.

The supposition that understanding is made up of social interpretations rather than awareness of a given external reality constitutes an essential premise in our context. Such a constructivist approach prompts a solid basis and relevant material for generalization (Stake, 1995). The emphasis is on the related variables such as things, places, events and people, not only in the sense of a commonplace description, but in the sense of Geertz's (1973) 'thick description'. Hence this approach is sensitive to the complexity and significance of local diversity, the relevance of particularity and the rhetorical power of oral reasoning so that 'the native's point of view'[14] is properly presented. Furthermore, the awareness, and employment, of 'local knowledge' is important to illuminate the relation between people's historical conceptions of community and their contemporary appeals for legitimacy. The ties and tensions between state sovereignty and forms of non-state authority emanated from kinship, religion or simply other factors, such as European colonialism (Turner, 1994: 85–6). To be sure, this approach is neither based on analytical particularism nor on outright relativism according to which reality is known in terms of the difference in how people perceive things (Stake, 1995).

This means that this method of accounting for and examining the society, politics or culture need not necessarily be peculiar to the Arab world. Rather, it is an attempt to substantiate an interpretation that aims to clarify the Arab world's special way of acting and reacting politically, and also how and in what way this peculiar make-up, in turn, conditions the behaviour of the various Arab states toward the outside world. The whole question of particularization would be fairly related with the uniqueness of the case, in so far as it helps to understand the course of the Gulf crisis. Therefore, the historical particularism of the modern state of Iraq, the Ba'ath polity and the Arab world is a necessary methodological formula for this purpose. The idiosyncrasies of today's Arab world can only genuinely be comprehended in the context of the historical experience of the societies and the formation of modern states in that region. Therefore the Arab world is peculiar, not because the categories of analysis applicable elsewhere do not apply, but rather because of the very special historical experience to which the Arab peoples have been exposed (Halliday, 1995: 12ff.; Bill, 1996).

The invasion of Kuwait, therefore, is approached here by an eclectic method that assumes that political behaviour can be comprehended when interests and power are incorporated with a rich understanding of peoples' beliefs. To be sure, most human beings embrace and adapt to religious faiths, or ignore and even turn them down, not on the presumption that they are logically, practically or even intellectually sound, but for their relevance (or lack of it) to people's day-to-day feelings, demands and aspirations, and on top of that, to the way people identify themselves. Islam, with a discourse of culture that is lived, maintained and held through the Arabic language, is part and parcel of the identity of the Arabs. This is very much the *vis vitae* (spirit) in which this book has been conceived. It is hoped that its diverse and multifaceted approach to the invasion of Kuwait and the Gulf crisis will reveal the extent of the changing forms and substances in the political process in the Arab world – events that covered a wide range of social constellations, political institutions and individual activities with claims and counter-claims of deeply rooted ideas of the collective self-image and prejudices about 'others'. By illuminating this differentiated and complex sociopolitical course, this book aspires to be an important step away from the literature of political Orientalism; literature that, unfortunately, still dominates the public discourse about the history and politics of the Middle East, despite the severe blow it suffered from the appearance of *Orientalism*, Edward Said's masterpiece, more than two decades ago.

2 THE REALIST PERSPECTIVE

INTRODUCTION

This chapter discusses the invasion of Kuwait through the premises of realism and, more precisely, examines the question of how Saddam Hussein reasoned and calculated the various alternatives when he decided to invade Kuwait. Iraq, so it seemed, had very few illusions when it came to the intentions of the United States and Israel. The invasion of Kuwait can be seen as a typical case for political realism's account of two states in a relationship in which the balance of power was asymmetrical. On the one side Iraq has a larger population, more territory and more powerful military forces. As a classically styled authoritarian state it used the traditional (though outdated) method of military conquest to gain spatial expansion, regional domination and territorial imperialism. On the weaker side of the balance is Kuwait. Even though it has been an important and more significant actor within the global framework of money, goods and power, Kuwait has fewer people, less territory and a smaller military force. Most important, it possessed all that Iraq needed in the way of economic assets and territorial access to achieve its much-longed-for regional hegemony in the Arab world and the Gulf region. American policy in the Middle East, particularly toward Iraq, and the lack of defence or security arrangements in the Gulf, or between Kuwait and the United States, assuredly worked to Iraq's advantage.

This analysis focuses on the shortcomings of the realist premises when discussing the Iraqi leadership's assessment and the implications of its conception of Iraq's national role. American–Iraqi relations and the question of deterrence are then discussed. As will be demonstrated, there was no American deterrence effort, and even if there had been it was unlikely that it would have been successful, first and foremost because of the peculiarity of inter-Arab politics, but also due to the

13

American historical political record in the region. The interaction and behaviour of Saddam Hussein, the Kuwaiti government, and other Arab and foreign decision-makers, subscribe only partly to realism's assumption concerning the political conduct of human beings in achieving foreign policy goals. Individuals make choices on the basis of their conception of reality and in intimate relation to the nature of power. The impact of sociological and cultural factors upon political behaviour inevitably determines the practices that guide the approaches of political leaders in measuring and managing power. In short, if there are interests, there also beliefs. Likewise, if there are material and power capabilities there are the intentions, perceptions, images and world views of leaders (Goldstein and Keohane, 1993; Smith, 1995). These two dimensions (i.e., discourse and reality) that account for political behaviour are central both to the study of international politics and to the practice of statecraft, and so it is within this framework that the assessment of the invasion of Kuwait through the scientific assumptions of political realism is to be viewed.

THE REALIST PERSPECTIVE: A THEORETICAL OUTLINE

There is no school in international relations that has exerted so much influence or elicited such enormous criticism as political realism. The main enterprise of the realist school is to grasp the interaction of human beings (primarily as decision-makers); the nature, distribution and the use of power; the formulation and the implementation of foreign policy objectives; and the likely influence of the natural and societal environment on political behaviour. The realist school has sought to advance and establish a standard (normative) theory about the purposes and practices that guide policy-makers. John Vasquez (1983) identifies five directions within realist thought in international relations as follows: 1) foreign policy research programmes that seek to highlight the concept of national interest; 2) emphasis on the concept of power in developing models of national policy-making; 3) the systemic research of the mechanisms that regulate international conflicts and the causes of war; 4) deterrence as a strategy for peace and bargaining; 5) international organizations, international regimes and multilateralism. Let us sketch briefly the main assumptions of the realist school in international relations.

The anatomy of the international system

The international system is anarchic and based on the principles of self-help – if you do not get it on your own, no one does it for you. In comprehending the international system – how states act/react to one another and, by implication, ensure security – the political realists view and assess the relative power of states acting 'rationally' on the basis of 'objective' knowledge. Only flesh-and-blood material resources are considered in the assessment of power. Linked intimately with this is the assumption that 'rational policy', identified and determined by certain conditions such as the ability to select favourable moments at which to promote one's own interests, presents the political edge for a self-aware decision-maker (Vasquez, 1983: 65–6). However, while it acknowledges the shortcomings and ambiguities displayed by games theories (non-zero-sum) and the speculative and conditional qualities of the concept of rationality, the scope and the limit of rationality have never been critically considered within the realist approach to world politics (Rapoport, 1982: 75; Vasquez, 1983: 205ff.; Nicholson, 1992: 4ff.). Within the realist perspective, the tension between internal conditions and international politics emerges in the form of contrasting subtraditions, with some evoking a Hobbesian account of the state of war, for example Kenneth Waltz's (1959) clarification of what it is seen as the three images of the discourse of *Man, the State, and War*. War is ingrained in human nature, in the sense that people are essentially social 'containers' in which, like water in a boiler, they are made to 'behave' in different ways. Gradually, this view evolved as a prevailing framework in identifying the international system as one of anarchy. The implication of this is a taken-for-granted assumption: 'wars occur because there is nothing to prevent them' (Waltz, 1959: 332). The core of this approach has become intrinsic in realism's assumptions of world politics as a perpetual fight for power.

The liberal school emphasizes elements of community, society, legitimacy and so on. In general, this perspective can be described in terms of a kind of international pluralism, through which individual actions and achievements are perceived in much less stark and clear-cut ways than those encapsulated in the realist vision. This does not mean that states become unimportant, rather that their position, their concerns and their methods of action need to be evaluated according to changing contexts. Martin Wight (1966: 17–34), one of the major historians within traditional liberal theory, has argued that 'where domestic politics is concerned with progress and convenient living, international politics is a realm of "recurrence and repetition," one where the highest value is survival'. International political theory reflects only universalist themes from both Christian natural law (Grotius) and the Enlightenment (Kant), as well as the pluralist realism of Machiavelli. Hedley Bull's (1977) use of the term 'anarchical society' points in the same direction, as do earlier accounts of the systematic or cultural (in this case 'European') coherence of international politics (Pasic, 1996). For both liberal and realism theory, these are all part and parcel of the international system and the way states act and react within it.[1] According to these classical liberal/realist accounts, the essence of world politics lies in its pluralism; war being the ultimate arbiter in the conflict between plural values and interests. Domestic political theory, by contrast, is said to be characterized by universalist values. For the realist, therefore, the transfer of domestic theory into the international context can lead only to naivety and wishful thinking.[2]

The state as the prime social organization

The state is the proper unit of analysis in world politics. Therefore international politics is to be understood on the basis of actions and interests of states. States, too, are the dominant and primary units of analysis in the international system and, thus, exclude domestic politics from the analysis of world politics. This assumption was modified by the neorealists. In this vein, Kenneth Waltz (1979: 93–7) asserts that states are unitary actors who, at a minimum, seek their own preservation and, at a maximum, drive for universal domination. States, or those who act on behalf of them, endeavour, in more–or–less sensible ways, to use the means available in order to carry out and attain policy objectives. Those fall into two categories: first, internal efforts, moves to increase economic capability, to increase military strength, to develop sound and skilled strategies; second, external efforts, moves to strengthen and enlarge one's own alliance, or to weaken and cripple (incapacitate) an opposing one. By the same token, Waltz (1979: 119, 1986: 339) 'freely admit that states are in fact not unitary, purposive actors. States pursue many goals, which are often vaguely formulated and inconsistent.' As the international system is essentially anarchical, this means the absence of an overall central mechanism that rules over states.

Ruggie (1986, 1993) argues that Waltz and his acolytes within neorealism have not only ignored changes in the density of interactions that usually occur in the international system and other regional systems, but have also assumed prematurely that the differentiation in the conditions of the states, and within systems, can be abandoned as unnecessary in comprehending the structure of the international system. In the short term, states may be the principal actors and function in an identical pattern. By the same token, other actors, such as multinational firms and international regimes, have since the late 1960s become more prominent, and the situation in world politics has been genuinely altered. Ruggie (1986) points out that neorealist theory is too static to explain the evolution of the international system. This situation came about with the rise of non-state social forces, as a consequence of the fundamental transformation of territoriality; the notion of sovereignty since the seventeenth century is yet another example of such fertile transitions.

The outright consequences of these two aspects (i.e. an anarchical world system and the centrality of the state in the analysis of world politics) of the realists' paradigm is the belief that once states have the objective facts, they (through their leaders) will act rationally. Actions are judged, more-or-less, rational by the degree to which they conform to the behaviour that, in one way or another, can be predicted by formal models (e.g. econometric analysis and games theory) that are based on objective facts. The data and knowledge that ought to be regarded and emphasized by decision-makers and, by implication, political scientists, must be well grounded on 'objective', that is 'scientific', facts. Most frequently, quantitative indices and tabulations of interstate relations are regarded as the hallmark of useful and, therefore, scientific knowledge (Rapoport, 1982; Nicholson, 1992: 4–5).[3] Consequently, the specification of the differentiation of historical experience and anomalies of sociocultural context that states normally experience are secondary, or at best remain hidden, since states practise and operate identical activities (Waltz, 1979, 1986; Gilpin, 1986). The same applies to decision-makers. It follow that the Pericles of Athens, the Caesar of the Roman empire, the Caesar Borgia of Florence, the Bismarck of Germany, the Saddam Hussein of Iraq, will act in the same manner in similar given circumstances that they may encounter. The realists claim that the specification of differentiation drops out because states as well as their leaders enact identical activities. Viewed in this way, the emphasis should be on what remains the same over time (Finnemore, 1996).

From a deeper perspective, Michael Williams (1992: 70) asserts that the epistemological implication of such an approach to the social sciences is that it identifies and treats cases of social realities as tangible facts. In order for us to grasp these facts, realism urges that we should follow the logic evolved for this purpose. At this juncture, realists are faced with a twofold dilemma: the first is the conception of the 'objects' of world politics in which it is determined by a self-evident stipulation that states are rational actors; the second is an ample postulation of this world of facts, where the postulation of the state as taken-for-granted actor, and the designation of the state as possessing a universal form of rationality, offer the epistemological basis for the assertion regarding objective science and knowledge. Such an approach defines and determines the standard of the essence and rationale of how world politics function and, thus, how states behave (or should behave). Following this line of theorization, the 'subjective' action (in that it is interwoven with many other variables unaccounted for by realism) of Iraq invading Kuwait is rendered objective. In a sense it can be understood by means of profit maximization logic in which there are no synthetic or empirical data requiring verification.

For example, questions of intergroup relations at levels other than the state, issues of meaning and symbolism and local-level views of the significance of crisis and conflict situations are almost completely ignored. The state, for realists, is the formal mechanism through which political power is exercised, and the organization which commands obedience (Gilpin, 1986). Yet if compulsory membership and the use of legal coercive power distinguishes the state from other organizations, the state is not the only organization that can compel behaviour or extract obedience. Many types of informal power may often be more binding than the formal kind. For example, despite the magnitude of its apparatus of violence and the dominance of public political and economic life, the state (or *dawla)* in the Arab world is not the focal point of loyalties – people are often more interested in their social, ethnic, religious groups. While not challenging the fact that the state (as a social organization) has an important role in world affairs, it is as such a phenomenon subject to political analysis. The 'state' is far from the sole social construct that influences world politics. In the Arab world less loyalty is felt towards the 'state' than is felt towards ethnic, religious or regional constellations on the one hand, and is secondary to the flood of emotion, affection and the linguistic unity of Arabism on the other.

On this level, there are a number of social, political, ethnic and religious units of analysis that have to be dealt with if we are to understand fully the nature of world politics (Anderson, 1987; Harik, 1990; Al-Azmeh, 1993).

The objectives and practices that ought to direct decision-makers

There is an often-repeated dictum that 'statesmen think and act in terms of interest defined as power' (Morgenthau, 1978: 5). *Realpolitik* contributes the principles for the methods used in such a paradigm: what statesmen conceive of as the state's interest provides the source of political behaviour. The necessity to promote, formulate and execute policy decisions originates from the inherently competitive structure of the international system, to which the state has to adapt itself. The assessments that allow for the complexion of the international system have to promote the state's best interest, and doing that successfully is the sign of success (Waltz, 1979: 117). Classical realists contend that human nature cannot sufficiently explain differentiation and so in order to develop a normative theory that accounts for political behaviour they seek to explain events in terms of goals and purpose. Waltz depreciates the controversial argument of classical realism that individuals seek power as an end in itself as disputable, even problematic. For him, individuals seek and pursue power only a means to an end, and this is a sufficient condition for a theory of world politics (Waltz, 1979; Keohane, 1986a). There are scholars who refute the claim that the injunctions of 'national security' have always shaped the source of national concerns and behaviour. And, by implication, the so called 'high politics' of the power struggle between states would be willy-nilly prioritized in the face of other issues in world politics also termed 'low politics' (Vasquez, 1983; Keohane, 1986b). On this point, Samuel Kim (1983: 15) notes that 'the concept of "power" in mainstream realism is excessively narrow and limited. Realism recognizes only material and physical power and is contemptuous of "normative power," and ... it denies the existence of the world normative system.' Furthermore, the realists' conception of 'national interest' is not as clear as they claim it to be. No one would dispute the fact that political leaders act and react in accordance with their nations' best interests. But, since the choices facing human beings are usually identified with their conception of realities, the question then becomes, whose interests? And in what context? Moreover, as is usually the case, national interest is dictated by historical legacy and previous political arrangements manifested in sociocultural realities with which decision-makers have to be familiar. In the Arab world the national interest and the way it is perceived must be related to the fact that political leaders are exhorted to preserve or promote it not only by their own people in a strict sovereign and state-centred sense, but also by other states in the Arab world.

The techniques for measuring and managing foreign policy goals

As was indicated above the bulk of the studies that have appeared on Iraq and the Gulf crisis have as their main study object the personality and behaviour of the Iraqi president, Saddam Hussein. By invoking such an approach they might have in mind an 'ideal type' of the rational (or for that matter the irrational) actor model suggested by Graham Allison (1971). Allison's rational actor model dominates the analysis of foreign policy decision-making and state behaviour in world politics. According to the model, the decision-making process is considered to be the outcome of unified and coherent decision units which function within political organizations that are structured to facilitate the execution of policy decisions in order to achieve clear, indeed, given objectives.[4] At one point Allison (1971: 5) recognizes that the rational actor model does not completely account for, or fully explain, the decision-making process. Therefore 'it must be supplemented, if not supplanted, by frames of references that focus on the governmental machine'. The first 'frame of reference' proposed by Allison is called the 'organizational process model'. It contemplates the actions of governmental organizations that are not fully controlled by the top decision-makers. For government, as Allison (1971: 67) puts it, '[can] not substantially control the behaviour of these organisations'. Governmental organizations in a modern liberal democratic society are usually regulated primarily by abstract and routinized operating courses of action. Only during major disasters do these organizations deviate from such procedures.

IRAQ'S ASSESSMENT WHEN INVADING KUWAIT

In line with the realist approach, when it decided to move against Kuwait the Iraqi leadership responded purposefully to what might have been identified as an external challenge and threat from 'those [Kuwaitis and by implication the United States and the 'Zionist entity'] who are stabbing Iraq in the back with poisoned daggers'.[5] Saddam Hussein, in this perspective, is assumed to hold a clear objective, to weigh thoroughly the costs of each option, to pick the best option and to implement it to the full. In this respect we can assume, in an immediate sense, that the benefits that Iraq anticipated would justify the attendant costs and risks. These were as follows:

1   by 'adding Kuwait's fabulous wealth to the depleted Iraqi treasury, Hussein hoped to slash Iraq's foreign debt and launch the ambitious reconstruction programs he had promised his people in the wake of the war with Iran' (Karsh and Rautsi, 1991: 213);
2   the occupation of Kuwait 'could enhance Hussein's national prestige by portraying him as a liberator of usurped Iraqi lands' (ibid.);
3   in geostrategic terms, 'the capture of Kuwait could improve Iraq's access to the Gulf and give it a decisive say in the world market' (ibid.).

In this way of viewing world politics all states naturally seek to enhance their power and all are motivated by security concerns.

Iraq's economic recovery after a destructive eight-year war with Iran looked remote. The only option left that could save the Iraqi government from the economic and social consequences of that war was the possibility of selling oil at favourable prices. Iraq's economic recovery was seen as dependent on its ability to sell oil at high prices, but a surplus of oil on the international markets had depressed prices. The situation in OPEC and the policy the organization wanted to pursue in regard to overproduction and oil prices dashed Iraqi hope of higher prices. At the same time, differences of opinion on oil-pricing policy within OPEC were beginning to surface. In brief, Kuwait and the United Arab Emirates, who had a higher production capacity than their export quotas, wished to maintain the existing oil price. As Iraq was producing well within its production capacity, it was keen to press for a price increase. Early in 1990 Iraqi officials lobbied the Gulf states to lower their production and to push the price up from $18 to $20 per barrel, which the Gulf states, for various reason, were reluctant to do (Terzian, 1991; Ibrahim, 1992; Joffé, 1993).

Kuwait's implicit reluctance to abide by Iraqi demands might have provoked Iraq to revive the age-old territorial claims to part and later on to the whole of Kuwait. Also, in the name of the security of the Arab nation, Iraq (since it considers itself the shield of the nation), dictated its demands for access to the islands of Bubiyan and Werba – thus Iraq would have, as it deserved, a deep water anchorage outside the Shatt al-Arab. Last but not least may have been the desire to discipline and even punish Kuwait for daring to request Iraq to repay some of their debts (Karsh and Rautsi, 1991: 212–13).

So far, things have been placed in a power preponderance perspective: economic hardships, territorial disputes and unstable political tyranny on the one side, and a small, helpless neighbour on the other. All the ingredients that unleash conflicts, crises, and wars are in place. Yet to approach the Iraqi invasion of Kuwait only within this framework would be inadequate and would overlook the most fruitful and interesting historical experience, the societal realities and the political discourse from which the invasion of Kuwait emanated. At this juncture let us elaborate on the political realities of the Arab world that already reflect the impact of historical experience.

Iraq and the Arabic praxis of foreign policy

Arab states do not have a foreign policy-making system and process in the sense defined in the standard and traditional classification of foreign policy analysis (e.g. Rosenau, 1966, 1981; Brecher *et al.*, 1969; Dawisha, 1983). It was due to the Western powers' interference and involvement in the Middle East after World War II that the Arab states became, in one way or another, part of the international system.

Arab foreign policies are mainly regional, between Arab states themselves. This regional orientation, argue Korany and Dessouki (1984: 2) is the consequence, among other factors, of the intensive preoccupation of the major Arab states with the Arab–Israeli conflict – Islam and pan-Arab incentives urge such interstate praxis. These 'inter-Arab relations are not really foreign relations but part of the politics of the extended family instead. Thus, Arab leaders tend to talk directly to the citizens of other Arab states. Pan-Arab issues (e.g., the Palestine problem) became a component of political legitimacy for many Arab regimes' (ibid., 1984: 28).

In the light of this environment and trapped within the frame of their own survival and self-interest, the Ba'athist leadership, understandably, have no choice but be engrossed in their immediate surroundings. Given the vertical social structure of the Iraqi polity and the kinship character of the organization of public life, Iraq is governed entirely by one family – the Abu Nasser family of the city of Takrit. This is what might explain the Iraqi leadership's unpredictable international behaviour and its inability to comprehend and deal with the intricacies of the global stratification system.

Another related and distinctive feature of Arab political discourse is the tension between the institution of pan-Arabism and the institution of state sovereignty. The realists' assumption that states behave in a unitary manner and are the principal and prevailing variable in the analysis of world politics is an illicit claim. The critics (e.g. Kratochwil, 1996; Pasic, 1996: 102) point out that the power of normative ideas about human communities, among other things, has exposed itself poignantly in the integration of the developed states in Western Europe and the disintegration of the state systems of the former Soviet satellites in Eastern Europe and elsewhere in the Third World, a phenomenon that has dominated world politics since 1989. It has vividly shown, sometimes even poignantly, that the once taken-for-granted claim that states are the perennial actors in the international system must be evaluated anew. In this regard, pan-Arabism highlights the limits of realism's approach to the analysis of Iraq's (and other Arab states') foreign policy. Emphasizing exclusively the role of the abstracted state leads us to overlook the way the phenomenon of Arabism can help us to understand how actors perceive and define the national interest and the content of state interest (Barnett, 1993: 292–3). In the case of Iraq, the definition of national interest expanded from the Iraqi territory to include the Arab nation, as when Saddam Hussein accused the Gulf rulers of being part of a 'Zionist plot aided by imperialists against the *Arab nation*[6]... Iraq had become the *Arabs'* one reliable defender'.[7]

During the spring and summer of 1990 the language used by the Iraqi leadership was increasingly inflamed, carefully chosen, it seemed, to convey metaphoric pan-Arab and Islamic sentiments. In the meantime, Kuwait, which was the principle object of the conflict, appeared very little in the four major speeches that Saddam Hussein delivered on 24 February, 1 April, 28 May and 17 July 1990, which prepared the way for the invasion of Kuwait and the war that followed. In the speeches, the Iraqi president attempted to exploit the frustration and anger at the *status quo* and whip up Arab hostility against the United States and Israel, employing political language replete with religious metaphors and symbolism. In order to unite and confirm his leadership as the crisis dragged on, Saddam Hussein tended to resort to vibrant pan-Arab and Islamic idioms, rhetoric and metaphors which loomed ever larger in his speeches (Heikal, 1992: 207).

The target was the West, and in particular the United States and Zionism which had been blamed in the long and abominable history with its disastrous implications for the Arabs. By the same token, the speeches were essentially coded, with the main target of dispute and conflict – Kuwait – almost invisible. In a review of the president's public speeches and statements between the speech at the Arab Cooperation Council Summit, on 24 February 1990 up to his statement of approving the 'merger' decision with Kuwait to the Revolutionary Command Council, the highest executive mechanism in Iraq, on 8 August 1990, we find that the United States, either alone or with Israel and Zionism, is mentioned 216 times against 26 times for Kuwait, only two of which named Kuwait as the nineteenth province of Iraq. A few days before the invasion, there were no territorial claims on Kuwait whatsoever. Afterwards the al-Sabah family, the otherwise legitimate rulers of the state of Kuwait, were perceived not merely as an imminent danger to the national interest and security of Iraq, but to the entire Arab nation. In the 'Victory Day' speech on 7 August 1990, Saddam Hussein declared that the invasion of Kuwait and the removal of the al-Sabah family were justified on the grounds that the family were:

non-patriots [in Arabism's sense] ... non-humanitarians ... In fact this is the only way [i.e. to eject them from Kuwait] to deal with these despicable *Qarun* who relished stealing the part to harm the whole, who relished possession to destroy devotion, and who were guided by the foreigner instead of being guided ... by the principles of pan-Arabism, and the creed of humanitarianism in relations between the sons of the same people and nation ... The authority of the honourable ... pan-Arab majority ... was absent and was replaced by the authority of the corrupt minority, which is connected with the foreigner. As a result, the nation was hit right between the eyes, and the damage it suffered was no less in its consequences than direct foreign rule (Bengio, 1992: 112, 114).

Although the majority of the Arab peoples live in poverty they are aware of the lavish and extravagant wealth of their Gulf brethren. The enormously rich families that rule in Kuwait, Saudi Arabia and other Gulf sheikhdoms were anathema to those Arabs who wanted to change the *status quo*. The bid that Iraq put forward was again simple. The age-old sentiments were pervaded about the haves, i.e. the Gulf Arabs, and the have-nots, i.e. the great majority, the north Arabs such as the Palestinians, Egyptians, Syrians and those from other North African countries. By comparison with these issues, the disputes between Iraq and Kuwait over the production and pricing of oil did not occupy the normal amount of space that is usually evident in state-centred approaches to interstate conflicts. In his public speeches from the spring of 1990 onward, Saddam Hussein relied heavily on the sentiments of the haves and the have-nots.[8] In his 'Victory Day' speech on 7 August 1990, Saddam Hussein argued in rhetorical and deeply sentimental language that:

[t]he wealth [of the Arab nation] centred in one place, in the hands of a minority lacking in cultural depth ... On the other hand, cultural depth and population density centred in a place remote from the sources of the new wealth ... This malicious act resulted in the minority becoming so corrupt that it was cut off from its nation ... The wealth in the hands of this minority did not come as a result of legitimate hard work. (Bengio, 1992: 114)

It is worth noting that powerful national affection and sentiments had been in the Arab world long before the rise of the Ba'ath Party to power in Iraq and Syria, and before Nassirism in Egypt. However, for the Arabs in the Middle East the earth-shaking events in Palestine, especially since 1936 after the Arab population in Palestine revolted against the flow of Jewish immigration, have had a rippling effect on the entire region. The problems of the Palestinians have always been viewed by Arab intellectuals as their own. Judging from the major works of the prominent Iraqi writers and intellectuals such as Mohammad al-Jawaheri, Nazik al-Malaeka, Badr Shakir al-Sayab and Abdul Wahab al-Bayati, to mention only a few, these phenomena did not concern Iraq alone, and from the 1950s onwards such concerns have been heavily exploited by the Ba'athist intellectuals and politicians. Saddam Hussein's strategy was to use pan-Arab and religious language and metaphors, from directly quoting the Qur'an, to referring to Muslim symbols and names in his speeches, to adding *Allah-u-Akbar* on the Iraqi flag. Such acts are not simply a rhetorical and desperate resort to history to legitimize unlawful or politically irrational decisions. For both Muslim fundamentalists and ordinary Arabs it does not matter who raised the banner of *Allah-u-Akbar*, if he is Saddam Hussein or even the devil, what matters was that the name of Allah was invoked which, for them, was/is inevitable.

It could be said that this was the most effective strategy the Iraqi leadership ever conducted. Among many other leaders in modern Arab history, President Nassir of Egypt used the same language in his political campaign and verbal attacks on Zionism, the United States and Western imperialism from 1956 onward. Nassir's successor, Anwar al-Sadat, used it during the Yom Kippur war in 1973. Such language, while it goes to the heart and mind of the average grass-roots Arab, had ultimately rallied the mainstream Arab intellectuals, Arab (and even Muslim) statesmen, politicians, Muslim fundamentalists, liberal and cosmopolitan humanists and leftist groups, all of whom were standing on the same terrain. Even they did not directly see the Iraqi president as the much-longed-for hero of the Arab nation, they were very critical of the United States' and Israel's intrusion in Arab affairs, and this was a stand which indirectly supported Iraq (see page 159ff.).

Even though the Iraqi Shi'ite fundamentalists – the Supreme Assembly for the Islamic Revolution in Iraq (SAIRI), the Islamic Daawa Party and the Organization of Islamic Action (Amal) – are staunch opponents of Saddam Hussein and the Ba'athist regime in Iraq, and had fought the Iraqi regime virtually since the early 1960s, they were compelled to confine their position to that of the mainstream Arabs in regard to the West and Zionism (Baram, 1991). They declared that once they had ejected Saddam Hussein and got the Ba'ath's clique off the Iraqi people's back, their regime would 'fulfil its national duty by fighting imperialism and Zionism and their schemes'.[9] They were even critical of the PLO chairman 'for his readiness to recognize Israel in exchange for the establishment of a Palestinian state alongside it. In their mind, the whole of Palestine is an Islamic land and not one inch of it can be conceded to the Jews' (Baram, 1991: 41).

It had been assumed that the Iraqi president's use of this language, which he otherwise would have abandoned earlier, would attract support and legitimacy from pan-Arab audiences during that spring and summer on the eve of the invasion of Kuwait. Again, while Saddam Hussein was in line with realism in pursuing his own political goals, it is difficult to explain why so many Arabs had been responsive to him through the premises of realism, since the political history and experience of the Iraqi president in power had been doubted by those constellations that supported Iraq or severely criticized Arab states for cooperating with foreign powers against an Arab brother. The Arab leaders' use of religious and pan-Arab language might be explained by the attributes of the Arabic language itself and its connection with Islam, and by the fact that it reveals more than anything else the identity and psychological union of all Arabs despite their differences.

Thus the language in the Arab context becomes the core of the idea of a sociologically *lived* as well as a phenomenologically *held* community tailored by Arabism. Even though it sometimes appears as a utopian and shapeless ideational framework of horizontal brotherhood with no concrete political objectives (Barakat, 1984: 50–1; Seale, 1986: 6; Al-Khalil, 1989: 229–53), as experience has shown it has been a powerful instrument in Arab politics. This vision of Arabism has always existed as an immediate and natural reaction to outside threats (real or imagined) from, primarily, Zionism and Western imperialism, and more specifically it emerges whenever there are conflicts between Arabs and outsiders, such as the Suez crisis, the 1967 and 1973 wars with Israel, and last but not least the Gulf crisis of 1990–91.[10]

The question of role conflict

This expansion of state and national interests was necessitated by various factors and forces and, again, by certain conditions that are peculiar to the Arabic political discourse. It will become comprehensible at a later stage as we examine the imperative of nation-building for the Iraqi population and for decision-makers, as well as for the surrounding states. As Barnett (1993: 284, n.

30) argues, the concept of 'national interest' is generally based on the assumption that 'the state whose mission is to promote the security of the nation, and the nation are circumscribed spatially by the same territory'. The fact that the Arab/Muslim identity is even more salient to the population than is the goal of a territorial sovereign state explains why Arab leaders are usually unable to use state-centred principles to justify their actions. Therefore, they often turn to the sentiments and aspirations of pan-Arabism to justify their policies as being in the interest of the Arab nation, and not only of their particular state. Consequently, this reality makes the realist and state-centric conception of 'national interest' irrelevant in the study of inter-Arab politics. National interest as it is articulated in the Euro-American discourse does not exist in the political language of the Arab states and leaders. They are obliged to speak to all Arabs, those living in their own states as well as others who live elsewhere; the notion of 'national interest' here in form and substance therefore ought to be confined to this context.

This role conflict among both political systems and leaders in the Arab world articulates the cultural and social dimension of power and interest. After independence during the 1950s, the societal and political expectations that define a particular political leader's role have often been highly generalized, ambiguous and contradictory. In a sense, an Arab leader may have a wide range of possible patterns of behaviour, while his publicly defined role is to work for the common good of his own people and to safeguard the national interest of his own country in accordance with his perception of the role expectations of other actors. The roles within a set (role set is a group of roles proclaimed by a single leader) often create contradictory demands (Walker, 1991: 1–3; Barnett, 1993). On the one hand they call for safeguarding the Iraqi national interest by adding the Kuwaiti wealth to the depleted Iraqi economy, by slashing Iraq's foreign debt, by improving Iraq's access to the Gulf and by giving Iraq an important position in the world oil market (Karsh and Rautsi, 1991: 213). On the other hand they may also call for action from him as a pan-Arab leader who is expected to conform and give a high priority to pan-Arab aspirations and to call for the expulsion of the imperial Western powers from Arab lands and the liberation of Palestine. Saddam Hussein's role enactment within the Iraqi political system is of interest here. His actual behaviour as a self proclaimed pan-Arab leader permits us to explain the decision to invade Kuwait by reference to his role expectations, interpretations and the competing demands of multiple roles (Korany and Dessouki, 1984: 12–13; Walker, 1991: 1–3). To a large extent, the Ba'athist leadership was inspired by the Nassirist duality of roles. This comprises viewing Iraq as a state and dealing with other Arab regimes, whatever their political ideology, in the Arab League, in the UN, and on bilateral matters like defence, and trade. It also comprises a revolutionary role that should ignore various Arab governments and deal directly with the people (Ahmad, 1991; Barnett, 1993).

The Iraqi leadership's assumptions about other actors' motivations and perceived interests (e.g., Arabs, Israelis and Americans), and their understanding of what role should be displayed to the world around them promises to take us a long way towards understanding these events.[11] The Iraqi decision to swallow the whole of Kuwait and not only the disputed areas on the borders might have been based on the assumption that the major Arab states such as Egypt, Syria and especially Saudi Arabia would respond in the manner of Arabism and adopt a role enactment that was typical of inter-Arab politics and one that had often been manifested in previous regional crises. The presence of both the powerful transstate institution of pan-Arabism and state sovereignty confers separate roles, preferences and expected patterns of behaviour on the Arab states (Viorst, 1991; Al-Gosaibi, 1993; Barnett, 1993: 275–7). Later on, the annexation of Kuwait may have seemed easier to legitimize than the appropriation of the disputed territory.[12]

The people in the Arab world have a strong sense of being Arab and/or Muslim – the whole regional system with its 22 sovereign states 'still paradoxically constitutes a single area of psychological, emotional, and intellectual resonance transcending state frontiers' (Khalidi, 1991: 58–9).[13] The behaviour of political elites within the Arab regional system is affected by the opposing roles derived from the powerful feeling of pan-Arabism and the political allegiances so essential to the modern sovereign state. Nevertheless, it is here that assumptions about taken-for-granted sovereign states with a given political leadership which has a preconception of the 'national interest' that is restricted spatially to a particular territory, prove to be questionable. Relating this aspect to the invasion of Kuwait, and beyond the Iraq–Kuwait tensions that were the immediate cause of the outbreak of violence, the Gulf crisis once again displayed and exposed a characteristic typical of the Arab political discourse. Arab leaders legitimize the promotion of their narrow state-centred interests and the consolidation of their personal base of power under the guise of advancing the Arab nationalist or Islamic ideals espoused by their population (Ibrahim, 1992: 12). Thus interstate Arab relations are characterized by a mutual lack of recognition and respect for state sovereignty. Interference in the affairs of other (usually weaker) states by manipulating part of the population against their own government, as well as direct cross-border activities, are distinctive hallmarks of Arab politics. Sayigh (1991: 490) recalls many examples:

the Saudi role in the Omani civil war of the 1950s, Iraq's assertion of its claim to Kuwait in 1961, Syrian and Egyptian policy towards Jordan in the mid-1950s and mid-1960s, Syrian involvement in Lebanon in 1958 and Egyptian in Iraq in 1960, Egyptian and Saudi intervention in the Yemen civil war in 1962–7, and the Moroccan–Algerian conflict of 1965.

The impact of a transstate institution (i.e. Arabism) on the formulation of foreign policy objectives is relevant to the invasion of Kuwait in many ways, and has serious implications for the decision-making process and the foreign behaviour of Arab states. Paul Noble (1984: 48–9) puts forward four factors that inevitably condition foreign policy decision-makers in the Arab world. First, the close scrutiny and sharp reaction of Arab states to each other stems from a strong sense of kinship. Differences over political issues are usually treated as harmful behaviour in many cases by depicting the opponent as traitors to the Arab cause. Saddam Hussein's attack on the Gulf states during the summer of 1990 was formulated in these terms. Second, when any segment of the community is in conflict with a non-Arab actor, the sense of membership in a larger family has led to pressures for Arab solidarity. During the spring of 1990 Saddam Hussein warned Israel against attacking not only Iraq but any other Arab country.[14] Third, a common Arab identity has become for some Arab regimes a justification for diverting attention away from domestic problems and seeking political legitimacy from other Arab populations. Since legitimacy is transstate in nature, the Iraqi leader justified the invasion of Kuwait by appealing to pan-Arab sentiments and Islamic consciousness. He stressed that Arabs had an obligation to control fully their sources and wealth and to drive out the West from the Arab world (Ibrahim, 1992: 12).[15] While pan-Arabism's rhetoric plays on the emotions as a mechanism for marginalization and protest, it exerts a powerful impact and becomes an instrument for instability both within states and on the regional level. It is often used as a pretext by leaders motivated by personal egoism to strengthen their power base. Fourth, due the sense of a common Arab identity and the identification and/or the direct affiliation of parts of the population with other Arabs, there is continuous external manipulation by leaders, political systems, and states of parts of or even whole populations. Leaders of particular states are usually exposed to intensive external pressures and manipulation. This might explain the late King Hussein of Jordan's support for Iraq, since there is a large Palestinian population in Jordan who enthusiastically supported Saddam Hussein.

Against this background, the Arab regional system cannot be treated as if it were a 'states-system', in Martin Wight's (1977: 129) assumption of international politics. This regional system lacks the discourse of historical development and 'the relatively protected position in time and space', in Charles Tilly's terms,[16] that characterized the development of the nation-states of the West. The fact that there are sovereign states that recognize each other in the United Nations and other international organizations and that there is regular communication through the diplomatic network should not, however, debase the realities of the internal dynamics that often violently expose and spill over with the first political crisis the state faces. Indeed, states like Iraq, Algeria, Libya, Sudan and Somalia, to name but a few, could quickly integrate into the international system but they would just as quickly destroy the 'would-be' social order in their societies (Sheth, 1989: 381–2). Having said that, there are three entwined factors (considered as sources for foreign policy decisions in the context of the Arab world) that might have induced Iraq to decide to invade Kuwait. First, the decline of the body politic and civil society (in the case of Egypt) and their collapse in the case of Iraq. By locating the state above and away from society, a new type of statism arose possessing a pronounced clannish, dynastic or military-dictatorial character. Second, the organic character of Arab politics, in the sense that foreign policy making is conducted in a familial manner.[17] In addition, Arab decision-makers' lack of information and knowledge necessary to comprehend the complexity of the global stratification system, for various reasons, result in them being almost completely immersed in domestic problems. This state of affairs renders the process of dealing with the outside world difficult. The Iraqi government's behaviour – reacting to outside pressures rather than acting according to preplanned policy decisions – during the crisis illustrates this point.

By the same token, states in the Arab world have often questioned and undermined one another's sovereignty for the sake of the ever-greater common resilience of the project of Arab unity, despite the existence of a regional balance of power system comprised of sovereign states who formally accept one another's sovereignty and legitimacy (Bull, 1977). There are both state and non-state actors that promote pan-Arabism and treat it as a political priority. This is what might give durability to the assumption that the role of the Arab state and the design of the regional system are still far from settled. Moreover, 'because of pan-Arabism, Arab states were in a constant search for legitimacy: their foreign policies often articulated, and at the least were couched in Arabism's designs, which only hindered the goal of institutionalising sovereignty' (Barnett, 1993: 289). Therefore the invasion of Kuwait could be approached as a consequence of the perpetual conflict between the institution of sovereignty in the modern Arab state and that of pan-Arabism – a reality that has dominated the Arab world since the formation of the Arab states after the collapse of the Ottoman empire at the end of World War I.

Nevertheless, sociocultural and political roles are not only appropriated or self-proclaimed by Iraq alone but have also been conferred upon Iraq by other states (e.g. Jordan, Algeria, Sudan and Yemen), groups (such as Palestinians) and other organizations within the Arab regional system. In this context, on 4 August 1990 King Hussein of Jordan referred to the Iraqi president as a 'patriotic man who believes in his nation[18] and its future and in establishing ties with others on the basis of mutual respect'.[19] Another example is that of the foreign minister (and later prime minister) of Algeria, Sid Ahmad Ghozali, who declared with great enthusiasm that Iraq and Saddam Hussein 'incarnate ... the spirit of resistance to those who wish to humble the Arabs'[20] (I shall return to this issue below). Since its creation in 1922, the rulers of Iraq had sought to benefit from the Palestine conflict which, at first sight, seems to have had little relevance to Iraqi politics, and yet the power struggle within a country so ethnically divided motivated the elite to seek engagement in regional conflicts to consolidate their power base inside Iraq. From the time of the monarchy right up to the Ba'athist government of Saddam Hussein, the Iraqi government has consistently exploited the plight of the Palestinians as a means of diverting public opinion away from domestic problems, to obtain control over Syria;[21] and most importantly to maintain political domination in the Arab world as well as regional hegemony. The perennial instability of Iraq – the struggle between Sunnites and Shi'ites, as well as other opposition parties – has also pressured the government to support the cause of the Palestinians (Eppel, 1994). The demonstrations by the Arab grass-roots in Jordan, Yemen and Algeria draw attention to the wide gap between rich and poor, and were triggered by anger, frustration with the *status quo* and by the tradition of misrule in the Arab world. They were also an expression of resentment against the United States and its unequivocal support to the Jewish state, and the widely acknowledged ill-treatment of the Palestinians by Israel, particularly during the *Intifada*. The logic on which Saddam Hussein had relied, like any other Arab leader in the same position, exploited the deep plight of the Palestinians' struggle against an all-powerful and omnipotent enemy.

By June 1990, the Middle East peace was deadlocked, leading to nowhere. The situation worsened with the United States' suspension of the dialogue with the PLO following a terrorist raid in Tel Aviv at the end of May. The PLO, disenchanted with the hopeless political situation, shifted the focus of its diplomatic activity to the radical Arab states.[22] The PLO switched from the moderate camp led by Egypt to the radical one in which Iraq was the most articulate proponent. Iraq, with its effective propaganda machine reaching all the Arab media, ingeniously transformed this situation into an activist policy flavoured with pan-Arab rhetoric.[23] At that time, the much disliked *status quo* of the Arab political state of affairs and regional system had come to be seen by the Arab grass-roots as the barrier to a more promising, helpful and forthcoming future (Heikal, 1992; Tylor, 1993; Mattar, 1994). Moreover, this shift was more than a just switch from a moderate to a radical state for support, it was also the opening through which Saddam Hussein could resume his quest for the support of the Arab grass-roots and constellations of civil society that were very responsive.

The idea of being the Arab world's new Abdul Nassir was necessitated by the political vacuum within the Arab regional order (Sayigh, 1991), an order that had been dependent on what Khalidi (1991) terms as the 'moral centre of gravity', in the style of Abdul Nassir (i.e. a father for the Arab family, who would take care of his own children). At this juncture, the Iraqi president actively presented himself as the longed for 'Hero of the Arab Nation'. Such a leadership image had a potential appeal as a counter to the political atmosphere of despair, and as the ultimate solution to the seeming inability of the existing regimes to deal effectively with the many problems facing the Arab world (Tylor, 1993). Expanding the warrant and threatening to 'burn Israel', thus deterring any likely Israeli aggression not only against Iraq but also against any Arab state, were steps along the way. Every single speech, literally from the 'Bazoft affair' in March 1990 (when the British, but of Iranian origin, journalist Ferzad Bazoft was killed), revived the memory of the 1950s and 1960s when, in the heyday of pan-Arabism, Abdul Nassir had appealed over the heads of governments to the people in the Arab streets.

After some fruitless rounds of diplomacy and political missions during the spring of 1990, designed to lay the foundation for a comprehensive settlement of the Arab–Israeli conflict, the US administration found itself unable or unwilling to pressure the hardline position and policy of the Shamir government, the principal obstacle to a peace settlement. At the time, the situation in the Arab world was volatile, even explosive. The prospect of a solution to the conflict had never looked so remote (Tylor, 1993: 88). Even so, and despite its extraordinary ability to benefit from events in Palestine, the Ba'ath regime fell victim to its own propaganda. In fact, Iraq, the Ba'ath Party and Saddam Hussein did very little to enhance this image in general through the history of conflict. In September 1970 Saddam Hussein, then the vice-president, prevented Iraqi troops, then deployed on Jordanian soil, from intervening to stop the bloodshed between the Jordanian army and the PLO. Similarly, Iraq's military support to the coordinated Egyptian-Syrian attack on Israel in 1973 was extremely limited, and was withdrawn at the first available opportunity. But engrossed in their plight and immersed in increasingly hopeless conditions, the Palestinians saw the Iraqi leader as a saviour, and did not care about the genealogy of such a tyrant. As Hanna Siniora, editor of *al-Fajr* put it, 'a drowning person does not care about the identity of the person throwing a rope to save him or her' (cited in Muslih, 1992: 115).

It is reasonable to claim that this popular support for Saddam Hussein was the decisive factor that motivated the Iraqi leadership to take over Kuwait despite the assurances to the contrary given to Arab leaders such as Mubarak of Egypt. Saddam Hussein might have decided to exploit the massive popular support for Iraq by Arabs and so utilize it politically to promote Iraq's regional ambitions. This reality makes Iraq and its leadership occupy multiple and conflicting roles that could easily lead to miscalculation in any given crisis situation. Role conflicts that arise even in a clear-cut and normal political state of affairs will understandably invite misconception and lead to an inability to act decisively, despite the fact that the role conflict is part and parcel of the societal and cultural reality that derives its relevance and strength from the past – a past, moreover, that is essentially also a present. This point is clearly illustrated by the Ba'ath leadership's assumption that, due to the norms and rules of pan-Arabism, all Arab states would never cooperate actively with the US and allow an American army on Islam's holy soil.[24] Saddam Hussein and other Iraqi officials never expected that the Saudis, or for that matter any other Arab regime, would dare to undertake a decision, whereby an 'infidel' Western army would be imported to fight an Arab brother, whatever the underlying reasons.[25] What Saudi Arabia did is act as a sovereign state that aspired to defend and secure its borders and national interest (Al-Gosaibi, 1993), though at a very high political risk and economic price. The Saudi decision to allow Western forces on the holy Muslim soil has engendered popular unrest and encouraged the opposition to resort to arms against the al-Saud ruling family; terrorist attacks on government institutions and on foreign (American and European) forces happen so frequently that they threaten to undermine the regime.

Pan-Arab identity and the self-image engendered by being an Arab is a matter to be taken seriously where political behaviour is concerned, not least by foreign policy analysts. Such a political atmosphere undermines a strictly *realpolitik* reading of a state's interest and of how states concretely display their interest.[26] Role theory particularly calls attention to the cultural and societal determinants of political behaviour, dimensions which are often overlooked in rationalistic theories of goal maximization in policy decisions, by favouring interests over beliefs and capabilities over intention, perception, images and world views (Smith, 1995: 23). After invading Kuwait, the Iraqi leadership refused to 'climb down' and 'save their skins'. They took the risk of being crushed militarily, rather than be ridiculed by other Arabs, especially by those who had huge expectations of Saddam Hussein and Iraq. Instead, the Iraqi leadership played the pan-Arab card and pleaded to their brothers against the conspiracy of Arab traitors and the American-Zionist plot to destroy the vanguard of the Arab nation (i.e. Iraq). Thus the assumption that behaviour that appears irrational may in fact be explicable by reference to a 'reflective' under-standing of the sources that generate or lead to role conflict. 'True rationality' Miriam Steiner argues, 'may require consideration of the "non-rational" world of emotions, desires, and feeling as well as the "rational" world of logic and facts' (1983: 392).

AMERICAN–IRAQI RELATIONS 1984–90

The American involvement in the Arab Middle East after World War II came as a result of the increasing importance of Arab oil, the creation of the state of Israel, and the United States' Cold War strategy of containing the Soviet Union in the Middle East region. The immediate implications for the invasion of Kuwait can be traced to the ceasefire after the Iraq–Iran war in July 1988. The full American military presence in the Gulf was one of the consequences of that war, and was initially directed against any Iranian threat to the rich Gulf states. Thereafter the United States modified its perception of the nature of danger in the Gulf region. This direct military involvement was the beginning of a new American military activism that the Iraqi leadership initially embraced, although Iraq was later visibly alarmed by the unusually large and unprecedented scale of the American presence (Ahmad, 1991; Mostafa, 1991). Was the Iraqi invasion of Kuwait really something that fell within a grand American design for the Middle East to get rid of Iraq once and for all, and therefore the potential danger that a strong and aggressive Iraq might mean to Israel and the rich Gulf Arabs?[27] For such an assumption to be acceptable would require a highly sophisticated plan in which the United States and Israel would command a watertight control over events. Such a scenario is utterly unrealistic given the historical pattern of American policy in the Middle East since World War II and the fact that vital policy-making during the last two decades was virtually orchestrated by America's 'lackeys' – Egypt, Israel and Saudi Arabia. The American policy and history of involvement in the Middle East is, however, undoubtedly relevant to Iraq's invasion of Kuwait. At this point it is important to touch on the subsequent popular interpretation of the Iraqi motivation being facilitated by the American invitation, or the 'green light' that Ms Glaspie (the US ambassador to Iraq) is alleged to have conveyed to Saddam Hussein in order to invade Kuwait. For a number of reasons the Middle East has always been fertile soil for all kinds of conspiracy theories: the lack of coherent regional security mechanisms that all states abide by (Sayigh, 1991; Barnett, 1996); the absence of established and regularly organized political institutions within states (Dawisha, 1977, 1990); the long history of foreign and colonial intrusion into the area to the extent that many states arose as a result of this (Corm, 1992; Ibrahim, 1992). In addition is the dependence and interdependence of the Middle East region in vital economic interests on the outside world; and finally the rise of the state of Israel in 1947 as the embodiment of the Zionist project and, to the Arabs, Israel's incomprehensible series of victories coupled with their own endemic feeling of being unable to stem the tide confronting it. Thus in the Arab narrative Zionism is a spearhead of imperialism and colonialism. After the military successes and political and diplomatic achievements of the Jewish state, and the fact that it became virtually a regional superpower, the scope of narratives became wider – imperialist nations (in Europe and United States) are only tools in the hand of world Zionism (Said, 1980; Lewis, 1986: 190ff.). The United States had to keep a low profile during the intensive pre-invasion days.[28] It was the policy that had later facilitated the swiftness of the American response when the invasion did occur. At this juncture, any attempt to deter Iraq could have been counterproductive. It could also have even intensified the anti-Americanism which is widespread in the area, since it could have been used by Iraq and other Arab states to claim intrusion by the United States in Arab internal affairs. It would, moreover, have ultimately made it difficult for the US to persuade Syria, Egypt and other states to join the international coalition to inhibit Iraq ambitions in the Gulf.

The division between the radical and moderate Arab regimes which had developed over the previous 40 years within the global context proved seminally important to explain the proportions reached by the Gulf crisis (Tschirgi, 1991: 15–16). The Cold War had not directly exerted a ubiquitous impact on the politics of the Middle Eastern region. Three specific aspects of the nexus between global and regional politics seem particularly significant. First, East–West rivalry during the Cold War was reflected in inter-Arab divisions, though the competition between the United States and the Soviet Union within the Middle East never resulted in a fully frozen regional polarization. Nor, for the most part, did it produce absolute realignments of Arab states with the contending superpowers. Instead the Cold War, ironically, provided Arab governments with a degree of manoeuvrability in pursuing their objectives through international politics (Ahmad, 1991). Second was the inordinately high degree of militarization during the previous 40 years in the region.[29] Third, the international atmosphere of the Cold War had an impact and constraining influence on the Middle Eastern actors. Mindful that regional conflicts might draw them into direct confrontation, the US and the Soviet Union were successful in restraining their respective clients within the Middle East regional system. Given the Middle East's violent recent history, it is obvious that the superpowers were not consistently committed to this end. It is also evident that even when they tried to promote restraint (e.g. Yom Kippur), their success was often incomplete. The American military presence in the Gulf was affirmed after the Reagan administration accepted a request from the Kuwaiti government to protect the Kuwaiti oil tankers from the Iranian threat. During the summer of 1987 the United States decided to protect the Kuwaiti and other Gulf shipping against any Iranian threat by an intensive naval build-up in the Gulf. However, the Iranians continued to harass shipping traffic despite the US military presence (Brown, 1992; Karabell, 1993; Telhami, 1994). It was, as the Iraqis perceived it, a weak response from a superpower claiming to have extensive interests in the Gulf region. So the Iraqi leadership might have anticipated a similarly weak response from the US if and when it considered invading Kuwait. The decisive difference here, of course, was that the major Arab states facilitated and supported the United States' policy of interference.

The Soviet Union, Melkumyan (1992) argues, adopted a very different policy in 1990 from that which it followed in the 1962 crisis sparked by the Iraqi claim to Kuwait. This was due in part to the

internal upheaval in the Soviet Union, the power struggle between
the political elites, and the problem of nationalities and the desire to
secede from the USSR. These factors were accompanied by the
Gorbachev regime's preoccupation with maintaining warm relations
with the West in the hope of economic assistance. All these Cold War
legacies seem particularly relevant to the Gulf crisis. The apparent end
of US–Soviet Cold War rivalry clearly altered the global environment
in a significant way. Despite both the Soviet Union's and the United
States' decisive assistance to Iraq in its war with Iran, the Ba'ath
government, by virtue of its very inward and secretive nature, distrusted
both of them.[30] However, Iraqi suspicions of the United States were
much more intense due to the US association with Israel. From early
1990 the Iraqi government was openly and constantly criticizing the
American involvement and policy in the region. On several occasions
the Iraqi president made speeches calling for the withdrawal of the
US forces from the Gulf region and urged the Gulf Arabs to boycott
and withdraw their financial assets from the United States and the
West (Mostafa, 1991). A key misjudgment, then, was the Iraqi
leadership's inability to assess the significance of the changing international system and decline of the Soviet Union and the implications
of its withdrawal from the Middle East regional as well as international
scenes.[31] The question to be posed, therefore, is that if the Iraqi
leadership had rightly perceived the fundamental alteration of the
structure of the international system and had foreseen the United
States' reaction, would it have invaded Kuwait? This leads us to the
question of deterrence.

The question of deterring Iraq

It has been argued that the Iraqi invasion of Kuwait was a consequence
of the unsuccessful American strategy of deterrence. That is to say,
the United States failed to make it abundantly clear to the Iraqi leader
that Iraq's threat to, and likely aggression against, Kuwait would not
only be opposed but that the cost of such an action would exceed the
gain. The strategy of deterrence is intrinsically aimed at maintaining
a peaceful condition. It is pursued to hinder eventual threats, or likely
acts of aggression, by convincing (through a supposedly clear form of
communication) actors or states who might envisage such actions that

the costs would exceed the gains. However, like several other extensively abstract concepts, deterrence has always been conceived by many scholars as 'an essentially contested concept'. This remains the fate of deterrence, despite the fact that it overshadows the analysis of security and foreign policy, whether in the form of academic textbooks or as an advanced theoretical discussion on strategy and policy analyses (Gray, 1986: 97; Williams, 1992). In the area of security, deterrence usually attempts to prevent a military challenge. The strategy of deterrence also has been utilized for the prevention of an unacceptable military deployment (e.g., the deployment of Soviet missiles in Cuba in 1962). This also applies to other actions that do not necessarily have military dimensions but which states might conceive as unacceptable behaviour. Deterrence, too, manifests the commitment to punish or restrain transgressors, and demonstrates that one has the resolve and possesses the capabilities to implement the threat – the whole question of credibility is intimately linked to deterrence (Lebow and Stein, 1990).

A reading of the Iraqi public statements during the spring and the early summer of 1990 would reveal a real Iraqi fear of an American–Israeli plot with the implicit backing of the rich Gulf states against Iraq. Therefore when it decided to invade Kuwait, Iraq expected an American reaction.[32] Having observed the US policy toward Iran and the Iranian threats to the Gulf states during the Iran–Iraq war, the Ba'athist government might have underestimated the circumstances that facilitated the United States ability to act. Although the US was intending, and committed, to oppose the Iraqi agenda in the Gulf, what was not understood by Iraq was the scale and the swiftness of the American reaction of using force and running the risk of incurring heavy casualties.[33] The Iraqi leadership's assumption of the US reaction and the means whereby any US or international involvement could be inhibited was based on its strategy to keep the whole matter 'an internal Arab affair', leaving Iraq with a free hand in Kuwait. Looking at the historical pattern of inter-Arab conflicts, Iraq might have reasoned that other Arab states would be either unable – in a power preponderance sense – or unwilling to wage war against Iraq over Kuwait, let alone cooperate with the US. Thus the serious miscalculation had to do with the Arab states' reactions, especially that of Saudi Arabia which, against conventional wisdom, allowed a massive US and Western army on Islam's holy soil.

To some, the US, like any other superpower, adopted a pragmatic course of action; this is also in tune with the domestic pressures the administration faces from time to time (Brown, 1992; Telhami, 1994). Both Iraq and the United States have their share of misperception, based on the historical record of distrust, but neither of them questioned its own assumptions. The nature of the relationship between the United States and the Arab world is one of the principal causes of the outbreak of the Gulf crisis (Tschirgi, 1991). The invasion of Kuwait provides a framework for examining foreign policy as an outcome not only of certain defined choices but also of the changing context of time, space and uncertainty affecting a given policy. Moreover, for the United States there is the requirement to act decisively to defend vital interests, usually within a framework of contingency and of uncertainty of time and space as events unfold (Telhami, 1994). In this context, the American reaction to the Iraqi invasion of Kuwait, as L. Carl Brown (1992: 18–19) puts it, conformed to:

a well-established pattern of American policy. This is not to argue a simple-minded determinism ... the United States ... approached the Gulf crisis assuming that the U.S. had a need, a responsibility, and a right to orchestrate political arrangements in the Middle East. Even if President Bush had chosen different options, he would have taken steps, sooner or later, consistent with this American policy of full involvement.

Like Brown, Telhami (1994: 153) argues that the American reaction to the Iraqi invasion of Kuwait 'was almost automatic; no matter who sat in the White House, or who had access to it, the decision would have been the same'. Indeed, one of the great puzzles of the crisis was just this quick and swift American reaction. To begin with the US administration had been willing to condone the Iraqi regime's aggressive policy in the region and the abuse of human rights inside Iraq. In fact, US policy towards Iraq was to accommodate in order to moderate, despite many skeptical voices including that of the powerful pro-Israel lobby (Karabell, 1995; Telhami, 1994).

The *Voice of America* (VOA) broadcasts,[34] the negative publicity in the Western media concerning the Iraqi government's treatment of the Kurds, human rights abuses and the attempts at smuggling technology related to an arms build-up and weapons of mass destruction, were all interpreted as an all-encompassing conspiracy against Saddam Hussein and, by implication, Iraq. Both the US and Iraq were unable to acknowledge the differences between their political systems.[35] Each tended to interpret the other's decision-making on its own terms. There was an overwhelming belief within the Iraqi leadership that US foreign policy towards the Arab world and Iraq in particular had always been based on a whole set of intended conspiracies. Policy-makers in Iraq and the US had studied each other very little. All the official statements by the US administration were designed for public consumption and the Iraqi leadership never distinguished between the various 'audiences' to which US policy-makers had to appeal. The VOA editorial fitted into this frame. There are, Edward Said (1991: 441) notes, no academic institutes or studies in the Arab world devoted to the study of Western societies, culture and politics, in spite of the fact that during the last two centuries the West has influenced and, to a large extent, shaped states, societies and the future destinies of states in the Arab world. Indeed, the United States has been almost indisputably the most powerful outside power in the Middle East, where it continues to be perceived by most Arabs as the new imperial and colonial power. More critical is the fact that:

it is difficult to explain to well-educated and experienced fellow Arabs that the U.S. foreign policy is not in fact run by the CIA, or a conspiracy, or a shadowy network of key 'contact' … This mix of long familiarity, hostility, and ignorance pertains to both sides of a complex, variously uneven and quite old cultural encounter now engaging in very unmetaphorical warfare. (Said, 1991: 441–2)

The role of projecting oneself, ignorance of the political institutions of others, the nature of the decision-making process, and differences in cultural and societal values may inhibit a realistic outlook by decision-makers of other states' common spheres of action and an understanding of their respective environments. At this juncture, how can we explain the US strategy of accommodation and the policy of constructive engagement to moderate Iraq that reached such an absurd level, and, whether the US had a deterrent intention, let alone a policy?[36]

Theoretical attention, however, has been largely devoted to the question of how the defender state can convince the offender that the costs of using force will be very high. To this end, there are two other related question: what types of military capabilities will effectively threaten the attacker with high costs, and what types of diplomatic and military actions strengthen the potential attacker's assessment of the defender's resolve to honour its threat of military retaliation. Theoretical attention should therefore be given to what variables outside of deterrence theory may have a consistent and significant impact on how the attacker evaluates alternative policy choices (Huth and Russet, 1990).

The deterrent actions of the defender will have little, if any, effect on the final decisions of the attacker in the case of what is termed 'extended deterrence', especially, as in the case of Kuwait and the United States, when there no political or security arrangements that form the basis for such protection.[37] Extended deterrence is concerned with the prevention of an aggression that a third state (usually in implicit or explicit alliance with one of the states in the deterrent interrelationship) might be subjected to. This was supposedly the case with the Gulf crisis, where the United States would have defended Kuwait against the Iraqi invasion. The United States pursued an ambiguous, even confused, policy called 'constructive engagement' towards Iraq up until the invasion of Kuwait (Karabell, 1993). The outcome of this policy lends credence to those who opposed such accommodation. Even when Iraq mobilized its forces along the border with Kuwait, the United States did not react with the same resolve and swiftness as was the case after the Iraqi forces poured into Kuwait. Perhaps this was inevitable. There was a fear of an Iraqi attempt to undermine moderate pro-Western Arab regimes through the exploitation of the plight of the Palestinians to cover Iraq's political ambition. Finally, public opinion in the US and Europe had hardened toward Iraq in the early months of the 1990s, particularly because of the arms build-up, the acquisition of weapons of mass destruction, human rights abuses in Iraq but above all because of world media reports of the maltreatment of the Kurdish minorities and other Shi'ite opposition groups.

The aim of general deterrence, Lebow and Stein (1989, 1990) contend, is to inhibit the outbreak of war by convincing other actors/states to keep down military escalation and, ultimately, not to resort to force and violence of various types. On the other hand, immediate deterrence is, indeed, precise in aiming to prevent military threats and/or aggression on specifically outlined assurances of protection through mutual agreements or other security arrangements (Morgan, 1977). In a departure from these premises, both the Reagan and Bush administrations had established an accommodative policy toward Iraq since 1984 after the resumption of bilateral diplomatic relations. For example, the Bush administration in 1989 had authorized credits worth $2 billion for Iraq. Moreover, up until two days before the invasion of Kuwait, the administration had granted a credit of $1,200 million for food purchases by Iraq (Karabell, 1993). The US administration had allegedly ignored warnings by the CIA and other military intelligence sources of imminent and unusually large-scale Iraqi troop movements towards the Kuwaiti border, so that the outbreak of the crisis caught it unprepared. On this point, several Middle Eastern pundits have argued that Iraq might have perceived the United States' approach as an encouragement to Iraq to go on into Kuwait, or perhaps that the United States' perceived weakness, or its inability to act decisively, could be a sign of indifference with regard to what Iraq was up to (Brown, 1992; Matthews, 1993; Karabell, 1995). This way of looking at the issues is consistent with Jervis's (1976, 1989) characteristics of deterrence in the face of an opponent who proceeds with his aggressive designs.[38] However, as Michael Dunn (1992) correctly points out, the fundamentals of a successful deterrent policy were not in place in the Gulf during the spring and early summer of 1990. The Gulf states had not created credible collective security and defence mechanisms. The incoherence of political institutions and security mechanisms and their structural vulnerability due to the crisis of legitimacy and domestic instability of the political regimes are factors to be considered at this point. After all, the Arab League is at best more a fragile alliance system for the Arab states than a reliable collective security arrangement. It does not include all the regional powers likely to be involved in regional conflicts – Israel and Iran, not to mention Turkey (Sayigh, 1991; Tibi, 1991; Ibrahim, 1992). Moreover, there is a long history of dependence on external powers both in terms of vital political and economic interests, factors that have had severe effects on the political structures of the states.

It has been argued so far that the source of deterrence, as well as the policy of reassurance, is the rational individual who is able to grasp it all, and who can 'stand the heat in his kitchen'. A decision-maker's options are determined by supposedly rational preferences among realistic and viable options (Allison, 1971: 166). In the theoretical framework of deterrence theory, Williams (1992: 73) rightly maintains that the rational individual who is both the subject and object of inquiry, who is both the locus of knowledge and its arbiter, is faced with the task of understanding deterrence. The core conceptual dispute revolves around the credibility of the rational threat to use diplomacy and/or weapons in order to achieve deterrence. The United States had the military capacity to deter Iraq, but, '[t]he diplomacy of deterrence was inconsistent, incoherent, and unfocused in the critical two weeks preceding the invasion. Had Saddam Hussein been deterrable, it is unlikely that he would have been stopped, given the confusing signal from Washington', wrote Janice Stein (1992: 155). The question is whether Saddam Hussein was 'aware' of the United States' intentions. The United States' 'double-edged' and confused policy, as Stein (1992: 149ff.) has described it, gave Saddam Hussein no hint of any decisive action if Iraq invaded Kuwait. What difference does it make?[39] Indeed, what was at stake was bigger than just Saddam Hussein's 'awareness' of the United States' intentions and military might. As far as the Middle East is concerned the United States has a well-established policy to defend at any cost any intrusion into its sphere of interest (Brown, 1992; Telhami, 1994). What is more important is that the Iraqi leadership, as is clearly indicated through its public statements and the deduction of events, knew that the United States would oppose any Iraqi agenda in regard to the Gulf states and other pro-American states in the Middle East. The most common forms of explanation regarding the apparent confusions in strategy centre around the claim that it is not the concept of deterrence that is itself at fault, but rather the misunderstanding by many scientists of its logic and meaning (Williams, 1992). These analyses stress the need for linguistic and analytical clarity regarding the nature of deterrence itself. If this clarity is maintained, pundits argue, then the conflicts over deterrence strategies will disappear and we will achieve the understanding necessary for the desired goal. For this purpose, Glenn Snyder (1983: 123) sought to sort out this enigma by making a clear distinction between the concepts of 'deterrence' and 'defence', since it is the relationship between the two which, in turn, construct the theoretical core in the analysis of strategy. As he succinctly puts it, 'perhaps the crucial difference between deterrence and defence is that deterrence is primarily a peacetime objective, while defence is a wartime value'.

This distinction, while it has long been the principal assumption in the analysis of strategy, is in fact mundane. By the same token, it overshadows the analysis of deterrence. In line with this approach, and perhaps with more vividness, Barry Buzan (1987: 135) argues:

[o]ne of the principal sources of confusion – and therefore of dispute – in the debates about deterrence arises from the relationship between defence and deterrence … This difference has major implications for what is meant by the term deterrence. It has both definitional and political roots, and one needs to have a very clear understanding of it before trying to tackle the intricacies of the deterrence literature.

The commitment of the real (or assumed) defender – the United States – to the Gulf states and to Kuwait in particular was vague and lacked the credibility essential to convey clearly the deterrent intention.[40] Following the norms and traditions of conflict management in inter-Arab politics, the Kuwaiti government urged the United States to keep a low profile and to let Iraqi, Kuwaiti and other Arab leaders sort out their differences.[41] They are, after all, 'brothers'. In line with that, the Kuwaiti state political and social structure and the media pursued an incredible state of normalcy. Even the Kuwaiti armed forces and other security and police agencies were doing 'business as usual' until the Iraqi troops poured into Kuwait. What is worth noting, moreover, is that the Kuwaiti as well as other Arab media did not report the invasion when it took place. Arab readers and listeners restricted to Arab media were not aware of the invasion of Kuwait until 5 August – the third day!

On the other hand, Williams (1992: 75) concedes that the connection between defence/deterrence and rational/logical has actualized the problem of credibility. The division of deterrence between defence engendered by identification and deterrence with retaliation is a fundamental error. The solution to this problem, Williams suggests, is to identify deterrence with the actual ability to actively defend. That is, to use military power in a defensive or denial capacity. Evidence accumulated from a wide range of historical sources illustrates the factors that contribute to the failure of deterrence, but not enough is known about the conditions associated with its success. Lebow and Stein (1990, 1989) and Stein (1991) put forward what they term as 'reassurance theory' as a more effective substitute for the strategy of deterrence in solving and defusing conflicts that arise between states. They argue that 'reassurance' departs from a different set of assumptions than does deterrence. While reassurance presumes ongoing hostility, unlike deterrence it regards the source of that hostility not in the adversary's search for opportunity, but in its needs and weaknesses. Reassurance strategies include not only the attempt to reduce miscalculation through direct communications and verbal assurances, but also a broad set of strategies that adversaries can use to reduce the likelihood of the threat or use of force.[42]

However, if there is a power that can bridge dialogue whereby the sources of misunderstanding and confusion can be sorted out, and thus conflict or war averted, then the United States is definitely the wrong power. Mainstream Arabs held a view of the United States as being manipulated by international Zionism, partially in favour of Israel and definitely against Arab interests. There is also a firm belief in the Arab world that United States' policy in the Middle East is not only influenced by the much-biased pro-Israeli lobby in the US, but is also completely manipulated by Israel and its powerful friends in Washington. Indeed, US officials and policy-makers throughout the history of American involvement in the region have never missed the opportunity to confirm this perception that is widely held by Arabs.[43] April Glaspie testified before the United States Senate that the whole Iran-Contra affair had once again proved that the suspicion of American ill-intentions toward Iraq and the Arabs was justified (Neff, 1991; Karabell, 1995). She said that the Iraqi leadership

believed we gave their order of battle to the Iranians ... The Iraqis were very, very worried about that. They complained about it all the time. They made formal representations to other Arab League states and to the European states, asking them to come to us – we should be off the Iraqi back. Day after day, the Iraqi media since February – literally every day – was full of these accusations ... I think it was genuinely believed by Saddam Hussein ... Whether we consider it paranoid or not – and I do find it paranoid – they believe we are trying to overthrow the government.[44]

The VOA editorial is also seen through this prism. Thus for Iraq and many other countries the United States' involvement in the Middle East is an episode which led to mutual suspicion and outright hostility.[45] The Iraqi president did not miss the opportunity during his meeting with Glaspie to convey such suspicions and sentiments. The transcript of the meeting is mostly a 17-page record of Saddam Hussein's monologue, of which the first eight and a half pages consist only of his remarks. In clear terms, Saddam Hussein focused on what he suspected as a hidden plot by Israel and the Jewish lobby.[46]

It was clear to us that certain parties in the United States – not necessarily the President, I mean, but certain parties who had links with intelligence and with the State Department, and I don't necessarily mean the Secretary of

State himself – and not like the fact we had liberated our land [from Iran]. Some parties began to prepare papers entitled 'Who will take over from Saddam Hussein?' They began to contact Gulf states to make them worried about Iraq, so they would not give economic aid to Iraq. We have evidence of these activities ... We do not accept threats from anyone because we do not threaten anyone. But we say clearly that we hope the US will not suffer from too many illusions, and that it will look for new friends rather than add to the number of its enemies.

Only one day before the meeting with Ambassador Glaspie on 25 July 1990, the Iraqi president reportedly voiced that he felt 'betrayed' by the deployment of the US forces in the Gulf and the military manoeuvres and exercises with the armed forces of the United Arab Emirates.[47] In the light of this perceived threat, Iraq saw the reluctance of the Gulf states to help it financially as part of an all-encompassing conspiracy, the roots of which Saddam Hussein later called 'that black conspiracy spearheaded by the rulers of Kuwait against Iraq'. Saddam Hussein perceived an attempt to manipulate the oil market in order to keep down prices and starve Iraq of resources.

On 11 September 1990, Iraq published the transcript of Saddam Hussein's meeting with Ambassador Glaspie. Even though the transcript was edited in such a way as to make it different in essential aspects from that published by the United States State Department more than a month earlier, Ms Glaspie and the American officials did not dispute the Iraqi version (or rather comment on its authenticity). Moreover, it contained no mention of the most important element in the Saddam Hussein–Glaspie conversation, namely, the emphasis on the conditional quality of Saddam Hussein's assurances that Iraq would not initiate any military actions against Kuwait if the Kuwaiti government submitted to Iraq's demands for debts forgiveness and the issue of oil quotas within OPEC.[48] The Iraqi manuscript of the famous meeting of 25 July 1990 between Ms Glaspie and Saddam Hussein is a good example in this regard. The emphasis on the conditional quality of Saddam Hussein's assurances to Glaspie regarding Kuwait's compliance with the Iraqi demands (that if Kuwait did not abide by Iraqi demands then Iraq would resort to violence, as was clearly stated by Saddam's public statement), did not appear in the US State Department's version, while it was very clear in the Iraqi version. It was in fact the very same text, since the US State Department has declined to comment on the accuracy of the text, which implies that the Iraqi text was not disputed.[49]

At this point, all the ambiguities and indifference in American policy towards the region were now surfacing. The so called 'constructive engagement', which was aimed at persuading Iraq to lean towards more realistic and Western-oriented political behaviour, became an illusive endeavour. American alarmism arose through their endemic misreading of the views of states and leaders in the Middle East. The culpability of the United States and the West in this was their ambivalence over issues such as Iraq's drive towards the acquisition of a lethal arsenal, their tolerance of the Ba'athist government's maltreatment of the political opposition and other ethnic groups, and the outright threats that Iraq openly demonstrated to the littoral Gulf states by associating their rulers with the American-Zionist conspiracy against Iraq and the Arabs. By tolerating these actions, the Western governments and, in particular, the United States, might have hoped that Iraq could be persuaded to acknowledge the need for political reform and moderate regional policies.

The Ba'ath government was convinced that the Soviet Union's irreversible decline from its superpower status had left the United States as the only power capable of jeopardizing Iraqi political ambitions for hegemony within the Arab order. The United States had never before engaged in a direct conflict within the Arab order or the Middle East the way it did in the Gulf crisis, so any attempt to combat an Iraqi scheme in the region would happen either via direct intervention or through pitting its Israeli or Arab 'lackeys' against Iraq. The Iraqi leadership, however, had good reason to anticipate such an attitude because despite the harsh criticism of Iraq following the Bazoft affair and the gassing of the civilian Kurds in northern Iraq, the US and the West had conducted business as usual with Iraq. In fact, the Ba'ath government had been puzzled by the international reaction to the execution of the British (of Iranian origin) journalist Ferzad Bazoft, compared with the gassing and killing of many thousands of Kurds two years earlier. In fact the Bush administration did not fail to signal its keen interest in cultivating bilateral relations. The US administration was keen to emphasize its interest in promoting bilateral relations with Iraq, and a group of five US senators – Robert Dole, Alan Simpson, Howard Metzenbaum, James McClure and Frank Murkowski – visited Baghdad on 12 April 1990. The declared aim of the trip was to denounce Iraq's quest for chemical and nuclear weapons at a time when the US Congress was probing the possibility of imposing sanctions on Iraq for the reasons stated above and Iraq's record of human rights violations. However, they privately reassured the Iraqi leader of the United States' support. Senator Dole assured Saddam Hussein in their meeting on the Iraqi city of Mousol that the

commentator for the VOA ... was removed ... Please allow me to say that only 12 hours earlier President Bush has assured me that he wants better relations and that the U.S. government wants better relations with Iraq. We believe – and we are leaders in the U.S. Congress – that the Congress also does not represent Bush or the government. I assume that President Bush will oppose sanctions, and he might veto them, unless something provocative were to happen, or something of that sort. (Cited in Sifry and Cerf, 1991: 119–21)

Ambassador Glaspie, who accompanied the delegation, had added that '[as] the Ambassador of the U.S., I am certain that this is the policy of the U.S.'. Senator Alan Simpson, after assuring the Iraqi president in a friendly tone of their support and how this support for Iraq would cost them popularity inside the United States, told Saddam Hussein that

I believe that your problems lie with the Western media and not with the U.S. government. As long as you are isolated from the media, the press – and it is a haughty and pampered press; they all consider themselves political geniuses, that is, the journalists do; they are very cynical – what I advise is that you invite them to come here and see for themselves.[50]

Later in April 1990 the US assistant secretary of state for near Eastern affairs, John Kelly, sought to block a congressional initiative to impose sanctions on Iraq by telling the House's Foreign Affairs Committee that such a move would be counterproductive to the US national interest and that the administration would not 'see economic and trade sanctions imposed at this point'. In June 1990, two months later, Kelly told the same committee that 'although Iraq had not relented in its quest for non-conventional weapons and continued to violate human rights, it nevertheless took "some modest steps in the right direction"'.[51] When the Iraqi leader firmly asserted Iraq's determination to ensure that Kuwait did not cheat on its oil quota, Glaspie sympathetically conceded that my own estimate after 25 years of serving in the area is that your aims should receive strong support from your brother Arabs. This was an issue for the Arabs to solve among themselves and the United States had 'no opinion on inter-Arab disputes such as your border dispute with Kuwait' ... and Secretary of State Baker had directed our official spokesman to reiterate this stand.[52]

When Glaspie finally asked Saddam Hussein, 'in the spirit of friendship, not of confrontation', what his intentions were regarding Kuwait, he reassured her of his preference for a peaceful solution to the dispute: 'We are not going to do anything until we meet with the Kuwaitis. When we meet and when we see that there is hope, then nothing will happen.' However, he stressed, since Kuwait's 'economic war' was depriving Iraq's children of the milk they drink, Iraq could not be expected to sit idle for much longer. 'If we are unable to find a solution, then it will be natural that Iraq will not accept death, even though wisdom is above everything else.' As a matter of fact, Ms Glaspie followed the directive of the State Department in settling an Arab/Arab dispute, which the Kuwaiti government urged the US administration to do.

At this point one may argue that the Iraqi leadership was convinced from historical experience of the United States in the region that the VOA editorial on 15 February 1990 was an attempt to undermine Iraq. Saddam Hussein simply put it within a context of long-standing attempts from the United States and its Zionist and Arabs 'lackeys' to plot against Iraq and the Arab nation. Having surveyed the Iraqi–American interrelationship and given the history, or rather the historicity, of the United States' association with the Middle East, as conceived by Iraq and other Arabs, the situation in the Arab world was escalating and explosive.[53] The question here is whether reassurance by the United States that they did not have any hostile intentions towards Iraq could have stayed and prevented the invasion of Kuwait. Let us round up this discussion from three different aspects, whereby it becomes clear that the strategy of deterrence and/or reassurance – as a normal and directly communicated political and diplomatic intercourse – had been a difficult task to perform as far as Iraq's pre-invasion behaviour is concerned.

First, traditional deterrence and reassurance theories stress the importance of credibility purely in terms of 'objective' national interests, and in executing the threat if necessary. In that sense, the 'seamless web of significance' in regard to the support offered by Arabs from all walks of life all over the Arab world would be invisible and meaningless. Such support was usually taken for granted, since it emanates from fraternal solidarity with the leader who challenged what is to the Arabs the evil triangle of the West/United States/Zionism. The discursive formation of the Arabs of the firmly held conviction (whether from Muslim fundamentalist or secular nationalist) that the West is immoral and corrupt is a factor to be assessed in this context. After all, this support constitutes the source from where foreign behaviour becomes legitimized by Arab leaders who seek to mobilize the Arab grass-roots – or simply to provide the backing for their decisions to go to war, however calculated or miscalculated. Judging from the way Saddam Hussein approached regional politics and from the tone of his speeches in the spring and summer of 1990, the Iraqi president intended to exploit the *status quo* and to present his leadership to the Arab world as the new Abdul Nassir. At this point, the apparent show of strength, together with a carefully chosen formulaic and metaphoric language of appeal to Arabs, made Saddam Hussein very popular in the Arab streets, with the intelligentsia and among certain radical political circles. The Iraqi president resorted increasingly to threats and pledges (i.e. 'burn Israel', and that the Israeli aggression not only against Iraq, but against all Arab states, would be severely punished), that turned out to have a powerful appeal in the culture of social and political despair that overshadowed the Arab political atmosphere. Every speech following the Bazoft affair in March 1990[54] was carefully couched in language aimed at larger audiences outside Iraq but within the Arab hemisphere. It was a pattern reminiscent of the 1950s and 1960s when Abdul Nassir had appealed over the heads of governments directly to the Arab peoples in the streets. The TV live coverage throughout the *Mashreq* of various Arab leaders summits with Saddam Hussein in the centre using language that was meant to challenge the United States and Israel had only strengthened such an image. As an Iraqi passer-by put it, the whole atmosphere seemed to suggest that 'Nassir made promises, but could not deliver. But, when Saddam speaks, he acts.'[55] When the cheering grass-roots population in the Arab cities reacted to Saddam Hussein's condemnations of Zionism and imperialism, the Iraqi president ostensibly sought to legitimize Iraqi political behaviour by these demonstrations of support, most notably in Jordan, Algeria, Yemen and Sudan. Along with the threat to Israel and warnings to the United

States, the Iraqi leader sharpened the tone against the conservative Gulf rulers. All this took place within an atmosphere of enthusiasm in highly publicized demonstrations, all in support of Iraq and, inevitably, of Saddam Hussein's quest for political and personal hegemony.

This reality justifies our examining the degree of knowledge of the decision-makers about one another's societies and their utilization of this factor, as well as the consequences of their ignorance of the strength of public opinion. It is often the case that policy-makers, whether in political or military spheres, focus far more on public opinion and in whipping up support in favour of military campaigns than on the political objective of promoting the conceived national interest. Indeed, it was these aspects that commanded more attention for both the United States and Iraq, though in different ways. The United States had experienced the so-called 'Vietnam syndrome' and there was formidable public opinion against violent conflict. This is what Saddam Hussein probably had in mind when it was reported that he had said to Ambassador Glaspie during their meeting on 25 July 1990: 'yours is a society that cannot tolerate 10,000 dead soldiers'. Within the Arab world the perception of external threats often automatically implicated the United States and Zionism.[56]

The underlying differences that often cause misconceptions, namely the discursive regime of identity (i.e. self-image) and cultural values, constitutes an important factor in the analysis of foreign policy decisions. Hence intentions signalled by the United States to deter Iraq would be a remote, if not impossible, task. Successful deterrence requires convincing adversaries not to undertake actions because their costs would be far greater than their benefits and any threat would be unacceptable. Deterrence will only work if one side can successfully signal to the adversary this simple message. This being so, it was even more difficult to determine just what constituted an acceptable cost for Iraq and the Iraqi leadership, bearing in mind the nature of American knowledge about Iraq. The lack of experience in dealing with a certain adversary (e.g. Iraq versus US), as opposed to the learning that comes from long-term dealings with another adversary (e.g. US versus Soviets), complicates not only the way their particular leaders deal with one another, but also inhibits the pundits' efforts to understand the nature of the relationship between the two rival states. This was especially true of the mainstream literature that saw Iraq as classical Third World tyranny (spiced with Arabophobia) and the United States as a value-free construct within the Arab world. Thus, the discursive regime of Arabism and the whole issues of discourses and perceptions, which otherwise were of fundamental importance in so far as the Iraqi invasion of Kuwait was concerned, were passed over in silence.[57]

Second, it is often the case that violence is practised with reference to a spatial as well as a time context. The act of violence retains symbolic and, indeed, metaphorical aspects that are akin to the object and the occasion of violence (Norton, 1988: 176–7). Therefore to identify the meaning, the significance and the implication of violence entails paying attention to history and to the evolution of political discourse and the nature of the myths that underlie the political and societal institutions. Gestures and signs that associate enterprises of violence with known mythic and historic symbols are usually invoked to grant them legitimacy and absolution through association. This is a dimension of fundamental importance, especially when the political institutions are fragile and incoherent. The meaning of the object in an act of violence is more often symbolic than literal. The object may derive its meaning formally, from its office or official significance, or informally, from its place in the network of meanings that form the cultural as well as the political discourse. Even though war can be initiated by rational conduct, conducting or managing a war quite often becomes an irrational enterprise.[58] Thus it is usually the case that decision-makers often find themselves in a situation where, against their wishes, they are obliged to contemplate war (Nicholson, 1992: 139–40). Therefore, the awareness of the political leaders, or what is known as the 'psychological disposition' – a cognitive understanding of the scale of devastation of the weaponry they and others possess – is an issue of an outstanding significance. The lack of awareness by both Iraq and the United States of the extent of the destruction that modern weapons can cause explains why Iraq's and Kuwait's infrastructures suffered extensively as a consequence of the Gulf War, not to mention the hundreds of thousands of dead. Conversely, that same awareness is what has so far prevented a nuclear disaster between the superpowers.

3 THE INSTITUTIONAL PERSPECTIVE

INTRODUCTION

The aim of this chapter is to discuss the role of the Iraqi polity in explaining the invasion of Kuwait. Its basis is an acceptance of the widely held assumption linking states' domestic instability to their international behaviour, so that the chilling Iraqi domestic state of affairs can be seen as one of the factors motivating the invasion of Kuwait. In line with this argument, Iraq's domestic environment – a crisis of legitimacy reflected in the regime's alienation from society which, in turn, provoked it to resort to exaggerated arms build-up programmes – disposed the regime to certain violent foreign policies. Beyond the issue of security/insecurity or economic hardship lies the intense relationship between the Iraqi state and the Arab order, the result of the ambiguous identity of the state of Iraq and which has led Iraqi regimes, since 1922, to seek to identify themselves with Arabism. The ideological affiliation with Arabism, therefore, is as significant as the impact of the domestic reality. Authority and governability, in an 'ideal-type' Third World state, are usually challenged by the political regime's narrow social base, though this problem is often bridged by facilitating cyclical political change through wars and *coups d'état*. Studies on foreign policy decision-making have asserted the causal link between authoritarian political systems and violent foreign policy behaviour (Korany, 1983; Korany and Dessouki, 1984; Morgan and Campbell, 1991). Domestic political and societal structures can be both sources of strength, liability or uncertainty for foreign policy decision-making, and in the case of Third World states, domestic instability and the regimes' lack of legitimacy often provide the motivation for foreign policy ventures.

After all, in probing decision-making processes special attention should be devoted not only to states as metaphysical abstractions, or to governments, or even to such broadly labelled institutions as 'the Executive', but also to institutionalized ideas and beliefs. This is of fundamental importance in highlighting the association between these forms of belief and the behaviour of the specific human decision-makers who actually shape governmental policy. The Iraqi decision to invade Kuwait is better illuminated through the following two aspects. First is the overlapping identity of the Iraqi state/regime and the imperative of nation-building, coupled with the difficulties encountered by successive Iraqi governments since the foundation of the modern Iraqi state to integrate different groups of the population into a modern nation-state. Second is the vertical character of Arab society and politics – the persistence of family, clan, and regional allegiances, all of which are elements in the modern political structure of Arab states. An understanding of this may shed light on the way Ba'athism deteriorated from being a vision of Arab awakening to being a degraded, sectarian one-man rule, as well as how this state of affairs affected decision-making and the way in which the invasion of Kuwait occurred.

The institutional approach taken aims to display in a comparative way the disparities and distinctive attributes of the way institutions are viewed in the Arab setting. As thoroughly organized and regularly routinized constellations of the body politic, political institutions are regarded as secondary factors in the politics of Iraq and the Arab world in general. Instead, institutions as concrete manifestation of cultural and societal realities are seen to exert a great influence on the decision-making process. It is the 'discursive formations' (Foucault, 1972: 32–9)[1] derived from these cultural and societal pan-Arab institutions that often become indispensable political factors in periods during which Arabs are in conflict with outsiders. In this case, even though Iraq acted within the traditional balance-of-power logic and wanted to maximize its economic and strategic leverage in a clear pursuit of hegemony in the Gulf and the Middle Eastern region, considering only these factors would leave the analysis incomplete. What matters in the case of wars and conflicts between states are not only what objectives motivate actors, but also how the actors set about achieving their objectives. The role of the Ba'ath Party and the Iraqi state in the invasion of Kuwait should therefore be examined within the wider context of inter-Arab politics.

THE INSTITUTIONAL PERSPECTIVE: A THEORETICAL OUTLINE

Political institutions[2] are designed to generate, organize and apply collective power in order to maintain social order and stability, defend society against external threats, resolve disputes and dispense justice. Political institutions are 'epiphenomena; that is they derive from social processes and especially those that crystallise in a society's pattern of stratification' (Gould, 1987: 291). All forms of institutional practice and bureaucratic organization are produced by the history and totality of the social experience of society. Political institutions, moreover, constitute the channels that bear the complex varieties of influences (e.g., the types of authority and power relationships) that ensue from the state as a social organization (ibid.). Political institutions and their routines are embedded in the political discourses and societal norms that are reflected in the way decisions are formulated. Over time, they become 'taken for granted by the people who are affected by them' (Keohane, 1988: 389). The character of institutions shapes the outcome of the decision-making process by reflecting the way political power is exercised, and by showing how the policy-making elite communicate and ultimately execute policy decisions, 'values, norms and [how] perspectives vary across cultures, and [how] such variations affect the efficacy of institutional arrangements' (ibid). The impact of institutions on the decision-making process can take two forms. First, an institution like the Ba'ath Party is taken here to be the *de facto* Iraqi political system. As such, the Party has a causal role both in contributing to the social and political changes and conditions that precede conflicts, on the one hand, and in the way conflicts are steered and managed, on the other. Second, key institutional structures of the political system shape the processes, procedures and other factors that affect the way decisions are formulated and executed. For example, the dominance of a closed, secretive and withdrawn elite, guarded by security services and surrounded by intimates (usually by kinship), generates patterns of oligopolistic decision-making. In addition to the distance between the ruling elite and the population, there is also another sharper and wider gap between this elite and the highly stratified and complicated global system. This is might give us a clue to the

incongruence in role conception and [how Arab leaders'] performance are sudden changes, zigzagging, and improvisation in foreign policy behaviour.

In some cases, this is caused by despair at the gap between capabilities and objectives. In others, erratic behaviour is due to an impatient leadership's incomprehension of the complexity of international politics, and the confusion between national dreams (which are by definitions of a long-range nature) and objectives that must be related to operational capabilities. (Korany and Dessouki, 1984: 328–9)

This state of affairs shapes future processes of political transformation. The chain of cause and effect that characterizes Iraqi political life would be as follows: an authoritarian political culture throws up authoritarian leaders who, in turn, strengthen and contribute to the continuity of authoritarian political culture by incremental adaptation. The outcome of the decision-making process, Koelble (1995: 242) argues, is inevitably affected by this political situation through the interaction between the intended consequences (e.g., formulating policy decisions) and the unintended consequences (e.g., authoritarian political culture).[3] The question, then, is how human choices and social preferences are formed, obtained, evolved and mediated by these social and institutional arrangements? Research on foreign policy-making, international conflicts and warfare frequently asserts the impossibility of grasping and comprehending such overlapping and complicated events simply through rational-actor-oriented and functional approaches.[4] While some concerns are evinced concerning how institutions emerge, most of the analyses treat rules and procedures as exogenous determinants of political behaviour. Approaches sensitive to the discourses from which institutions emanated are more promising for the prospect of understanding human choices and their social meanings (Pasic, 1996). The Weberians' emphasis on cultural constructs offers appropriate procedures for a scientific understanding of human and social phenomena.[5] Weber (1968: 404–8) – and later his acolytes (e.g., Geertz, 1980) – conceptualize culture as an internally emanated and interpretive symbolic universe that responds to powerful ideational and discursive needs, for example, religious idioms, ideas, and identities to define the essence and the fate of human collectivities by virtue of mythical schemes (e.g., Weber, 1968: 11–12). For the purposes of this book, the significance and impact of cultural constructs (i.e., identity formation) needs to be examined within domains that lie beyond issues of rational conduct (Shweder, 1986). Similarly, an examination of their effect on social institutions needs to extend beyond the narrow concern with economic systems and cover issues of broader social and political concerns, such as the problem of identity and difference, and the question of governance and what it means for both rulers and the ruled.[6] It is important, therefore, to distinguish between institutions as a legal or formal set of rules and their concrete manifestation in social and political realities, just as government can be distinguished from the state.[7]

It is, therefore, necessary to be aware that the political process in the Arab world differs from that in the West. In capitalist liberal democracies, political institutions are inscribed and designed to perform and carry out the wishes of often tolerant majorities, but in the Arab world the purpose of political institutions is to facilitate the constant unfolding or revelation of a popular consensus, regardless of the dimension of legality. In understanding political institutions, one is required to examine the societal values they embody and the culture they manifest. In the Arab/Islamic setting social values are Platonic – that is absolute.[8] This is a dimension reflected in the lack of pragmatism in dealing politically with the outside world (Barakat, 1984: 328). Arab leaders who find themselves in conflict with Israel or the West act as if they are working in the name of the Arab nation. Indeed, from a political standpoint an Arab leader cannot make any concession or give-and-take in an outright manner with foreign powers on issues that are held to be the concern of the Arab nation.[9]

This divergence between the Arab and Western views of institutions goes even deeper. The Arab perceives a single community of faith and language as the ultimate political and social objective within which many ideologies and movements seek fulfilment (e.g., Ba'athism, Nassirism and Islamism). This reality contrasts sharply with the Western emphasis on competing but mutually adjusting political factions. In the West politics has a taste and pattern of controlled conflict that the Arabs reject, even abhor, as being destructive to the community (Lewis, 1984: 9ff.). During the tense days before the Iraqi army marched into Kuwait, Arab leaders and the Arab media pretended that nothing was going on, and a reader restricted to Arabic newspapers would not even have known that Kuwait had been invaded as the media (and particularly the press), including the Kuwaiti media, were silent and did not report openly on the events. People had to read and listen to the Western media to know what was going on. Known for its skilled diplomacy and having always trodden carefully between the greater and often unfriendly powers of the Gulf region (Assiri, 1990), but still in conformity with pan-Arab norms, Kuwait insisted, at least publicly, that the whole matter was between Arab brethren and had to be solved within such a framework.

In liberal democracies (e.g., Western polities), politics depends on a network of abstractions that people seldom encounter in the real world. The concept of the state is one such abstraction (Turner, 1994: 23ff.). The ideal-type Western modern state was historically grafted on to the culturally coherent ethno-religious or ethno-linguistic political entities called nations (Gellner, 1983; Anderson, 1991). In the Arab world, however, the nation-state came about as a deformed creation of Western colonial policies and their direct control over and organization of non-Western societies. Following independence, their status as nation-states meant no more than membership of the United Nations. In reality, they had yet to build, as required by the theory, a truly sovereign state and a 'national' society out of a myriad of linguistic, cultural and religious pluralities operating within their new-found states (Sheth, 1989: 379–82). Further, in liberal democracies abstract values serve as the basis for the formation and regulation of political institutions in the state. The political systems are organized and function in accordance with a defined set of rules. The legitimacy of political actions is assessed according to abstract and ideal as well as concrete principles, and society is sanctioned by a secular contract embodying human-made laws that provide rules and procedures, and also legitimize authority. In addition, individuals are presumed to be acting on behalf of and for the good and benefit of themselves (Turner, 1994: 24). The organizing principles of Arab societies, on the other hand, are firmly embedded in a concrete social context where the family and the network of kinship are the Archimedean point to which individuals always relate themselves. Even the idea of political action originating with the individual is regarded as abstract in the extreme since it implies that the social environment in which he or she is supposed to act has been disregarded. Arab states and their polities are also organized according to radically different principles from those in the West. Politics and power relationships are defined not by abstract values, but by kinship and the regulation of social relations. Identity and loyalty are determined by one's place in a tight-knit, vertically structured social network, and it is the control over that network that guarantees the power basis for the political elite and the holders of power.[10] Within this political order, where kinship is the principle that organizes political relations and determines identity, control over the means of production is central to the political authority (Barakat, 1984: 219–24, 1993; Sharabi, 1988; Al-Azmeh, 1993: 71ff.). Furthermore, in Arab societies individual action is sanctioned and legitimized through two closely related premises, namely the god-given law and the immediate social network (usually kinship) that encloses the individual. The point of reference that Arab leaders usually consult in cases of conflict (including inter-Arab conflicts) is to require conformity with traditions, i.e. that actions conform to a familiar and accepted social pattern and to cultural norms (Barakat, 1984: 37ff., 1993; Sharabi, 1988). When Iraq invaded and annexed Kuwait, Arab leaders who condemned the Iraqi action did not do so on the basis of international law or the United Nations Charter. Instead, they referred to analogies drawn from Islamic history, the Prophet's teachings and practices, and quotations from the Qur'an to enforce their view of the invasion and annexation.

But, in a modern world where certain cultural modes (i.e., Western rationality) exert and dictate the power on others unilaterally, Arab societies today exist in a state not only of social but also political turmoil, in which the whole of social life – the body politic, economic and cultural activities – is changing more in reaction (under pressure) to external influences than to processes and mechanisms within the society itself. The state emerges as an artificial entity that becomes disarticulated in the face of any political crisis (e.g., Algeria, Iraq, Somalia and Sudan, to mention only a few). Politics becomes a reign of coercion and direct administrative intervention by regimes, rather than rule through mutual consent. The state itself becomes the embodiment of a civil group (e.g., the Ba'athist polities in Syria and Iraq, Libya and all the Gulf states) based on a social web of cousins and friends of friends (Batatu, 1985; Al-Azmeh, 1993: 72–3). Such circumstances constrain the choices open to the elite by limiting the information available and the knowledge necessary to formulate and execute foreign policy decisions.

In a country like Iraq, the government in reality provides the leader with unlimited and unchecked power. Indeed, the personality cult is a phenomenon of Middle Eastern politics. In the highly personalized politics of the region, where leaders often count more than state institutions, the famous dictum '*L'état c'est moi*' has extraordinary political implications. Yet – and even by Third World standards –

Saddam Hussein carried the idea to an incredible level of propaganda and compulsive flattery (Al-Khalil, 1989: 110–24).[11] Foreign policy decision-making is the exclusive monopoly of the top leader. In such a state, parliaments 'when they exist, ... act merely as a rubber stamp for executive decisions' (Dawisha, 1977: 66). The leading political party is a *de facto* state bureaucracy, and exercises a monopoly of violence that performs primarily by mobilizing the citizens and legitimizing the leader to them. Iraq's deeply segmented ethnic groups and divided society, its geographic vulnerability, and its unstable political institutions characterized by considerable violence, all are factors that influence decision-making in fundamental ways. This is in line with the assumption accepted at the start of the chapter that links states' internal instability and their international behaviour. The emphasis, then, is on the importance of domestic sources for foreign policy decision-making and how, owing to their highly destabilized domestic environment, authoritarian states usually seek foreign (often violent) engagements. This could take two forms: either as a simple process of projecting one's own fears on the others, or as a means of diverting attention away from the internal problems. Added to these is the prevalent factor in the ability of Arab leaders to disguise their own domestic disturbances in Arabism and the fact that the grass-roots cherish such Arabic sentiments.

Consequently, going beyond the focus on individual actors it is important to take into account the character of the state. As a social organization, the domestic politics of the state determine how it interacts with and reacts to external political pressures. The role of the institutions in the formulation and execution of foreign policy objectives will reflect the place of the leader in the political landscape, and the leader alone, although maybe as part of a political system, translates societal values to the outside world. As the prime representative of the state, the importance of his/her position places him/her under enormous pressure and scrutiny in a crisis situation (Robinson, 1994: 418). Further, Robinson (1994: 426) argues, what is at stake is how actors project their political commitments and seek to fulfil them. Such commitments reflect the political salience of the state, its political culture, its relation with its adversaries, and the way it defines its international prestige. Robinson (1994: 426–7) also notes that:

crisis involves issues perceived to be of great national importance. The implications and dangers of manipulating or exploiting such issues in the pursuit of foreign policy should not be underestimated. For an unstable regime or government the crisis issue may become a matter of life and death.

The Iraqi invasion of Kuwait and the crisis that followed have been a matter of life or death for the Iraqi leadership. If they succeeded and incorporated Kuwait in what had to be the political core of the Arab nation, then Saddam Hussein would realize his dream of being the Bismarck of the Arabs. But if the entire plans of the Iraqi leadership were shattered, then the existence not only of the Ba'ath regime but also of the Iraqi state as such would be in great peril. It was the latter fate that lay in wait for them.

THE OVERLAPPING OF IDENTITIES

States are embedded in a myriad of institutions (Barnett, 1993: 273; Keohane, 1988; Wendt, 1992). In understanding the values and norms within which political institutions operate, history is a useful tool. It provides important clues to an understanding of the evolution of authority, power and legitimacy, and also of how individuals conceive their roles as political actors. Institutions, Keohane (1988: 286) writes:

are embedded in practices. In modern world politics, the most important practice is that of sovereignty. To understand institutions and institutional change in world politics, it is necessary to understand not only how specific institutions are formulated, change, and die, but how their evolution is affected by the practice of sovereignty.

All Arab states put special emphasis on their Arab identity. Modern Arab history has witnessed that all states, regimes and ordinary people experience that the state's identity is interwoven with that of pan-Arabism. This process takes place with various degrees of intensity, but one of the preconditions for it is an Arab regime's lack of internal political legitimacy, a reality that motivates that regime to obtain its legitimacy instead from a pan-Arab domain. Arab leaders who experience social, economic or political troubles at home always seek pan-Arab legitimacy,[12] but both Abdul Nassir (throughout his political career) and Saddam Hussein (primarily during the Gulf crisis of 1990–91)[13] have been exceptionally successful in attracting such support. Endemic domestic instability and a political culture of violence have been the prime reason for all Iraqi regimes (who are of Sunni origin) since the inception of the modern Iraqi state in 1922 to associate themselves with pan-Arabism and its paramount question – that of Palestine (Eppel, 1994). The decision to invade Kuwait can be seen as an outcome of that domestic instability, even though the Iraqi leadership sought to acquire pan-Arab legitimacy as a cover for their otherwise egoistic power maximizing policies. In short, the eagerness of the Iraqi regime to relate itself to the idea of Arabism (to legitimize the Kuwait decision) came about as a consequence of the tenuous nature of the state and its domestic constraints (that motivated the decision) and its failure to develop a durable national community out of the myriad Iraqi ethnic groups and their religious diversity. During the Gulf crisis, Iraq claimed that the rulers of the Gulf states were agents of American imperialism and international Zionism. Having said that, there are two points that might illustrate the interrelationships between human choices and their social meanings and the issue of overlapping identities between citizens of states and adherence to a pan-Arab community that have always been an important factor in the analysis of the foreign policy behaviour of Arab leaders.

The first point is related to the fact that the Arab peoples are highly politicized (due to certain historical and political circumstances) and, therefore, usually have a decisive role in pressing, urging or legitimizing the foreign policy decisions of their leaders. They can be mobilized almost spontaneously and without much effort by regimes, though their political activism cannot be considered as a contribution to open and free public debate, nor to the process of consolidating a civil society in a liberal democratic sense. Rather it reflects an Arab collective request for self-definition in the face of what they perceive as the enemy and an evildoer. By the same token, it is a phenomenon related to the social and political alienation of politically illegitimate authoritarian regimes and their politically indifferent populations.[14] This is the paradox of the Arab people's involvement in politics: passivity and activism.

Passivity refers to the individual's lack of opportunity to influence the political process – deciding power transfer or rotations, for example the peaceful removal of political elites that have lost the confidence of the people. If the citizens are to be active and aware of the need to preserve political freedoms there needs to be open sociopolitical debate that reflects the coherence of a civil society with firmly established political institutions. The lack of coherent and stable mechanisms of power relationships is explained by the long history of authoritarian political rule that puts emphasis on obedience to rulers in order to avoid anarchy.[15]

Activism refers to the other side of the coin, namely, that the very same politically passive people have demonstrated a colossal show of support for Arab rulers who are in conflict with non-Arab actors. Paradoxically, the people have always played a decisive role in times of crisis, especially when a non-Arab actor is involved. Examples abound: the Suez crisis in 1956; when Nassir declared his resignation after his defeat in the 1967 war; the second Gulf crisis, where the Arab peoples played a major role in the political process by giving a sense of legitimacy to their leader's action. The people also support leaders' policies – whether right or wrong, just or unjust, planned or gratuitous – in so far as these symbolize a sense of strength and resistance to the West and Zionism, or any other imagined or constructed enemy. This is similar to the 'national identity dynamic', the sociopsychological dynamic by which a 'mass national public may be mobilised, in relation to its international environment' (Bloom, 1990: 79; Barnett, 1993: 284). The history of the Arab–Israeli conflict, the rise of pan-Arabism as a challenge to Western dominance in the Arab world and, most importantly, our case study – the invasion of Kuwait – are all part of a pattern that fits into this framework. The demonstrations and the impressive show of support for Iraq and Saddam Hussein by ordinary people, intellectuals, interest groups and Muslim fundamentalist movements throughout the Arab and Muslim worlds on the eve of the Gulf crisis was an essential ingredient in the decision to invade. Saddam Hussein was supported by these different groups not because he had violated the Charters of both the Arab League and the United Nations by invading a helpless and much weaker neighbour state, but because for all those Arabs Saddam Hussein and Iraq symbolized a spirit of resistance against and, ultimately, revenge on a much disliked enemy of the Arab nation – morally corrupt West and its protégé, Zionism.

The second point is related to the meaning of the state in the day-to-day life of ordinary Arabs and the invisibility of its presence in the discourse of politics. While the Arabic *Maghreb* (North Africa, Libya, Tunisia, Algeria, Morocco and Mautania) is relatively homogeneous in religious terms and while identification with the state does not necessarily contradict with ethnic origin (i.e., Arab and Berber) and religion, the *Mashreq* (the Arab world from Egypt eastward to the Arabian Peninsula, Mesopotamia – Iraq – and the Fertile Crescent – Lebanon, Jordan, Palestine and Syria), with Iraq as the prime exemplar, is 'an anthropologist's paradise' (Dawisha, 1990: 284). It is inhabited by many diverse ethnic and religious groups with unmistakably parochial communal loyalties that are often in conflict with the loyalty demanded by the state. Thus, the projected image of the Arab regional system is one of bewildering complexity (Hermassi, 1987: 76–80; Bayomi, 1995: 14). Every political crisis in the Arab world reveals the fragility of the state and its incoherent political institutions. Since 1936, when the Iraqi officer Bakr Sidqi masterminded the first ever *coup d'état* in the Arab world, it is estimated by Salinger and Laurent (1991: 223) 'that there have been eighty-one *coups d'état* in fourteen Arab countries, twenty-four of them successful. The two countries with the most *coups d'état* have been Iraq and Syria: thirty-two attempts, fourteen successes.' However, since 1970 many Arab regimes have remained in power and have created stable, or rather solid, organizational structures around them, though many observers would contest the impression of stability and would claim that 'the state is a house of cards, its stability more apparent than real' (Luciani, 1990: xiii). The modern history of the Arab states has witnessed frequent attempts by regimes to achieve cooperation, integration and unification, but these attempts have often rapidly collapsed due to poor planning/execution and, more fundamentally, owing to the lack of the preconditions of the process of integration. Despite the pan-Arab and/or pan-Islamic vocation of Arab states it is ironic that they pursue a policy of isolation that 'makes it difficult to cross an inter-Arab border, to call another Arab city by telephone, to get a work permit here, an export licence there, and a travel visa to almost everywhere' (ibid.; Barakat, 1984: 54).

It is at this juncture that the question of the 'Arab peoples' as a national group (suprastate) belonging to one civilizational *imagined community* (no matter if they are exposed, or merely subjects of absolutism[16]) as opposed to being citizens of state (Iraq, Jordan, Syria etc.) comes into play. When nationhood and affection for a nation extends to repudiating that nation's own ideal, then it becomes an issue of use and misuse of political power. The irony is that Arab nationhood is firmly implanted in the minds of individual Arabs, who, if the occasion arose, would fight their governments on a very localistic basis

– be it based on tribal, ethnic or even regional allegiances. This situation is most evident in Iraq among the states in the *Mashreq*. The social, ethnic or even political groups that are opposed to various central governments and are able to express political opposition to the state under propitious conditions are, in their turn, using the same Islamic/pan-Arab symbolism (Halliday, 1995). The example of the Iraqi Shi'ite Islamists fierce opposition to the Ba'ath is a case in point. They are as hostile to the West and Zionism as to the Ba'ath itself, for the equilibrium between loyalty to a territorial sovereign state and the civilizational 'imagined community' that must be guaranteed first and foremost by the state is being disrupted and corrupted by the very same state. Because the leaders of Arab states have exalted political goals that stretch beyond the borders of their states and, paradoxically, are required to aim at such goals for the sake of their legitimacy, it is within this context that we should approach the role of the Iraqi polity in the invasion of Kuwait. Considerable progress has been made towards maintaining and respecting the reciprocity of the sovereignty and the integrity of the Arab states since the heyday of pan-Arabism in 1950s, when Abdul Nassir talked directly to the Arab people and bypassed their political leaders. However, the discrepancies between the institutions of governance under which Arab citizens directly live and which they encounter in their day-to-day social and economic affairs, on the one hand, and the national aspirations, goals and expectations that they hope will be fulfilled, on the other, are still the most salient traits of political life throughout the Arab world.[17]

The conception of Arabism versus the idea of an Arab state

The grand process from the sixteenth century onwards of stretching out national communities in Europe, the rise of the vernaculars on the ruins of Latin, and the emergence of the book and printing technology using merely local languages were all the outcome of painful, but also of pristine *imagination* (Anderson, 1991). There was, moreover, time and space to enable these great transformations to be worked out and to become durable. American, British and French nationalisms are often considered durable and perennial processes of human and social progress because they were the articulation of broad movements in a quest for liberalization that was rational and also provided a humane definition of the framework of political power that seeks to guarantee the political rights of all citizens. Such liberal nationalism, insufficient as it was, laid down the norms that would guarantee continued progress towards the objective of creating rational, mature and viable social and political institutions (Pocock, 1975; Greenfeld and Chirot, 1994).

The lack of similar social and human developments within the context of the Arab world draws attention to the weak and incoherent political ideologies in that world, a state of affairs reflected in polities that lack the ability to create an open and equitable public sphere that embraces all citizens, recognizes their rights and makes them feel equal, even in a theoretical sense. This has always been the hurdle that Arab states have been unable to overcome due to their superficial approach to the questions of governance and nationalism (Tylor, 1988: 114).

In the Arab world there was no need for the invention of new vernaculars, only for the revival of the Arabs' living past. The great Arabic Renaissance, or *nahda*, from the 1830s onwards had more or less created a mass-reading public and printing technology that was oriented to reach readers on a pan-Arab scale. The entire process of people's *imagination* is the same as Anderson's (1991) idea, but the objects of imagination were (are) not the territorial sovereign state, but rather, the 'imagined community' of the 'Arab homeland'. In this context, Bernard Lewis (1993a: 157) notes that terms like *'watan'* (homeland) and *'qutr'* (country) for nations such as Iraq, Jordan, Lebanon, Syria and so on, usually symbolize sentiment and nostalgia, but not loyalty, allegiance or even a source of the individual's self-identity. As discussed by Anderson (1991), Gellner (1983), Kedourie (1961), Smith (1986) and others, the idea of nation and nationalism – comprising an ethnic group of people, defined by language, culture and real or imagined descent – which crystallized in Europe, gives a geographic imperative and a spatial dimension to a preconception of culture – tradition, habit, faith, pleasure, ritual – dependent on enactment in a particular territory (Malley, 1996: 30). Moreover, territory is the place which nourishes rituals and contains people like oneself, people with whom one can share without having to explain. Territory thus becomes synonymous with identity, and in an even deeper sense it also encompasses the morality of kinship and the aptitude and calibre, in Anderson's sense, to *imagine* kinship beyond its immediate concrete manifestation, the family, the clan and the sect.

A national identity manifests in the idea of a nation-state which is predicated on an organically developed political discourse that serves as the vital cement of continuity and coherence of any state. However, it is not merely, as Kedourie (1961), Gellner (1983), and Anderson (1991) argue, through the appeal of nationalism that national identity becomes articulated, but rather through the ability of people to imagine a collective of equally like-minded individuals all dedicated to the idea of loyalty to the 'imagined community'. The concept of the nation-state – a sovereign with an imagined/real territory as the cradle of national identity and the sole object of loyalty – has no history in the Arab world (and the Middle East), because it has had to compete directly with a much more powerful partner (ideology), namely, the deep-rooted and ever-renascent cultural identity and loyalty towards Arabism and Islam. For, Arabism (i.e., Arab nationalism) is not a feature of the state; Arabism is the attribute of a people – the Arab people.[18]

How can such an imagined construct like the Arab nation be constituted out of normative power relationships? Of even greater importance is, how does the Arab nation constitute, reproduce and maintain such relationships despite the absence of the material pre-conditions for such an objective? For Gellner (1983) the precondition was the self-aware modernization process administered by the state; for Anderson (1991) it was print capitalism and the administrative capacity of empires; or it was simply the need for self-definition by certain groups (Kedourie, 1961; Smith, 1986) – factors that were all essential for the national project to take shape. Again, the story is different with Arabism than with Western nations. With the common language and culture of the Arab states, they recognize who they are, albeit within the Islamic context. The nation does not correspond to the state. In conventional politics the state serves as the instrument of power that completes the process of nation-building (e.g., Kedourie, 1961; Gellner, 1983; Smith, 1986; Anderson, 1991) and in such context the purpose of Arab nationalism would be tenuous, even ambiguous. Arab nationalism is rooted within the Islamic identity and to a lesser extent within the Islamic faith. Arab nationalism is, therefore, indistinguishable from Islam (Yassin, 1981b: 100–2; Barakat, 1984: 37–45; Tibi, 1990b).

The Arab national identity is firmly implanted in a discursive formation that relies exclusively on the authority of the past for its assertion. Essentially, politics has become an expression of the tension between the polities of the individual states and the drive for national (including 22 different states) unity. In this often emotional, sentimental and sometimes even realistic encounter, each Arab leader is either eager to portray himself the exalted leader of the Arabs or, harbours suspicions that fellow leader is plotting to take over his country and annex it into the larger 'imagined community'. After all, this has always been the declared aim of Arab unity, and the invasion of Kuwait can be seen within this context. So, to many Arabs Saddam Hussein was simply enlarging the 'imagined community' by invading Kuwait. This explains the fact that despite the great fragmentation of many Arab societies, they have sufficient solidarity at the grass-roots level to make any protest or action against outside powers, and for political leaders it is a viable strategy and even a taken-for-granted objective.[19] A glance at the Iraqi narratives in appealing to pan-Arab audience and presenting the case against Kuwait during the spring and summer of 1990 confirms that.

Having said that, what does the shift from a local (family, tribe, ethnic or regional) to a national (pan-Arabism) level imply? It is the decisive shift from relations to images. In fact, Anderson has suggested one important difference that lies precisely in this convergent and even merging scale and kind. Human collectives are 'imagined', Anderson (1991: 15) argues, 'because the members of even the smallest nations will never know most of their members, meet them, or even hear them, yet in the minds of each lives the image of their communion'. This transition to images requires and, indeed, leads us to expect one radical difference between national and local levels. In this vein, Anderson's focus on the act of 'imagining'[20] raises the thought-provoking prospect of comprehending the transition and/or the switch from local social relations to their large-scale embodiment in terms of cultural identity and interests. According to Anderson, the process of constructing nationhood in Europe during the seventeenth and eighteenth centuries depended essentially on the rise of the mass book-reading public and of print capitalism. Conversely, the process of imagining being an Arab, and the deep emphasis on the scale of nationalism's appeal, is related exclusively to the Arabic linguistic unity cemented with Islam. Unlike, conventional (e.g., European) nationalism, where one has the ability to convey one's own version of imagination through the limitless ability of modern technology to communicate signs and, by implication, assert and express feelings of unity and cohesion, Arabs maintain that their conformity is to something that need not be explained. Moreover, the social categories that pan-Arabism commonly uses to emphasize identity and cultural bonds is the family, kinship and ancestry, not to the imperative of a territory – fatherland or motherland (Aflaq, 1958; Yassin, 1981a: 86–8, 173–5; Barakat, 1984: 33ff.; Al-Khalil, 1989: 197–201).

The imperative of Iraqi nation-building

How is the Iraqi national identity conceived and imagined? The development of Arab awakening (i.e., nationalism) is not, as has been argued by (e.g., Kedourie, 1961; Gellner, 1983; Smith, 1986), a simple process of coming to self-awareness. It is rather the outcome of political interactions among emerging internal social forces, on the one hand, and between domestic, regional and international political forces, on the other. As argued above, Arabism is not the same as the other models of nationalism that arose in Europe and were rooted in nineteenth-century racism and Orientalism. Arabism is an attempt to elaborate a more layered and multiple sense of political identity not exclusively determined by the geographical boundaries of the classical nation-state, but by the larger cultural community – the Arab nation. At the end of nineteenth century, when the Western colonial powers, France and Great Britain, scrambled into the Middle East, the Arabian peninsula and Mesopotamia were wastelands which had been neglected for centuries by world history. No one would have imagined that a hundred years later this area would be the scene of the dramatic episode of the Gulf crisis (Corm, 1992). By the same token, the fictive nature of contemporary nation-states in the Arab world was severely exposed by the Iraqi experience in the Gulf crisis. It was held that the Iraqi state was a modern alternative to the Gulf oil patrimonial states with their premodern feudal political and social structures. Since 1958, Iraqi society and politics have witnessed changes that have clearly taken place on a number of important levels, even though much of what has happened was only on the surface. In fact, the transformation has consisted of no more than a facade of modern consumerism through the import of Western technological commodities rather than a genuine transformation of premodern forms of production based on primordial values and political societal interrelationships. Beneath this facade of modernism, patriarchal values, connections of family, clan, tribe and sect are always present in almost all walks of life (Batatu, 1978; Stork, 1989; Farouk-Sluglett and Sluglett, 1990; Zubaida, 1991). Moreover, localized ties continue to be reproduced and, since 1968 in Iraq, form the core of the most repressive and tyrannical regime in the Middle East. This is very ironic, as the Ba'athist revolutionary philosophy set out to foster and encourage people to leave such primordial arrangements and ultimately bring about their disintegration. However, despite its 'modern' facade of progressive socialist revolutionary ideology, the Ba'ath Party *de facto* degenerated from being a theory of Arab renaissance to becoming a quasi-religious despotism of one-man rule (Stork, 1989; Farouk-Sluglett and Sluglett, 1990; Zubaida, 1991). In Iraq the basic structure and rationale does not differ from that in other neighbouring states: with the leader's charisma, the concentration of state power in the hands of one family, the coercive interaction among the various spheres of life – religion and politics, public and private, society and the state. Thus, as Sami Zubaida (1991: 209) contends, '[t]he "orientalist" picture of Islamic societies as communalistic, religious and impervious to modern ideologies has actually been realised as a modern phenomenon under totalitarian regimes in Iraq and elsewhere'. From its inception, the modern Iraqi state was characterized by weak structures and by political institutions that were external and imposed upon the society. The sheer arbitrariness displayed in the formation of the modern Iraqi state, together with the absence of a stable and centrally organized polity and its religious and ethnic heterogeneity (in a sharp contrast to Egypt), created a situation in which a stable state was a virtual impossibility. Iraq's endemic political instability and its propensity for violence and fragmentation have posed particular problems for the creation of an Iraqi identity, of a coherent political culture and universal political legitimacy. Iraq has been characterized as the least coherent of all Arab states and perhaps even the least governable (Zubaida, 1989; Gown, 1991; Bromley, 1994: 137ff.).[21]

The Iraqis, with all their great interest in culture and literature, have always been hampered by ethnic and religious fragmentation. Iraq is a country of great imaginative extremes, and hidden in the folds of one wild extreme there is the possibility of another.[22] A culture of civility and mature political governance cannot be invented or imposed. The only institution that can substitute for such a tradition and create a stable and coherent public sphere which, in turn, forms the point of departure toward such an objective, is a wise and strong leadership. The approach of the colonial powers and the Ottomans before them to the issue of governance was that they had to look for a leader who would command the widest possible allegiance. The British colonial administrators, inevitably, leaned toward the settled Sunni groups when recruiting the ruling political elite. It was the tragic fate of many states in the Middle East, and especially Iraq, to be saddled with the tradition of 'the one and only strong leader', and so the history of Iraq — from Bakr Sidqi, the leader of the first *coup de état* in the Arab world in 1936, to Saddam Hussein — is a perfect example of the continuity and tenuousness of the integrity of Iraqi state and its national identity (Kedourie, 1970; Farouk-Sluglett and Sluglett, 1990; Gown, 1991; Mathews, 1993: 28).

The Ba'athist government claims regarding the integrity of a precolonial Iraqi state that predated the British mandate in 1922, and even Ottoman suzerainty, are contestable, since like many states in the Middle East Iraq came about as a result of Western imperialist and colonial arrangements. It was a handful of British colonial administrators who by endlessly dealing with different tribes and, in many cases, by employing outright deceptive diplomacy, created the modern Iraqi state out of a host of conflicting social and ethnic groups (Finnie, 1992; Bromley, 1994: 134ff.; Mathews, 1993; Schofield, 1993). The persistence of premodern values and social norms into modern times, Farouk-Sluglett and Sluglett (1991: 1411) assert, was part and parcel of the politics of the Sunni-dominated governments between 1920 and 1958, with the helping hand of the British. While intending to promote the formation of an integrated and new-found Iraqi nation-state, these governments reconstructed and preserved the premodern social and tribal arrangements through their land tenure, agricultural and other social planning policies.

Historians and social scientists of the Middle East chime in with the assumption that Iraq does, sometimes in fundamental respects, deviate from other Arab states on a variety of levels.[23] Within Iraqi society the importance, on a daily basis, of a person's family, clan, tribal affiliation and regional background is often acknowledged and is much more apparent and pronounced, not only in the rural areas, but even within the long-established, settled urban population of Baghdad, Basra and other major cities. This is not the case in other states with a similar historical experience, including the exposure to foreign rule. British policy has been instrumental in creating a powerful ruling elite of feudal landlords drawn exclusively from the tiny Sunni ruling group. In a wider perspective, it is the social and economic consequences of this policy that are to be blamed for the failure to form a modern and governable Iraqi society (Stork, 1989; Farouk-Sluglett and Sluglett, 1991: 1409). The failure of the process of state-formation and nation-building and the absence of a civil society in Iraq led inevitably to the evolution of a Stalinist state marked by a violent and repressive bureaucracy. But in this respect, Iraq is no different from many other Third World states. In contrast to many other such states, however, Iraq was a major oil producer during the critical period of the 1960s and 1970s and so, due to the highly organized and disciplined Ba'ath party, the state's authority was finally imposed. The 'rentier'[24] aspects of the Iraqi polity further increased its ability to opt for coercion instead of less brutal forms of mobilization and control.

Benedict Anderson (1991) clearly points out that the 'imagined community' can be established by dominant, but self-aware nationalist elites,[25] though it is the people who are the decisive component that gives the modern nation its special historical and cultural peculiarity. Be that as it may, this issue raises two different yet related questions. The first is the question of 'who is in' and 'who is out' of the polity, or the public sphere – inclusion and exclusion, and this determines the question of the evolution of a durable and homogeneous civil society. The generic portrait is of multiethnic polities with socially narrow bases (Arab and Third World states) that are always compelled, as a security measure, to choose to draw the lines of metaphorical kinship in such a way as to exclude other groups, such as the Shi'i, Kurds and others in the case of Iraq. The state manifests its existence principally by virtue of its repressive capability. For example, the problem of the state versus civil society is recognized as society only negated by the state's polity. Another related issue is that of authority in a body politic bent on the presumption of violence against the population as a taken-for-granted discourse (Al-Khalil, 1989: 129ff.). In Iraq, the body politic controlled by the Ba'ath Party has swallowed the civil society.[26] The second question is that of the identification of the state and the nation (especially so in the Arab political discourse), i.e., the distinction between, so to speak, the Iraqi nation and the Arab nation. What links these two questions is that their definition of the domain of influence and power of both the state (Iraq) and the Arab nation overlaps.

Arab states recognized the vital importance of modern printed technology and mass communication in extending regimes' views, ideologies and control over their populations. In the case of Iraq the process of fabricating and manipulating all media communication through the Ba'ath Party organs and the state machinery had reached a peak matched only by the impressive control once wielded by Nazi Germany's and the Soviet Union's propaganda organizations (Al-Khalil, 1989: 89).[27] To illustrate this point I will show how the Iraqi propaganda presented the invasion of Kuwait. Ever since Iraq's creation after World War I, there have been attitudes and sentiments among its ruling elites to the effect of that it ought to own Kuwait. This started with King Ghazi's outright claim to all of Kuwait in 1938 and with an aborted military campaign, intensified with President Qassim's threat of a military invasion of northern Kuwait in 1962, and culminated in the invasion and annexation of Kuwait in August 1990 by President Saddam Hussein's Ba'athist regime. Despite all this, the textbooks in Iraqi schools did not teach children that Kuwait was a natural part of Iraq. Maps printed in Iraq showed a clear border between the two and listed Kuwait as a separate entity. Saddam Hussein referred on several occasions to Kuwaiti sovereignty as not only given but also to be protected, especially against the Iranian threat. Indeed, during the Iraqi campaign which preceded the invasion of Kuwait, there was hardly any reference to Iraq's claim to Kuwait in general, or to the Werba and Bubiyan islands in particular. Even in the immediate wake of the invasion the Iraqi media made no mention whatsoever of Iraq's 'historic rights' concerning Kuwait. Conversely, the Iraqi official discourse presented the invasion as a temporary emergency measure taken at the request of the 'liberal regime' of brothers that had been established in the sister state of Kuwait against the 'reactionary' al-Sabah family (Freedman and Karsh, 1993: 45). During the sweeping preinvasion period the Iraqi media claimed that Iraq had responded to an appeal by 'The Provisional Free Kuwait Government' which had revolted to overthrow the family of Croesuses[28] (a metaphor for the al-Sabah family). The news of the invasion of Kuwait, which became public in a broadcast on the Baghdad 'Voice of the Masses' radio, was announced in these words:

God has helped the free and honest men of Kuwait to depose the traitor
regime in Kuwait, which is involved in Zionist and foreign plots. The free
sons of dear Kuwait have appealed for a brotherly help from the great Iraqi
people ... [which], represented by the Iraqi leadership for support to prevent
any foreign interference in Kuwait's affairs ... They have urged us to restore
security, in order to protect the sons of Kuwait from harm ... We will
withdraw when the situation becomes stable and when Kuwait's Free
Provisional Government asks us to do so. This may not exceed a few days
or weeks.[29]

By the same token, geographical and political maps and books
produced and distributed by the Iraqi educational institutions have
never claimed any rights to the whole or parts of Kuwait. With their
sentimental pan-Arab propaganda and rhetoric, the Ba'ath Party, at
least from 1963 up until 8 August 1990, had been referring to marked
and clear boundaries between Kuwait and Iraq. The intensive Iraqi
propaganda campaign, Saddam Hussein's speeches, official statements
by the Ba'ath party, the government, etc., gave no indication of any
preparation for annexation prior to the invasion of Kuwait.[30] Indeed,
in the official handbook *Iraq – 1990,*[31] produced by the ministry of
information and published a few months before the invasion of Kuwait,
there was no reference to the claim to Kuwait. In reviewing the
Ottoman history of Iraq, there was no mention of Kuwait as once
having belonged to Basra *vilyat* (province). The only reference to
Kuwait in the book is that it is one of the states on the southern border
of Iraq. Equally important in the course of reviewing the Iraqi Ottoman
history, there is no notice or reference to the fact that Basra *vilyat* had
any connection whatsoever with Kuwait (Simpson, 1991: 83–7).[32]
Within months of the publication of *Iraq – 1990* the Iraqi ministry of
information produced a booklet entitled *Kuwait – Historical Background,*
intended to provide evidence that Kuwait had always been an integral
part of Iraq.[33] The Iraqi president received the Amir of Kuwait, Jaber
al-Ahmed al-Sabah, twice on official visits to Baghdad within the
course of eight months: the first a state visit on 23 September 1989,
where he was given the Medal of Mesopotamia, *Wesam al-Rafidain,*
by the Iraqi president. What is interesting about this medal is that it
is only conferred on heads of other states, Arab and foreign. According
to the presidential memorandum number 472:

It is out of our appreciation for all of that [the help of the Amir to Iraq during
the war with Iran] and out of recognition of, and gratitude for, Kuwait's

noble stand and support, and according the Law No. 1, Article No. 5 of the Law of Medals and Decorations No. 95 issued in 1982, We have decided the following: To give His Highness Shaykh Jaber al-Ahmed al-Jaber al-Sabah, the Amir of the State of Kuwait *Wesam al-Rafidain* of the First Class and a Civil Type.[34]

The second visit was on 28 May 1990, at the Arab League summit in Baghdad, where he was received, like everybody else, as head of a member state of the Arab League.

THE DOMESTIC SOURCES OF THE IRAQI INVASION OF KUWAIT

The foreign behaviour of states reflects the character of their social and political institutions, as well as the historical experience, social practices and cultural values they embody (Korany and Dessouki, 1984: 12–13; Goldstein and Keohane, 1993). There are durable connections between authoritarian domestic political structures, on the one hand, and regional stability and international peace and security, on the other. The fragility of the Iraqi state (a mixture of ethnic and religious minorities), the incoherence of its political institutions and the dominant role of Saddam Hussein using the Ba'ath party as an instrument for personal domination further aggravate these problems and intensify their effects. This is why Iraq's unstable domestic environment might have disposed the regime to violent foreign behaviour. For example, the excessive militarization that emanated from an acute feeling of insecurity reflected the regime's alienation from Iraqi society rather than a desire to safeguard the security of the state from outside danger (Al-Khalil, 1989). The arms build-up in Iraq and other major states in the region during the 1980s certainly affected the Iraqi economy and the infrastructure of its civilian sectors. On the eve of the invasion, Iraq had one million men under arms, a huge military structure for a country with the size and the strategic needs of Iraq. This state of affairs, in its turn, pressured the regime from within and, ultimately, compelled it to divert attention away from home (Regan, 1994; Workman, 1994: 145–63; Ayoob, 1995).

This situation was accelerated, moreover, by the tradition of inter-Arab politics leading those regimes whose social base is narrow and who lack political legitimacy to resort to pan-Arabism, radicalism, manipulation and the manufacture of foreign enemies as a means of covering up their weakness at home. The fragile social and political base of the Ba'ath Party and Saddam Hussein within Iraq provided the prime motive for resorting to transstate institutions (i.e., pan-Arabism) to seek legitimacy. Thus, the process of projecting the regime's own fears on to its surroundings was often disguised in pan-Arabism. This phenomenon reflects the peculiarities of inter-Arab politics, where leaders fully legitimize themselves not only in the eyes of their own population but also to those living in other Arab states, who quite often permit leaders to do just that. This state of affairs, however, becomes problematic since pan-Arab legitimacy leads to role conflicts involving both regimes and leaders (Noble, 1984; Seale, 1986; Barnett, 1993). The Iraqi invasion of Kuwait can be seen as an outcome of the domestic/regional intercourse.

Why and when do states use military force to achieve national objectives? It has been suggested that we live in an age in which brinkmanship – the deliberate creation of a recognizable risk of war which is not a completely controllable operation – is the main feature of crisis management. This emphasizes the importance of deterrence and coercive diplomacy as a strategy for achieving foreign policy objectives and maintaining peaceful conditions. Therefore, military forces are mainly utilized for peacetime manipulation and threat rather than directly in violent conflicts and wars (Garnett, 1991). The frequent use of military force by Iraq highlights the growing alienation of the Ba'ath from Iraqi society and how the ruling Ba'ath projected its own fears about itself on to its surroundings (Al-Khalil, 1989). Any emphasis on the use of the military, both in the form of physical force and psychological strength to achieve foreign policy objectives should, therefore, extend beyond the use of force in the traditional sense. In this vein, John Garnett (1991: 77–8) makes a distinction between military power and military force:

military power depends to a large extent on the availability of military force, but conceptually it is quite different; it emphasises a political relationship between potential adversaries rather than a catalogue of military capabilities. In a nutshell, the difference between taking what you want and persuading someone to give it to you. In a sense, therefore, the use of military force represents the breakdown of military power. The physical use of deterrent power shows not how strong a country is but how impotent it has become.

Indeed, analysts have played down the importance of military capability when assessing why decision-makers contemplate the use of force.[35] Therefore, the decision to initiate war and violent conflict should not be treated as a self-contained episode suspended above the social and political struggle within states. These are events that are closely linked up with the structure of domestic settings. There is, then, a causal link between high military build-up – states acquiring more arms than their security requires – and resorting to violent foreign policy behaviour. Dawisha (1977: 59–66) emphasized the high level of militarization as characteristic of states in the Middle East and, therefore, of decision-making in that region. A military build-up and increased armaments constitute a dangerous process that, apart from reflecting the regime's alienation, also increases dramatically the likelihood that it will resort to violent foreign policy behaviour. It is indicative that during the 1980s, average defence expenditures in the area varied between 14 per cent and 26 per cent of GNP, which is extremely high by international standards.[36] The majority of states in the region have large military establishments and armies that exceed their immediate security needs. This excessive militarization constitutes a source of pressure and dictates the outcome of foreign policy behaviour (Sid-Ahmad, 1984; Workman, 1994: 107–10; Ayoob, 1995). A glance at the military expenditures of the major states during the period 1985–90 illustrates this point.[37]

	Conventional weapon	Total military expenditure[38]
Iraq	$11,989 billion	$89,066 billion (26% of GNP)
Saudi Arabia	$8,764 billion	$96,356 billion (22% of GNP)
Syria	$5,876 billion	$10,878 billion* (15% of GNP)
Egypt	$5,795 billion	$30,856 billion (6% of GNP)
Libya	$3,186 billion	$10,353 billion* (2.9% of GNP)
Iran	$2,940 billion	$44,956 billion (3% of GNP)
Israel	$2,687 billion	$30,089 billion (14% of GNP)

While emphasis is placed on the domestic situation, the pressures exerted by the international system should also be taken into account, and these pressures can take political, economic or public relations forms. Most notably within the course of our analysis, the international media and world opinion may have had a clear effect on Iraq before the invasion of Kuwait. The gassing of the civilian Kurds in Halabja in February 1988, the Bazoft affair in March 1990, the *Voice of America* editorial of prodemocracy and the condemnation of world tyrants in February 1990, the assassination of the Canadian ballistics expert Dr Gerald Paul in Brussels on 22 March 1990 and the threat and counterthreat regarding Israel – all these were highly publicized in the Western media and, filtered through the lens of the popular Western–Zionist conspiracy theory, and might have strengthened Saddam Hussein's belief that the US, Israel and the Gulf rulers were implicated in a plot to get rid of his regime. This view, combined with assessments of an adversary's intentions, of the political elite's own responses, and of the probable outcome, reflects the way Iraqi leaders deal with the outside world. However, the process of understanding the adversary often embodies both reality and distortion. It might be argued that both US and Iraqi decision-makers had failed, for different reasons, in properly judging each other's plans and intentions.[39]

Another related factor is that the consequences of wars pave the way for new ones in a vicious circle of violent conflict. For example, the real losers of wars and violent conflicts are usually the marginalized and oppressed groups and the poor. In Iraq, these groups are the Shi'ites and the Kurds who constitute the absolute majority of the population, and contribute, in turn, to regional instability (Regan, 1994; Workman, 1994: 157–63). To understand the circumstances that generate war, we should emphasize the social, economic and political struggles inside the state and how these condition interstate patterns of behaviour and norms, set in the international arena or by a regional system. When these occur in a state such as Iraq, which has no such contractual legitimacy and which claims for itself complete societal power (a power which, in one way or another, it acquired through the obedience of the citizens), it will inevitably have to evolve mechanisms that are inherently fragile. Thus, any crisis would reveal the state's fragile basis and this in turn will compel the regime to resort to violent political practices in a natural quest for survival. Lacking legitimacy in this highly interdependent modern world, and aware of how legitimacy is so essential to their stability, Arab regimes have three strategies to pursue.

First, there is what Luciani and Beblawi (1987) termed 'rentier' politics whereby regimes (mainly the rich Gulf states) use their oil wealth to bribe a part of their society to purchase the support of allies in order to strengthen their power base at home. At the regional level this policy is pursued to buy the goodwill of rivals, which often are stronger regimes. The Iraqi demands on (or extortion of) Kuwait and other Gulf states to write off debts and provide additional financial aid, fit in with this pattern of rentier politics. By the same token, one could assume that these politics triggered the conditions that ultimately generated the process of escalation that led to the invasion of Kuwait. Second, leaders (e.g., in Egypt and Tunisia) are eager to have the acquiescence of their populations in their leadership. Their strategy is to create an image of the leader as meritorious, through the media they control and the state bureaucracy they dominate (Dawisha, 1990: 284).

The third strategy is a combination of the former two, though on a more vicious scale, and here Iraq is a perfect example of this combination. The emergence of a common nationhood in a multiethnic society like Iraq involved a tortuous process of constant manipulation among different ethnic groups. The classical way to solve this problem is that the tribe which holds the economic resources and political power bribes other smaller or weaker ones (al-Naqeeb, 1987), but when religious, ethnic and historical enmities are deep and economic growth is slow, a classical (and often-practised) solution is to rely on authoritarian and dictatorial solutions to the problem of social, political and economic development (Sheth, 1989). Related to this strategy, though in a double-edged manner, is the popularity of the elusive and distant objective, Arab unity. But as a political ideology pursued by various regimes, pan-Arabism remains as yet more an emotional feeling and sentiment than of articulated political notions and objectives (Seale, 1986: 4), and the result is that it constitutes a source of political instability both within states and on the regional level. Regimes use pan-Arab sentiments to justify their foreign policy behaviour, and it constitutes the most effective way of legitimizing their political actions. The Ba'athist government and Saddam Hussein have justified the invasion of Kuwait not because Kuwait was a 'historical part of Iraq', but by appealing to pan-Arab and Islamic awareness and by calling on Arabs to control their sources and wealth and drive the West out of the Arab world (Saddam Hussein's speech on 17 July 1990; Ibrahim, 1992).

This emphasis on a narrow and severely restricted Arab nationalism, Greenfeld and Chirot (1994: 109–17) argue, urges and stimulates embittered Arabs even more to view the others as anathema, a deadly enemy, even when many of these prejudices are already in place. These ideas are enforced by the Ba'athist emphasis on freedom (from Zionism and Western imperialism). Thus, radicalism, intolerance, obstinate narrow-mindedness combined with suspicion become an everyday preoccupation and an essential component of Ba'athist politics. Indeed, the manipulation and construction of perceived external threats by the Ba'ath nurtures the broadly held and resentful view of the West, on the one hand, and mobilizes the people behind the Ba'ath's violent foreign policy behaviour and enhances its power structures, on the other. Since 1958, Iraq has literally been at 'constant war [with all its neighbours], and with itself, because its fragile and artificial identity is based on a larger conception of nationalism than can be accommodated within its borders' (Greenfeld and Chirot, 1994: 116; Farouk-Sluglett and Sluglett, 1990). The effect of these political realities on institutional arrangements is that the ruling elites quite often choose foreign engagements to divert and defuse their domestic problems. Nicole Ball (1988: 40) points out that the term 'internal security' in the context of the Third World in general is misleading since its objective is rarely to make all citizens equally secure but, rather, to enable the ruling elites to remain in power by enhancing their power bases, usually at the expense of the majority of their populations. This preservation of sovereignty and territorial integrity should no longer be understood as a function of military strength. The security of the Iraqi polity has always been threatened more by forces exclusively within Iraq than by the outside world. Indeed, safeguarding territorial integrity and security in the modern age is emphasized more by economic, political and diplomatic means. The impressive military arsenal and strength of the former DDR and Soviet Union alone proved insufficient to preserve them as states, and even the mighty Iraqi army was unable to stop the *de facto* territorial disintegration of Iraq. Again, this process is accelerated by the fact that 'security' in pan-Arab terms, Barnett (1993: 278–80) argues, is transstate in character, and that the conception of 'national security' includes literally the entire Arab world. The crux of this conception of security thus differs from that of the realist and *realpolitik* approaches in two essential respects. First, power politics and the balance of power in the Arab states do not derive from any imminent threat to the security of the state from an external power. The threat that Arab states pose to each other, therefore, is not as a rule military in character, though the great irony here, perhaps, is the Iraqi invasion of Kuwait as the exception to the rule.

Second, since the political legitimacy of regimes is related to the norms of Arabism, what is more feared is the loss of autonomy and sovereignty over their defined territorial state because pan-Arabism urges Arabs to give up their own state sovereignty and embrace Arab nationhood instead. Rival regimes often intimidate each other by accusations that they are working against the common good of the Arab nation, and the Iraqi leadership had consistently adopted this strategy before the invasion of Kuwait and throughout the Gulf crisis. As such, it went home with the intended audience, and this audience did not only consist of the angry and frustrated grass-roots in Palestine and Algeria, but also contained mainstream social and political constellations all over the Arab world. These elements, in their turn, expected their leaders to act in order to safeguard vital pan-Arab interests, not merely the individual interests defined by their respective states. Viewed in this way, 'power translates into threats only within a certain set of understandings and presentations' (Barnett, 1993: 279). Armed conflicts in the Arab world are rarely cross-border,[40] rather, they are an outcome of domestic challenges to the legitimacy of political regimes frequently supported by outside intervention, usually another rival regime. Recent wars in the Middle East being the exception, security threats more often arise, not from outside aggression, but from the failure to integrate diverse social groups into the political process. Deterrence against external attack is not an adequate representation of security goals when it is the internal security that is the greatest threat. The state in the Arab world has never trusted the capacity of the people to be active participants in social and political processes, but has always placed its trust in money, surveillance technology and arms (Ajami, 1981; Al-Khalil, 1989; Regan, 1994).[41]

The assumption that weak and/or illegitimate regimes usually govern without popular consent and rule by repression is applicable to the Ba'ath regime in Iraq. The absence of a central state, combined with deep communal traditions, internal strife and a continuous history of foreign rule, are factors to be blamed for Iraq's failure to develop a mature civic culture. An unmistakable attribute of public life is its essentially 'anti-social' behavioural reflexes towards authority and disorder, disobedience, and favouritism by government as regards its own kin. This is what makes Iraq, of all the states in the region, the most difficult to govern, and has led to the most controlled and repressive society in the world. In addition, the comprehensive and deep processes of modernization in the social, economic and cultural spheres increased the institutional penetration of society by the state through direct economic intervention, education, conscription and policing. Alongside these changes, the various tribes and other social arrangements were allowed to continue to observe their own practices and traditions (Farouk-Sluglett and Sluglett, 1990; Bromley, 1994: 138; Workman, 1994: 67–71). The downside of the process of modernization and the state institutional penetration of the civil constellations has had disturbing consequences ever since. As Al-Khalil (1989: 44) puts it, '[o]il revenues and terror have been the mainstays of Ba'ath rule'. The spectacular oil wealth became central to the economy and the state, as did the systemic and incredible levels of repression that characterized the political order. All this is true, especially after Saddam Hussein consolidated his power through the security apparatus of the Ba'ath party from the mid-1970s onwards (Workman, 1994: 103–11). The highly centralized and brutally repressive Ba'ath polity, with its narrow social and ethnic base, make its key role within the huge and efficient security services and the armed forces a logical conclusion. Moreover, the absence of an established indigenous bourgeoisie and of non-state civic networks, culminating in the destruction of the only organized political force – the Iraqi Communist Party – allowed the Ba'ath to straddle a society that consisted of many diverse ethnic and religious groups (Batatu, 1978; Farouk-Sluglett and Sluglett, 1990, 1991; Zubaida, 1991).

Since 1968 the Ba'athist regime has had the doubtful honour of having increased the level of violent repression beyond belief, even by Iraqi standards (Zubaida, 1989: 121–82; 1991: 197–211). The Ba'ath Party leaders worked industriously, and with ultimate success, to infiltrate and control the Iraqi army and make the entire military corps subservient to the realization of the party's political goals, and in this way finally destroyed the institution of the officer corps as an independent authority within the Iraqi polity. Theoretically, decision-making (in both high-level and day-to-day politics) was the business of the party's Revolutionary Command Council (RCC), but the truth is that, the party and the RCC are purely a facade behind which the politics of clan, family networks and regional allegiances has always prevailed. There are, for example, the clan of the brothers Arefs aj-

Jumailah and, after the coup of 1968, the clan of Abu Nasser to which Ahmed Hassan al-Bakr and his successor Saddam Hussein belong. The tribal, religious, ethnic and regional (usually related to tribal and religious affiliations) fragmentation of Iraq is taken to be the fundamental factor in public life and politics, even though such communal divisions represent the main obstacle to the governability of Iraq and, by implication, to the formation of a common national entity with which all of the population can identify. This division, too, is the rationale of, and even the justification for, the incredible culture of political violence and repression that has been almost a normal feature of the modern history of Iraq. Al-Khalil's (1989) demonization of Ba'athist Iraq as an 'ideal-type' Stalinist state is, somehow, pertinent.[42] Yet, his tone of indignation and his condemnation of the Ba'ath polity as a 'totalitarian universe of terror' undermine the objectivity of his superb analysis of the history and society of modern Iraq. The vanguard of the Ba'athists of the second coup in Iraq in 1968, like many other middle-class nationalists of the Third World, were not necessarily a group of daredevils. Like many other Third World political elites, they were vulnerable to patronage and corruption. Indeed, Ba'athists like Aflaq and al-Bazzaz and others combined poetic and passionate language with unrealistic social or political visions, especially in the highly unstable and excessively sectarian Iraqi society. The Ba'ath wanted to avoid the mistakes made by the regime of the Aref brothers in Iraq, and also that made by Nassir in Egypt of creating an organizationally loose populist dictatorship, but they inevitably sought to follow the path of other Leninist-style polities elsewhere in the world. The nature and the make-up of the party leadership and the social and political realities of Iraq, 'urge them against the course of one-party dictatorship. If their middle-class nationalism made the regional imperialist temptation irresistible, the Stalinist experience made their domestic course equally so' (Farouk-Sluglett and Sluglett,1991: 1412).

Ba'athist domestic planning, Zubaida (1991: 208) argues, has been introduced with the sweep and ruthless elimination of the authority and the power basis of the traditional landlords, merchants, tribal and religious leaders. If they remained it was only on condition they accepted complete subjection to the party, which for the most part consisted of the clans and family members of the Ba'athist leadership. Consequently, patronage, clientelism and the special position of those of the Abu Nasser clan, the religious-ethnic Sunni minority and the regional networks of Takrit, have been the mainstay of Ba'athist rule in modern Iraq (Batatu, 1985; Farouk-Sluglett and Sluglett, 1990). Naturally, this state of affairs, Zubaida (1991: 209) argues, maintains and breeds a perennial and ceaseless social and political atmosphere of threat, fear and collective insecurity, and in a vicious circle that fosters a network of kinship, religious-ethnic and regional solidarity with patrons who arrogate to themselves and their groups the rights and privileges of power and authority. In other words, Ba'ath rule in Iraq can be described as communalism not only in terms of the historical resilience of primordialism, but also in the sense that the Ba'ath have abused and corrupted the power and authority of the state. Inevitably, the entire apparatus of the state is directed towards, on the one hand, money, surveillance technology and arms, and, on the other, towards depriving its citizens of the chance to participate in societal and political engagements. Thus, people can never feel secure in their day-to-day survival.

In such a situation of deeply rooted insecurity, Putnam (1993: 171–4) argues, distrust and an atmosphere of suspicion between citizens in the society have become normal conditions of life. In the cause–effect chain, this societal setting makes it impossible for people to participate actively and cooperate on the basis of common interest, simply because the gain of one individual would necessarily entail a loss for his fellow citizen, in a cynical zero-sum game. In a parallel with the emergence of a highly militarized regime ruled by a presidential monarch and party seeking total domination of all walks of life in the state, the Iraqi government turned the whole of the people into state employees (Al-Khalil, 1989: 105ff.). Societal institutions and the middle classes were overwhelmed by a draconian process of Leninist-type political mobilization of the rural populations into the Ba'athist state organization. The Ba'ath effort to penetrate society was achieved through the centralization of the economy and the creation of a huge public sector comparable only with those of the former socialist states of Eastern Europe and the Soviet Union. This rapid mobilization of the rural population into active politics, the design of a party of the Ba'ath calibre, is a long-standing thesis for the instigation of populism and authoritarianism as in the case of Nazi Germany and fascist Italy during the 1930s (Moore, 1967).

Through an unusually rapid modernization process (due to the spectacular increase in oil incomes after the 1970s), the Ba'ath polity has been able to organize its own social base by the virtue of being the largest employer in a new phenomenon of state capitalism (al-Naqeeb, 1978), and this has been achieved despite the high level of violence in society. Al-Khalil (1989: 105) asserts that in 1980 the Iraqi government managed to employ within the state bureaucracies some 677,000 people who, by implication, became subject to mobilization and recruitment to the Ba'ath Party (other figures suggest some 853,000 state employees). In 1980, the Ba'ath Party's membership was estimated at about one million, a figure that increased during 1984 to 1.5 million (an incredible figure seeing that Iraq had a population at that time of 12 million). While this macrosocial transformation had some positive impact on the living standards of a majority of the population that had previously lived in great poverty, the overall consequences were negative. Moreover, the distribution of wealth in a society that lacked social settings characteristic of European and even some Middle Eastern societies, was vastly uneven. The common wealth did somehow become balanced between various social groups, though it did not change the Ba'ath position as an essentially alienated, secretive organization distanced from the mainstream of Iraqi society (Farouk-Sluglett and Sluglett, 1990: 108–11, 1991; Zubaida, 1991). Over and above that, the degree of Ba'ath alienation, Al-Khalil (1989) argues, reached a peak with the internal conflict that accompanied Saddam Hussein's elevation to the presidency to the extent that the culture of violence during the 1980s was injected into the details of day-to-day life that make up all state-mediated relationships. Thus, the artificial social base created by the Ba'ath and the state-organized middle class is a reminder of the transitory and ephemeral mass-basis of totalitarian one-party states, where this can vanish in one day as has been shown by the experience of Nazi Germany in 1945 and the large communist parties of Eastern Europe and the former Soviet Union.

In the Arab world, a wealth of experience in political authoritarianism together with a weak, even moribund civil society are the ingredients whereby the state bureaucracy naturally manifests the deformed character of the body politic. Mustapha Hijazi's (1980) analysis of the relationship between the ruling bureaucracies and the populations in the Arab states and of what these bureaucracies inflict in terms of psychological damage on their citizens, indicates that the latter are so routinized and regulated that with time they identify themselves with the framework of state violence.[43] By virtue of its unquestioned authority, the entire political administration hangs together in regarding the citizen as a helpless outsider to be left at the bottom of the societal pyramid (Hijazi, 1980: 134–5; Ajami, 1981; Al-Khalil, 1989: 42–5).

According to Al-Khalil (1989: 45ff.), the maltreatment of citizens by the state and even the violence its bureaucracies inflicts on them was facilitated, not because of a break with a civic tradition and rights that were guaranteed in the past but no longer exist, but mainly because the Ba'ath succeeded in uprooting people from their only safe social domain – the tribe and the family – without creating a public sphere that enabled citizens to go on with their lives. State mobilization and the bureaucratization of a traditional society like Iraq was so severe that people found themselves psychologically driven to become totally conformed and immersed in the Ba'ath and its ideology. Such a state of affairs motivates people to resort to a kind of transcendental rationalism in order to create for themselves a secure space that provides a measure of psychological equilibrium and so enables them to go on with their daily life. It is a necessary measure of

self-defence in Ba'athist Iraq [is oneself] to identify wholly with the powers that be: people join in party activities, become Ba'athists, make contributions, and believe in the righteousness of what they are doing. Even when the first gesture is calculated to be a deception, complicity makes the final act one of wanton abandonment. Stepping back and pretending one does not know what is going on, as people in Argentina did under the terror in the late 1970s, is not enough. (Al-Khalil, 1989: 45)

The distressing condition of Iraqi society and politics that we have just reviewed has become a taken-for-granted fact about Iraq. It is not by any means a new discovery or finding. It is the tragic fate of the modern state of Iraq and its peoples since 1922 if we are to believe Elie Kedourie (an authority on Iraq and the Middle East), when he claims that the Iraqi regimes before 1958 were similar and no better than that of the Ba'ath. Kedourie (1970: 260) states that:

Iraq under the monarchy faced two bare alternatives: either the country would have plunged into chaos or its population should become universally the clients and dependents of an omnipotent but capricious and unstable government. To these alternatives the overthrow of the monarchy has not added a third.

Thus, the assumption that these domestic conditions become the fertile soil and provide the prime motives for projecting them into outside spheres might be accepted. One can argue that the decision to invade Kuwait was brewed and framed out of the grotesque milieu we have just reviewed above, though to be sure, what is at stake is much greater than the institutional input to decision-making in the form of projecting their own domestic difficulties on others abroad. Indeed, the whole issue is intricate and puzzling. At first glance Iraqi domestic realities were exported to cover the entire regional order, as was the case in September 1980 when Iraq suddenly invaded Khuzistan, the western province of Iran. But the difference in the present case is that Kuwait is not Iran. Iraq's domestic difficulties were glossed over by a pan-Arab veneer, and as such acquired a powerful momentum in the hands of the Iraqi leadership. The striking presence of the United States and Zionism in the Iraqi narratives was in line with their strategy, and this factor was entwined and strengthened by the role conferred upon the Iraqi President by many Arabs to destroy the *status quo* that dominated the region during the period preceding the invasion of Kuwait. The *status quo* was a state of affairs loaded with frustration, steeped in political repression and provoked by economic misery, the incompetence of the Arab regimes and anguish at Israeli policies in the region. It so happened that this same *status quo* went (or was deliberately made to go) hand-in-hand with the Ba'ath pursuit of power and regional hegemony.

THE GENEALOGY OF THE POLITICAL ELITES IN THE ARAB WORLD

In the Arab world the prime social values and moral responsibilities in both the private and the public domain are still located in the family and its social extension such as the tribe, a reality that is especially strong in Iraq and the Arabian peninsula (Barakat, 1984: 219ff.). There are great variations between Arab states as regards natural resources, geography and even historical experience, including exposure to the West and colonialism, but since the creation of modern states following the advent of Western colonialism after the disintegration of the Ottoman empire, Arab leaders have conducted themselves in the way they govern with a striking conformity that makes their roles in practice so alike as to be interchangeable. This is the case irrespective of their title of sovereignty – marshal, president, Amir, or king – and despite the fact that they usually have very different personalities and have no common denominator that links them as regards background or education (Karawan, 1992).

What are the sources of legitimacy that Arab leaders and political elites rely on? Weber's (1947/1964) insights are apt in this context. The legitimacy of any body politic is quite often attained by depicting itself as consistent with societal traditions, by displaying positive, sentimental and emotional attitudes, by rational belief in the political system's absolute value, and, most important of all, by being recognized by others as representing the legality of the political order. In modern societies, Weber (1947/1964: 131) suggests, 'the most usual basis of legitimacy is the belief in legality, the readiness to conform with rules which are formally correct and have been imposed by accepted procedure'. A fair guarantee that such an outlook will be workable is the fact that control over political authority and power is essential for the regulation of the conditions that facilitate human existence. But, with their outright authoritarianism and also by making great efforts to resist democratization, all Arab leaders are equally intent on using religious symbolism and the norms of Arabism (often the two are entwined) to gain legitimacy (Karawan, 1992).

Legitimacy and conformity to lawful rules can be reviewed differently in this context. In the Arabic political discourse, the narration of the succession of leadership from the Prophet Muhammad to Salah Eddin to Gamal Abdul Nassir to Saddam Hussein to whoever comes next, the fundamental obligatory item of leadership has always been institutionalized hitherto by the virtue of reiteration, argues Ann Norton (1988: 109). The connection of piety with military prowess, she goes on to say, is marked by the exalted traits of leaders who came about by way of this reiteration, a tradition that is embedded in the supreme glorification of the symbolism of Arab glory in the advent of Islam. The persistent personae of leaders in folk mythology endorses and, indeed, affirms the continuation of the outlook they embody in political life. For this reason, it is crucial at this point to make a distinction between political and societal institutions in their concrete manifestations, and to separate government from state. The famous declaration *'L'état c'est moi'* has extraordinary political implications in the sense that, in the Arab world, leaders essentially identify themselves with major components of their society, and tend to position themselves to transcend the limitations that would otherwise play to their behaviour and consolidate their bases of power relationships.[44]

In developed capitalist states, where the political institutions are regularly bureaucratized, the requirements of role enactment as regards the political leadership are often clearly defined and tend to be more rigorous, and an environment exists in which the structure of government resembles Allison's (1971) depiction of the decision-making process within the organizational model as 'pulling and hauling'. There is competition and bargaining between the different state bureaucracies that function according to defined operational procedures. In many Third World states, the bureaucratic influence is often neutralized by the direct control of the top decision-maker, who usually asserts himself vis-a-vis other subordinate political institutions (Korany, 1983). This 'presidentalism', to use Dawisha's (1977: 62–5) term, has historical roots in the societal traditions and political culture of the patriarchal nature of Arab societies and has originated and evolved from the Islamic conception of power and authority. This rulership tradition has always referred to *one man* as the embodiment of fatherhood to the community. This father figure must be confirmed in his role by the ruled – all follow in the path of the Prophet, and after him the Caliph, the Sultan, the President, etc., (Barakat, 1984: 179ff., 1993; Sharabi, 1987, 1988). It follows that in the Arabic public and political discourse, rulers become more than just sovereigns who, as heads of polities, govern the affairs of states. They tend rather to acquire a semiotic quality that stretches beyond such a limited role. Halim Barakat (1993: 117) succinctly depicts this state of affairs:

[r]ulers are cast in image of the father, while citizens are cast in the image of children. God, the father, and the ruler thus have many characteristics in common. They are the shepherds, and the people are the sheep: citizens of Arab countries are often referred to as *ra'iyyah* (the shepherded).

Here is the essence of what Hisham Sharabi (1988: 7) termed as the 'neopatriarchal society' with the unmistakable attribute in

the dominance of the father (patriarch), the centre around which national as well as natural family is organized. Thus between ruler and ruled, between father and child, there exist only vertical relations. In both settings the paternal will is the absolute will, mediated in both the society and the family by a forced consensus based on ritual and coercion.

Both the father and God here are cast in two ideational extremes: promise and a threat, or *wa'd wa wa'id*; grace and suffering, or *rahma wa adhab*. In the two cases, punishment is grace, and this representation is infused and quite often taken as a theme in literature and in works on popular culture.[45] Let us sketch the historical background of this social and political phenomena.

The politics of kinship in Arab history

The structure of pre-Islamic Arabian society, like all other premodern human collectivities, was established on the basis of blood kinship, and was a community that originated from a common real (or imagined) ancestor and was united by common worship, customs and habits which had mutual defence as its ultimate objective. It was the bond of blood that constituted the source which gave coherence to and emphasized the idea of brotherhood in Arab culture. The tribe in Arabian society is synonymous with the great family.[46] Islam banned ethnocentrism (*asabiyya* or *qawmiyya*), though the organism of *asabiyya* was preserved for various reasons, and the new *asabiyya* was incorporated into the new conception of Muslim collectivity – *umma*, the moral community of the Muslims. Thus, the advent of Islam had transformed Arabian society from being a collection of primitive, segmented and ungovernable tribes into a well-organized social and political structure cemented by faith. Yet, within the *umma* there were appeals to the deep sense of kinship, *asabiyya*, a reality that is so well-articulated in the compelling historical narrative of the fourteenth-century Arab philosopher Ibn Khaldun's *Muqaddimah* (De Santillana, 1961; Hitti, 1970; Rodinson, 1971).[47] The authority of the Prophet emanated from the belief in divine revelation, and a combination of divine knowledge, wisdom (*hikma*), science (*ilm*), and authority (*mulk*), all were attributes of his. For Muslims, Muhammad is the seal of all prophets. Despite the fact that the Prophet has always been the 'ideal type' and the timeless exemplar of succession and the requisites of leadership in the Arabic political discourse, the combination of prophethood and the worldly statesman was not passed on to political leaders after him.[48] Hereditary nobility (the first to convert to the Islamic faith and with nearness of kin to the Prophet),[49] qualities which were held to belong to *Quraysh* in general and the *muhajirun*[50] in particular, were the crucial factors in the debate at the time of the Prophet's death. The authority of the First Four (known as the orthodox) Caliphs emanated from their primogenitore (first-to-convert) in Islam and from the common consent of the community of Muslims.[51]

There is almost a consensus among historians that the Islamic polity had not been able to alter the social structure of pre-Islamic Arabia into a truly socially homogeneous community (Watt, 1968; Rodinson, 1971; Hjärpe, 1985; Hourani, 1991). Conversely, this nearness-in-principle has become the taken-for-granted rule within Islamic polities and public functions, and, argues Ira Lapidus (1990), it was on this basis that Islam as a faith functioned as a force for empire-building throughout Islamic history from the Umayyads to the Ottomans (between 661 and 1918). This is what gave the empires both an unequivocal basis for legitimacy and an awareness and a recognition of interrelationship with the tribal identity. The structure of government was always centralized in both bureaucratic and military terms, though the dynastic character of the governments required that deliberations and consultations on important policy matters were always conducted within a close kinship network which usually occupied the highest governmental functions.[52]

The principal characteristics of the modern Arab state are that they have a flimsy internal sovereignty and political structures dominated primarily by networks of kinship with local and/or communal commitments. The structure of governments in the Arab world formed from certain tribal, ethnic or social groups has actualized Ibn Khaldun's (1967) classical theme on the state in Islamic history as *de facto* tribal alliances with the powerful tribes as states in miniature. Recent events in Iraq, and elsewhere in the Middle East, confirm this theme as topical. Though *asabiyya*[53] is essentially a kinship phenomenon, Ibn Khaldun (1967: 247–327) saw religion as being of fundamental importance to its explication, for it seemed to him that Arab/Muslim rulers needed religion in order to achieve the levels of *asabiyya* essential for royal authority and in order to expand the Islamic polity because the suspicious nature of premodern societies made mutual trust and reciprocity impossible. Islam and the foundation of a new community based on common faith had created the conditions in which individuals restrained themselves and cooperated for the sake of the common purpose. Religion supplemented family loyalties and so created a wider, more encompassing feeling of solidarity (Lapidus, 1990). Arabism, Arab nationalism and modern Arab intellectuals sometimes tend to reject and downgrade the reference to tribalism, or *Qabaliyya*. However, beneath the facade of ideology, modernism, nationalism, revolutionary radicalism, Gellner (1990) and Tibi (1990b) argue, the world of the Middle East as Ibn Khaldun depicts it in the late fourteenth century is fully in place, civil society is unable to proclaim and assert itself vis-a-vis the state and political conflicts within the state polity reflecting the rivalry of patronage, regional, tribal and communal networks are as resilient as ever. This type of political tribalism commands more expression in states such as Iraq, Syria, Libya, Sudan and the entire Arabian peninsula. Their political behaviour is marked by the persistence of an essentialist and rigid attitude combined with a strong sense of religion, and an all-powerful and omnipotent state governed by frail *asabiyya* of quasi-kin, quasi-territorial patronage. By the same token, after it was transformed from being a mere system of dogma into a symbol of belongingness and a fount of identity, Islam as a religion has retained a powerful political force that contains sufficient solidarity at the grass-roots to enable it to be used by regimes in order to legitimize their political actions (Barakat, 1984: 45–9; Gellner, 1990; Sharabi, 1971, 1988). Thus, political allegations and social loyalties in Arab societies (primarily those of the *Mashreq*) are divided between support groups (i.e., quasi-kin of *asabiyya*) and those on the larger scale (i.e., *al-umma al-Arabiyya*, the Arab Nation). In the Ba'athist and other pan-Arab ideologies the Arab nation is the exemplar, and modern states are founded and establish their identity on the same basis (Batatu, 1985; Tibi, 1990b; Harik, 1990).

The majority of the population within the Arab world believe that the Arabs are one people and should remain so, and that the various Arab societies from the *Mashreq* to the *Maghreb* are one and the same (Ibrahim, 1980). However, in spite of the imaginary nature of such an assumption, there are common features and unmistakable primordial traits that have survived into modern times, among them the prevalence of tribal forms of organization, not only amongst the nomads of the Arabian peninsula and the Gulf littoral states, but also in the sedentary agricultural regions of Mesopotamia, the Fertile

Crescent, North Africa and Sudan. When certain tribes or families take over the reins of government, they fundamentally transform the entire body politic along with them. Modern-day tribes are part and parcel of the state population, whether in Iraq, Syria, Sudan, or Libya or the Arabian peninsula, though I am far from claiming that the national populations in the Arab world are still organized into tribes. In the course of the last 200 years, the modern Arab world, like every other region in the world, has experienced fundamental, rapid, even staccato social, political and cultural changes. This is partly a result of the process of (or, rather, coercive) integration into the modern world system, and Arab societies and their populations, including the tribes, have inevitably been involved in this process (Batatu, 1985; Tibi, 1987, 1990b).

Despite the effects of evolution and developments (sometimes called modernization) the imperative of nation-building is far from accomplished, save in the process of integrating various ethnic and social groups into the public sphere, which is usually established and instituted by the modern nation-state. In Iraq, and elsewhere in the Arab world, tribal and other varieties and forms of primordial and prenational arrangements, where the allegiances and loyalties are not to the state but to these arrangements, are as resilient as ever (Tibi, 1987, 1990b: 129). So, the difficulties confronting Arab societies are obvious. First, Arab society is no longer traditional in the sense that any significant sectors can be swayed by appeals to custom, status or superstition, because too much has happened in this century to disrupt customary authority relations and the status of old elites; too much social mobilization has occurred in the last few generations for primitive superstitions or fatalism to remain as reliable bases for rule (Eisenstadt and Roniger, 1984: 44, 48–9). But if contemporary Arab societies are no longer traditional, they are far from being fully modern. Rather, they are, in Eisenstadt's (1973) terminology, 'post-traditional' – an obscure, ambivalent condition conducive neither to traditional legitimacy nor to rational legal legitimacy in the Weberian sense (1947/1964: 130–2). Arab society is a combination of patterns, a flow of modern legal modes interwoven in primordial structures.[54] Tribal mergers, alliances and affiliations play essential roles in economic systems, in social arrangements and in the body politic of the states in the Arab world. Thus, royal families, presidents, modern parties, come all from the very same primordial social webs of clans and families disguised in a modern facade of power interrelationships, as is aptly noted by Clifford Geertz:

Structure after structure – family, village, clan, class, sect, army, party, elite, state – turns out when more narrowly looked at, to be an ad hoc constellation of miniature systems of power, a cloud of unstable micro-politics, which compete, ally, gather strength, and very soon over-extend, fragment again. (Quoted in Somjee, 1984: 153)

A glance at the immediate political structure of the Arab states gives us a striking account of the tribal dimensions of the governing elites. In Saudi Arabia, the ruling family, estimated to include more than five thousand individuals with a royal title, rules the state bureaucracy and dominates the economy and public life. In Kuwait, the al-Sabah family have been in power since the late eighteenth century. Likewise, in Jordan, the Hashemite family; in the United Arab Emirates the family of al-Nahyan; in Bahrain the family of al-Khalifa; in Qatar the family of al-Thani etc. This state of affairs is not, however, limited to the sheikdoms of the Gulf. It is a reality of life in more radical, revolutionary and self-professed modern progressive Arab states as well, and the example of the Alawites ethnic group in Syria,[55] is a case in point. The members of the Syrian body politic, whether the civilian establishment or the majority of the military, police and other control mechanisms are, according to Hanna Batatu (1981: 331):

chosen with extreme care and it seems unlikely that preference in selection would not have been given to men with close tribal links to Hafiz al-Assad's Matawira tribe and more specially from his own clan, the Numailatiyya. Many of them are even said to be from al-Assad's birth place, the village of Qardaha.[56]

The genealogy of the political elite in Iraq

As far as the politics of the organic family is concerned the case of Iraq is interesting, since the tribe of Abu-Nasser, from which almost the entire current governing elite originates, lives in the predominantly Sunni city of Takrit in the north-east of the country. Throughout the history of their rule in Iraq the Ottomans had preferred the Sunni minority to the Shi'ite majority when choosing the political administration, and this was a tradition that the British kept and even strengthened. Whenever a Sunni group or region takes over state power in Baghdad it ensures and guarantees its authority via its family members and nearness of kin. The regime of general Abdul al-Kareem Qassim (1958–63), who like many Iraqis was the son of a mixed marriage (Sunni father and Shi'ite mother), had its roots in the predominantly Sunni village of as-Suwairah in south-eastern Iraq, and all government officials, aids and associates came exclusively from as-Suwairah. As is usually the case, the government had a support base in the military, Qassim's own nineteenth brigade. It is worth noting that the Qassim regime was probably the one and only government in modern Iraqi history that had enjoyed the sympathy and support of the Shi'ite majority, including the Iraqi Communist Party which was also dominated by Shi'ite notables (Batatu, 1978: 1003–76; Farouk-Sluglett and Sluglett, 1990). The regime of the brothers Arefs, Abdusalam and Abdulrahman (November 1963–July 1968), which succeeded Qassim through a bloody *coup d'état* were supported essentially by the notorious military brigades of the Republican Guard and other military establishments controlled by Arab Sunni officers from the Arefs' own home region of al-Anbar (Dulaim), a province in north-western Iraq. Along the lines of the vertical bond of clientalism and strong interpersonal ties all of the political and key security appointments in the military, in intelligence and in the internal police forces were exclusively granted to members of the tribe of aj-Jumailah, the Arefs' own tribe (Batatu, 1985).

The reliance of the present Ba'ath regime on kinship of even closer family members and interpersonal intimates from among Sunni Arabs has been even more conspicuous and striking. This is specially true of their overrepresentation in the state bureaucracy and the group of men surrounding the Iraqi president are all from the village of al-uja, Saddam Hussein's birthplace, in the north-western town of Takrit in the province of Salah Eddin. The presence of an influential power behind the throne consisting of Takriti men in the armed forces, the government apparatus and the party organs with Takriti connections, has been on an overwhelming scale. Tribal loyalties to the Abu-Nasser clan and connections with the Al-Maguid family have been the only merits one could point to in order to occupy any prominent post and to make a political career under the current Ba'ath regime (Batatu, 1985: 379–93). The former president of the Republic, the introverted and withdrawn Ahmad Hassan al-Bakr (1968–79) belonged to the same tribe. After being the regime's day-to-day helmsman and

kingmaker between 1968–79, his cousin Saddam Hussein has been
president since then. Incidentally, Saddam Hussein's cousin and
brother-in-law Adnan Khairallah Tulfah was, in the meantime, the
son-in-law of al-Bakr and Minister of Defence until his death in an
aeroplane accident in 1989. This accident was rumoured to have been
arranged by Saddam Hussein because of Adnan's growing popularity
at that time. Saddam's half-brothers, Barazan Ibrahim, Dr Sabaawi
Ibrahim and Wathban Ibrahim, hold key positions in the regime's
political and security apparatuses. Saddam Hussein's cousins, Hussein
Kamel Hassan and his brother Saddam Kamel, were both married to
Saddam Hussein's daughters. The former held a senior position as
the head of the Military Industry Authority and as coordinator of
Iraq's much exaggerated military build-up during the 1980s until his
defection to Jordan in September 1995 and his death in Baghdad in
March 1996. Saddam Kamel was one of Saddam Hussein's
bodyguards. All these people mark the primordial attribute of how
modern political institutions in Iraq are in fact a political structure that
bears little resemblance to the political structures that have emanated
from popular consent and which function in rationally prescribed and
regulated routines.

The networks of kinship as a decision-making unit

Within authoritarian cultures where the political system is immersed
in patron–clientalism and coercive interrelationships with the
population, individuals who may be alienated by the state always seek
to find refuge from oppressive political structures. In such circumstances, Robert Putnam (1993) asserts, it is usually difficult for people
to pursue the impossible dream of cooperation in the absence of social
capital, the most effective precondition for civic engagement and
cooperation for mutual benefit. Civic engagement is an emanation
from the social and human capital of the society that, ultimately,
becomes a personal attribute of individuals within the same society.
As such, people are capable of being socially reliable, simply because
they are implicated in these norms and in the trustworthy civic networks
within which their behaviour is internalized and ingrained (Eisenstadt
and Roniger, 1984: 81–4). Further, Putnam (1993: 187) argues,

[s]tock of social capital, such as trust, norms, and networks, tend to be self-enforcing and cumulative. Virtuous circles result in social equilibria with high levels of co-operation, trust, reciprocity, civic engagement, and collective well-being. Defection, distrust, shirking, exploitation, isolation, disorder, and stagnation intensify one another in a suffocating miasma of vicious circles.

By the same token, oppression and coercion combined with the outright favouring of kinship in the public life, to use Putnam's (1993: 157) words, 'provide a primitive substitute for the civic community'. This equilibrium, or lack of it, has been the attribute of modern Arab societies. In this Hobbesian dilemma the only option available is the oppressive state which inevitably prevails. Thus, the whole social system is destined to remain in a state of self-perpetuating stagnation, though this state of affairs is far better than the Hobbesian nightmare of an anarchic 'state of nature',[57] where the war of all against all becomes the natural condition. This logical outcome, which Hobbes deplored, can enable people within social settings that are exploitative and devoid of mutual trust to attain the minimum level of security to get on with the business of living. This disturbing condition, inefficient and defective as it may be, is the only choice open to the powerless and marginalized citizens in Iraq and elsewhere. Yet, while acknowledging this shortcoming, Hobbes (1967: 232) severely reproached people who accept such settings because 'every particular man is Author of all the Soveraigne doth; and consequently he that Complaineth of injury from his Soveraigne Complaineth of that whereof he himself is Author; and therefore ought not to accuse any man but himself'.[58]

The attitude toward authority, authority-subordinate relations and conformity or its opposite are important ingredients that give unmistakable insights into the political discourse, as does also the encouragement of intellectual independence manifested in the readiness to challenge the evaluations and judgements made by a higher authority and to present alternative interpretations.[59] This has significant implications as regards the ability to accelerate a collective decision-making process. In the Arab world, of course, these Hobbesian conditions are evaluative and critical in their long-term implications, in the sense that they are frequently evoked in public life,[60] though they remain embedded at local levels between different conflicting social, ethnic and regional constellations (Eisenstadt and Roniger, 1984: 81–4, 271–6). This Hobbesian apathy, Norton (1988:

85) argues, originates in and arises from the daily encounter with and experience of misrule that make this conclusion a realistic judgment:

[S]ince those in power cannot be trusted, one must seek more intimate bases of reliance. If the state have proved unable to fashion a perfect national universe, people have grounds for seeking self-exonerating explanations of their own failures to deal with the tyranny of misrule.

Saddam Hussein exerts and commands a unique kind of political power that has evolved to become an institution into itself. This remarkable absolutism makes his person an essential variable to the analysis of Iraq's political behaviour since 1979. The absence of pressures from within Iraqi society, from both the Arab world and the world at large, leaves the analysts facing a double-edged paradox. On the one hand, we have a leader with this unique political power; on the other, it would be insufficient to concentrate only on the leader's idiosyncratic and perceptual variables. As a political and leadership phenomenon, Saddam Hussein has attracted an impressive body of analysis (Al-Khalil, 1989: 110–46, 267–9; Miller and Mylroie, 1990; Karsh and Rautsi, 1991; Khalidi, 1991; Simpson, 1991). A case in point is the circumstances that unleashed the war with Iran. When Saddam Hussein wanted to find an accommodation with the Ayatollah's regime and so avoid going to war, his associates stood firmly by his side and pronounced on the grave consequences of waging war. But as the then newly installed Iraqi president, Saddam Hussein assumed that the Mullahs represented threat to the Ba'ath regime[61] and so changed his mind and decided to resort to violence in order to eliminate this threat. His associates readily abandoned their previous moderate views and insisted on the advantages of invading Iran (Karsh and Rautsi, 1991: 135–49). It might be argued that this situation can be extended to the case of the invasion of Kuwait. There are reasons to believe that Saddam Hussein's world view has been genuinely shaped by the Byzantine culture of flattery and self-abasement surrounding his leadership. Wafeeq al-Samaraai, the former Iraqi chief of military intelligence during the Gulf War (he later defected to Syria), has pointed out that how it was virtually impossible for even a high-ranking official like himself to suggest an independent point of view to Saddam Hussein, nor even utter something that Saddam would not like to hear. This was the required code of conduct even when it came to very important and essential policy matters.[62]

This pattern of leadership has been facilitated by the absence of a cohesive and vibrant civil society, of free political debate, and of reliable internal political and societal institutions that are able to restrain the tendencies of leaders who are eager to wage war. All these factors are relevant to the regime's aggressive foreign behaviour (Morgan and Campbell, 1991). As a dominating leader, like other totalitarian leaders such as Hitler, Stalin, Kim Il Song and Nikolai Ceausescu, Saddam Hussein saw himself as the source of authority and political power by virtue of his control over the Ba'ath Party, a control that penetrates and pervades every detail of the day-to-day life of Iraqi society. Since 1968, when the Ba'ath took power, Iraq has developed into a mass society (Arendt, 1951), in the sense that it involves a modern political party that adopts a chiliastic ideology using modernist myths and advanced means of control through propaganda and the sophisticated technology of violence and surveillance. All these are hidden in a veil of primordiality – a group of individuals related to one another by kinship, a tight vertical social network that permeates all facets of the state's public life (Karsh and Rautsi, 1991: 176–9), as is sorrowfully, but correctly put by Al-Khalil (1989: 110):

Saddam is the president of the republic, chairman of the Council of Ministers, Commander-in-Chief of the armed forces, chairman of the RCC, general secretary of the Regional Command of the ABSP, chairman of the Supreme Planning Council, chairman of the Committee on Agreements, chairman of the Supreme Agriculture Council, and chairman of the Supreme Council for the Compulsory Eradication of Illiteracy, among other things. In addition to these party and state functions, an impressive array of honorific titles and forms of address include the leader-president, the leader-struggler, the standard bearer, the Arab leader, the knight of the Arab nation, the hero of national liberation, the father leader ... and the daring and aggressive knight (*al-faris al-mighwar*).

Moreover, through the network of brothers and cousins Saddam Hussein is the absolute and sole ruler of Iraq. During the Gulf crisis the most difficult aspect when dealing with the Iraqi leadership was the total absence of Saddam Hussein's political advisers. There were no persons or key contacts to discreetly influence, and there were no channels through which to convey messages or suggestions for solving and finding a way out of the conflict. No public figures, no single individual in the Revolutionary Command Council – which is the highest official political institution in Iraq – no ministers, no Ba'ath

Party member, not even the army had any real authority or power at all (Simpson, 1991: 94–5). For example, during the critical moments before the allied war campaign in February 1991, the foreign minister, Tariq Aziz, had to travel back and forth between Moscow and Baghdad by land through Iran to consult Saddam Hussein on the Soviet Union's initiative to solve the deadlock with the United States-led international coalition. The Iraqi foreign minister, it seemed, had not been delegated any power nor any kind of independent authority usually granted to these at a lower level to accept or reject political initiatives and proposals; this is certainly very odd indeed, especially in the context of brinkmanship crisis management. This institutional attribute of Iraqi polity and the prominence of Saddam Hussein's position in the political landscape may give him a free hand to act without accountability, but this interferes with the efforts of those who have the vital interest of the state at heart. The way the Iraqi leadership approached the economic issues and obtained the necessary financial leverage needed is clear evidence that they did not understand the intricacies of the international system. Ironically, they would have been better off economically if they had not ordered soldiers into Kuwait, and this leads us to the question of the economy and the invasion of Kuwait.

THE QUESTION OF MITIGATING IRAQ'S ECONOMIC NEEDS

Territorial, geostrategic and economic considerations have been important factors in the motivations behind foreign policy decisions, though the way decision-makers perceive a state's interests is also set within the framework of societal and political practices that have accumulated from a society's historical experience. Therefore, in the analysis of economic considerations the emphasis will be on how these were involved in the Iraqi decision to invade Kuwait, as well as on the assumptions of the Iraqi leadership concerning how the difficulties facing Iraq would be mitigated, since the 'real environment' in which decision makers operate is, in turn, shaped by their 'psychological predisposition' – the screen through which they perceive the world around them (Brecher *et al.*, 1969; Brecher, 1972). In their attempts to deal with shortages and to bridge the gap in economic and other material resources, states naturally search for ways to compensate for the shortages, or at least to moderate their effects on themselves. The economic hardships that Iraq was experiencing after eight years of war with Iran were assumed by many (Miller and Mylroie, 1990; Simpson, 1991; Stein, 1991; Ibrahim, 1992) to be the prime motivation for the invasion of Kuwait. Iraq's serious economic condition provided the background for the quarrel between Iraq and Kuwait, a quarrel that had gradually come about because of the issues of frontier delineation, Iraqi access to the Gulf, the oil production and pricing policies of Kuwait, and the Iraqi debt to Kuwait. To those pundits familiar with inter-Arab politics involving prolonged demands, stiff bargaining and ultimate concessions, the Kuwaiti government, quite unusually given the pragmatic political policy it had been pursuing over the years, had displayed an unprecedentedly defiant attitude in regard to the issues of financial aid to Iraq and territorial concessions (Draper, 1992: 51). As it is virtually impossible to obtain reliable figures that enable an accurate assessment of the true state of Iraq's economy and, thus, of the effect on Iraqi society, the need for territorial access to the Gulf may have been an important issue that motivated Iraq's action, since there are reasons doubting the assumption that Iraq invaded Kuwait to acquire economic gains (i.e., increasing Iraq's oil reserves or obtaining quick financial assets). It was reported that the Iraqi leadership was offered an immediate aid package of $10 billion by Saudi Arabia and Kuwait during the meeting in the Saudi city of Jeddah on the eve of the invasion, provided that the boundary issues were addressed and settled once and for all. Iraq refused the offer and demanded $27 billion.[63]

Having said that, at this point we should ask the question: how do states go about protecting their geostrategic interests and coping with economic shortages? Studies of both the direct and indirect influence of economic factors on the causes of war indicate that they have been much less important than, for example, political ambitions, ideological conviction, legal claims, irrational psychological complexes, ignorance and an unwillingness to maintain conditions of peace in a constantly changing world. 'The fact is', Aristotle asserted, 'that the greatest crimes are caused by excess and not by necessity.'[64] War, moreover, is the most uneconomic social and human enterprise in which humankind has ever engaged. The majority of studies on the cost and the consequences of war demonstrate that the economic gains from victory seldom compensate for the costs of war and the losses in trade

and other economic activities (Wright, 1986: 463). Although
economic issues and the wellbeing of states are of central importance
in the process of foreign policy making in the modern world, it is hardly
the case that such issues alone ever motivate states to go to war.[65]
Kenneth Waltz (1979: 88–9) explicitly plays down the influence of
economic factors in shaping relations among states, let alone as
providing the motivation to go to war. For him a system, whether
international or domestic, is determined by three characteristics: first,
the system's ordering principles; second, its differentiation of functions
among members; and third, its distribution of capabilities. Since
domestic political structures are based on hierarchical organizing
principles, the differentiation of functions in the internal political life
of states goes hand-in-hand with the differences between states in
terms of material capability or power. At the extreme, however,
differences of the third type lose political and, by implication, analytic
relevance. Waltz's (1979: 115) explanation for this development is
that, '[i]n hierarchies the complete differentiation of parts and the full
specification of their functions would produce a realm wholly of
authority and administration with none of the interaction of parts
affected by politics and power'.

In a similar vein, Robert Gilpin (1981) focuses on two problems:
first, the governance, and the impact on (within the international
system in general), the economic concerns and objectives of individual
states; and second, the probabilities and the consequences of warfare.
Gilpin contends that military and economic powers are two different
sides of the same coin, and that this is so because history has shown
that less fortunate and less wealthy economic powers have frequently
and systematically plundered wealthier ones. It is this systemic
evolution and transformation that fundamentally and consistently
influences the stability or instability of the international system and
the probability of conflicts and warfare. Relating the precondition for
peace only to the stability of the international system, Gilpin (1981:
10–12, 50–1) argues that states (through their rationally prone leaders)
always endeavour to bring about a change in the existing setting of
the system, providing this would be to their benefit. But if the cost
of the change outweighs the benefit, then states will refrain and the
system will remain stable. For example, had the Iraqis accepted Saudi
Arabia's and Kuwait's offer in Jeddah, it would have eased Iraq's
desperate economic situation, at least in the short run. As their
economies depend on the worldwide oil industry, the rich Gulf Arab

states are *de facto* an extension of the advanced world capitalist system (i.e., the world economy), and their resources and wealth are part and parcel of the world economy. Regardless of what happened at the meetings that preceded the invasion of Kuwait and the Iraqi acceptance or refusal of offers from the Gulf states, Iraq has always benefited economically from generous assistance provided by the Gulf states. When Iraq was at war with Iran and needed hard currency to finance its war machine as well as its war-torn civil economy, it received, according to reliable estimates, between $60 and $80 billion in hard currency from the Gulf states during the 1980s (Fisher, 1993; Joffé, 1993). So, the structure of the oil economy that was dominated by the leading OPEC members such as Saudi Arabia and Kuwait during the 1980s has been to the benefit of Iraq, and there were no indications of any crucial change. Having this in mind, and also given the nature of the international oil market, Iraq would have been better off economically by not invading Kuwait. Since the beginning of 1970s the rich Arab Gulf states, as the major producers of oil, have become dependent on and are even extensions of the advanced capitalist economies of Europe, North America and East Asia. The Gulf states produce capital surpluses that are invested in the worldwide capitalist system. For example, Kuwaiti assets are invested and placed outside Kuwaiti territory (Assiri, 1990).[66]

None the less, it is unthinkable to exclude or reject the thesis that economic factors, in one way or another, do matter in the process of warfare, though there is no hard evidence to suggest that any of the existing economic systems have in any direct and decisive manner generated or led to war or aggression. It has been almost consensually contended that wars are the outcome a complex set of factors that quite often include economic excess and/or necessity. As Quincy Wright (1986: 463) asserts,

[w]ar springs from irrational illusions or unreasonable fears rather than from economic calculations. Wars have not arisen, as is sometimes said, from the struggle among peoples for the limited resources provided by nature. Even animals of the same species maintain their existence more by co-operation than by lethal struggle. Among men with great capacity to relate means to ends, competition for economic resources, if not influenced by political loyalties and ambitions, ideological commitments, has led to co-operation in larger groups and larger areas.

Wright's analysis of the economic motivations to go to war is relevant if we are to understand the Iraqi invasion of Kuwait. An analysis of the economic shortages that may have triggered Iraq's decision to invade Kuwait is related more to the inability of its leadership to comprehend the complexity of the international system and its mismanagement of Iraq's vast resources than to a classical Third World problem of a 'resources gap', where the effect of external political pressures and economic constraints dictate the outcome of policy (Rothstein, 1977). In the Arab world, political processes are articulated in two different dimensions – conflict and poverty – and these factors are usually caught up in a cause–effect chain leading to a highly destabilized domestic political order and a fictionalized society of tribal, ethnic, religious and regional allegiances; in other words, an unstable polity. Here, economic deprivation and security threats are highly interdependent and Ball (1988: 163–7), for example, argues for an expanded definition of security on the basis of this interdependence: internal military conflicts often arise because elites are unwilling to alter exploitative social and economic conditions and political arrangements which work to their advantage. The trade-off between military and economic security becomes severe when resources are diverted from development to exaggerated armament programmes. In addition to the fact that such programmes have a destructive effect on the structure of the economy and economic growth, they do not provide people with their basic material needs.

Unlike many other Arab and Third World states, and due to climate and an ample supply of water from the Tigris and Euphrates rivers, Iraq has a relatively large agricultural sector that not only provides self-sufficiency in food, but can also generate a surplus for export. Iraq's oil reserves – estimated to be second only to those of Saudi Arabia – have made Iraq wealthy, equipping it with great financial leverage in the area. Proven published oil and gas reserves in the six OPEC members (and therefore the largest in the world at least when it comes to oil) on 1 January 1992 were as follows (in billions of barrels):[67]

	oil (billions of barrels)	gas (billions of km^3)
Saudi Arabia	257.5	5,184
Iraq[68]	100.0	3,107
UAE	98.1	5,157
Kuwait	94.0	1,394
Neutral zone	5.0	–
Iran	92.2	17,010

One further point in regard to the figures of oil reserves is that Iraq is the least exploited of all countries with vast oil reserves, so the real extent of its oil reserves is simply unknown. The reason for this is that the Iraqi government is not in effective control of the Kurdish area near Kirkuk in the north of the country, an area with great potential for oil reserves. Moreover, Iraq has been in a *de facto* civil war with various Kurdish opposition groups and rebellions almost ever since 1961. The other areas with great potential oil reserves are in the south, which were the scene of military operations against Iran after September 1979. Iraq oil revenues started at only $19 million in 1950, by 1968 they were $488 million, rising to $575 million in 1972, to no less than $5.7 billion in the first year after Iraq had nationalized the petroleum sector, then to $9.6 billion in 1977, rising to $12.8 billion, a figure that was high by international standards. As a result of these oil incomes the Iraqi gross national product had risen to about $30 billion a year by the late 1970s.[69] During the 1980s, Iraq, like other OPEC members, benefited from the dramatic increase in oil prices. For example, Iraq's oil revenues were estimated to be $9.8 billion in 1981; $10,250 billion in 1982; $9.7 billion in 1983; $10,000 billion in 1984; $11.9 billion in 1985; $6.8 billion in 1986; $11.3 billion in 1987 (Fisher, 1993: 491).

There has been a rapid transformation of Iraqi society in terms of an improved civilian infrastructure, better communications and greater investments in industry. However, since the nationalization of oil industry in 1972, this spectacular oil wealth has been placed in the hands of the governing elite, and has been used systematically for an arms build-up and for the establishment of one of the most repressive and violent state apparatuses in the world (Workman, 1994: 103–11). With careful and thoughtful economic planning and by balancing imports against exports the government could have put things in order by instituting the measures that normally have been taken after such a destructive war. Governmental control of expenditures would have accelerated a steady economic recovery even at an oil price of $16 a barrel. However, policies for mitigating the economic problems were not adopted, though rebuilding the almost totally destroyed cities of Basra and al-Amara, and restoring the civilian infrastructure and industry were certainly necessary objectives. Instead, the Ba'athist government allocated $5 billion for an arms build-up for the year 1988–89, and it also spent $2.5 billion on constructing prestigious and extravagant projects, such as the victory monuments and presidential palaces throughout Iraq. Owing to the Gulf Arabs' generous financial assistance the Iraqi economy had been relatively successful as a war economy, and some efforts were made to restructure the economy and invest in civilian projects, but to no avail. Instead, the process of restructuring led to incredible rises in the costs of basic commodities such as food and other items, resulting a rate of inflation that was estimated at 45 per cent in 1990. This affected those on fixed incomes hardest, particularly government employees (Fisher, 1993; Joffé, 1993; Workman, 1994: 145ff.).

Moreover, the attempted rationalization of the state bureaucracy since 1987 had resulted in an army of unemployed citizens which, in turn, made a swift and speedy political demobilization virtually inconceivable, something that might have worried the leadership and the Ba'ath party. All these factors combined to produce a deep sense of dislocation and economic insecurity among the state–employed middle class. These were politically important social categories who had grown up used to the habit of the state providing them with secure employment and subsidizing the most essential commodities of consumption ever since the 1960s. After eight years of economic misery and suffering there were legitimate expectations and hopes that the ceasefire and peace with Iran would bring results in the form of stability, prosperity and security, but such hopes or wishful thinking still remained unfulfilled by the summer of 1990 (Khalidi, 1991; Ibrahim, 1992; Joffé, 1993; Regan, 1994; Workman, 1994). Instead of investing in the infrastructure and other civilian sectors, the Iraqi government's 1984 five-year economic plan envisaged spending $14.2 billion in hard currency on military-related high technology imported from several European countries, mainly the United Kingdom, France, Germany and Italy as well as the United States. Estimates of high- and low-technology exports to Iraq between 1984 and 1989 from five Western countries were as follows: West Germany, $5 billion; United States, $4.5 billion; United Kingdom $4 billion; France $3.2 billion (or 25 billion francs plus 4 billion francs in interest); Italy 3$ billion.[70] Between 1975 and 1983, Iraq's arms purchases from abroad were estimated at $23.3 billion, of which $7.2 billion came from the Soviet Union; $3.8 billion from France and $1.5 billion from China (Fisher, 1993). During the war with Iran, Iraq spent $42.8 billion on military equipment between 1982 and 1985, and $15.5 billion between 1986 and 1989.[71] It was estimated that some 60 per cent of Iraq's gross oil revenues were indirectly (through assigning material to be used on the military industries to the civilian budget), and directly spent on a military build-up and on initiating a highly publicized weapons manufacturing programme (Miller and Mylroie, 1990: 111; Freedman and Karsh, 1993: 37).

The devastating consequences of the Iran–Iraq war had firmly set the stage for the later Gulf crisis, and the war that followed, through the social and economic hardships the population had to face (Workman, 1994: 145–63). At the time of the ceasefire in 1988, Iraqi finances were in complete chaos. For example, in 1990 Iraq's debt to OECD countries were estimated to be between $31 and $35 billion (Joffé, 1993: 10). Another version of Iraq's total foreign debt is the figure of $65 billion in September 1990, as supplied by the Iraqi government (Fisher, 1993). However, Iraq's economic situation after the war with Iran could not be described as desperate, as was the case with Egypt, Yemen, Sudan and many other Arab states. After all, Iraq had very substantial oil reserves, and had also received vast sums in financial assistance from the rich Gulf states during and after the war with Iran. For example, Saudi Arabia had provided Iraq with $25.7 billion, according to official Saudi sources in January 1991; Kuwait had donated the equivalent of $16 billion and another $9 billion in cash at the beginning of the war with Iran, and had, moreover, sold petroleum worth $6.7 billion for the benefit of Iraq during the second half of the 1980s. The United Arab Emirates had provided between $3 and $5 billion to Iraq, so the total sum of Arab financial aid to Iraq during the 1980s reached about $50 billion. Neither Iraq nor its Arab creditors felt there was any need to repay it since these were legitimate Arab donations to Iraq's efforts to defend the Eastern flank of the Arab nation (Joffé, 1993: 10).

By February 1990, the Ba'athist government had recognized that it needed to do something drastic to loosen the economic stranglehold which had gripped Iraq. In terms of Iraq's economic viability, the massive Iraqi military machine with 1 million men unproductively under arms, along with some 5,000 tanks and 500 aircraft, had become a liability that was sapping the economic vitality of Iraq. There was also the huge expenditure on imports of sophisticated weapons, which only added to the overall insecurity of the region, and not least to that of Iraq. For example the value of Iraq's imports of such weapons were as follows: Iraqi dinars (ID) 990 million in 1980 (one Iraqi dinar was the equivalent of $3 at 1988 prices); ID 1.4 billion in 1981; ID 2.4 billion in 1982; ID 3.2 billion in 1983; ID 4.3 billion in 1984; ID 4 billion in 1985; ID 3.6 billion in 1986; ID 4.3 billion in 1987, ID 4 billion in 1988.[72] Other figures were also given by SIPRI regarding Iraqi military expenditures in the same period as follows: $12,306 million in 1980; $14,007 million in 1981; $21,952 million in 1982; $28,596 million in 1983; $31,590 million in 1984; $23,506 million in 1985; $16,531 million in 1986; $17,073 million in 1987, $12,868 million in 1988.[73] Other figures provided by SIPRI on Iraq's imports of only major conventional weapons quote the sum of $11,989 million between 1985 and 1989 as follows: $2.8 billion billion in 1985; $2.4 billion in 1986; $4.2 billion in 1987; $2 billion in 1988; and $418 million in 1989.[74] Before they embarked on the Kuwaiti adventure the Iraqi leadership had estimated that it would have to spend $14 billion on defence in 1990, almost three-quarters of Iraq's total revenue. But by that time Iraq was no longer receiving generous financial assistance from the Gulf states to bridge the gap (Joffé, 1993). It is reasonable to assume that the Iraqi leadership simply had to be aware of that fact that by invading Kuwait Iraq could not get the immediate financial leverage it needed, and had sought to obtain, to ease what it claimed were the severe conditions in the country. Moreover, is as mentioned above, if Iraq had been seeking to control oil fields or reserves, then it had enough within its own borders to control and utilize for the purpose of its political ambitions as a regional power. In this context, the Lebanese Pierre Terzian (1991) an expert on OPEC and oil research and the head of the Paris-based Petrostrategies, Inc., was interviewed and asked, if 'Iraq wanted to control all the oil reserves in the Gulf?' His reply was that:

Iraq has no need of other oil reserves; its own reserves are very large and its potential production capacity is far from being exhausted. And even though it has a relatively long oil history, Iraq is still for the most part practically unexploited for oil – only a very small part of Iraqi territory has been explored relative to its potential. The Iraqis really don't need the oil of neighbouring countries. If they had, or have, such ambitions, they would be absolutely senseless.

On the question of whether Iraq aimed at 'controlling the market?', Terzian replied that:

What Iraq needs is not more reserves, but oil prices that allow it to meet its financial needs – to import goods, to pay off the enormous debt contracted during the Iran–Iraq war, and finally to boost an economy that had suffered greatly during the war. From the purely Iraqi perspective, the influence on prices – Iraq had moreover obtained at the OPEC meeting in Geneva … July 25, 1990 – should have been sufficient since it could guarantee acceptable revenues.

The idea of Iraq's severe economic crisis and the conflict over oil prices or quotas had actualized the territorial claims which, in turn, have attracted the majority of the works on the invasion of Kuwait and the Gulf crisis. The fact that Iraq's oil reserves are among the highest in the world, second only to those of Saudi Arabia, gave Iraq, at least up to 1980, enormous financial leverage in the Middle East. However, since 1970 a significant part of this wealth had been systematically used for an arms build-up and for strengthening the violent apparatus of the Ba'ath government. If Iraq was in need merely of financial leverage, it could have obtained it as it had always done in the past during the war with Iran. In a newspaper interview, the Kuwaiti foreign minister, Sheikh Sabah al-Ahmad al-Sabah, stated during the Jeddah meeting on 1 August 1990,[75] that Kuwait had agreed to cancel Iraq's oil debts – according to him it was $14–15 billion – and lease Werba Island as an outlet for the Rumayla oil field. Sheikh Sabah also said that Iraq had asked for Bubiyan Island.[76] Moreover, the members of the Kuwaiti Cabinet at their meeting on 18 July had taken the Iraqi military threats and the mobilization of a 300,000-strong force on the Kuwait border as an economic issue and as a show of force to compel the Kuwaiti government to continue with 1980s-style financial aid. They simply recognized the overheated Iraqi military threat as a form of extortion on the eve of Jeddah meeting, and thought that worst Iraq could do, or could be expected to do, was to mount a limited operation at the Ritqa and Qasr areas on the border between the two countries.[77]

Iraq has always been the largest recipient of financial aid and generous loans from the Gulf states, though the sum that it had received before the Gulf crisis has not been revealed by Saudi Arabia, Kuwait and other states. They have all been silent about that, but a moderate estimate varies between $60 billion and $80 billion in hard currency, a truly huge amount. So, by invading and holding Kuwait's territories, Iraq also hoped to gain and keep its electronically accumulated wealth, but Kuwait's riches were not accessible. Thus, one could argue if Iraq had been merely in need of financial leverage, it could have obtained it, as it always had done in the 1980s during the war with Iran, and without ordering any soldiers into Kuwait.[78] When it come to this particular problem of money between Iraq and Kuwait, still 'there is a difference between taking what you want and persuading someone to give it to you' (Garnett, 1991: 77). The Iraqi president's narratives on this issue did not indicate any plea for economic assistance, or generous loans, or help from the 'haves' to the 'have-nots', since the rich have the right to decide to whom they will give in a way that is consistent with their sovereignty. However, Saddam Hussein put it in terms of sharing the common wealth of the Arab nation and accused the Kuwaitis and the Gulf Arabs of squandering that wealth, and this theme was music to the ears of 95 per cent of all Arabs (i.e., the have-nots). During the weeks preceding the invasion of Kuwait Saddam Hussein had become increasingly irritated by the boldness of the Kuwaiti government. The Iraqi president's pursuit of political hegemony and economic interest was cloaked in symbols of Arabism and in the absolute terms of Islamic idioms. He had committed himself to a certain objective in such a way as to ensure that any softening or compromise from Iraq would be taken as capitulation and thus humiliation for him, Iraq and, by extension, for the Arab Nation, too (Simpson, 1991: 101; Freedman and Karsh, 1993: 62).

4   THE REFLECTIVE PERSPECTIVE

INTRODUCTION

The overriding objective of this chapter is to integrate the questions of identity in the politics of the Arab states. Realism and other traditional approaches to world politics take the individual (i.e., Saddam Hussein) as a point of departure for their analysis. Consequently, Islam, Arabism, political culture, norms, ideas, shared meanings and values are all epiphenomena to this *homo politicus*. In essence, in such approaches the individual creates any unit of analysis regarded as germane to the study of international politics, for example, states, international regimes, organizations (Finnemore, 1996: 333). Earlier in this book I highlighted the necessity of integrating the peculiarity of inter-Arab politics into the analysis of the invasion of Kuwait. By the same token, focusing exclusively on the Iraqi president to the exclusion of the sociocultural values and historical experience of Arabism and emphasizing only the individual (Saddam Hussein), as the prime maker of events would be shortsighted and inadequate. So, the institutional setting of the Iraqi polity has to be included in the analysis.

However, treating the Iraqi polity as a structure or a group of purposeful social actors with identical predesignated interests is inadequate for gaining an understanding of its proper role in the invasion of Kuwait. For example, other relevant factors that must be included in the Arab context in an analysis of the invasion include the national interest in expanding economic wealth and safeguarding state security, and the politicians who function within, presumably, clear institutional frameworks as self-interested egoists.[1] The basic element of Arabic political discourse is the overlapping of identities and, therefore, of political allegiances to the otherwise universal modern sovereign nation-state. Ethnicity, as well as social and ideological

113

backgrounds, overlap without by-passing the state (as a social and political organization such as Iraq, Jordan, Libya, Syria, etc.), with Arabism and Islam. In political discourse there is no emphasis on Iraqi national interests – the security and absolute sovereignty of the state of Iraq overlap with those of the Arab nation. We are not, therefore, faced with a Euro-American political discourse, which is usually articulated in sovereign and clearly state-centred language, but with an Arabic political discourse which cherishes pan-Arab identity.

The interconnectedness and relationship between Arabism and the Iraqi polity as an institution are so vividly manifested in this latter discourse that they must be described in detail. Despite the Iraqi ethnic labyrinth, in which a considerable percentage of the population are not ethnic Arabs, the intertwining of Iraq and Arabism is demonstrated in the overlapping identity of the Iraqi polity with that of the state. The way Iraq and its polity identify themselves and relate with others is part and parcel of the discursive social structure of Arabism, and the genealogy of the political elite, together with the entire issue of security, are, to some extent, explainable only in relation to Arabism. Within the domain of Arabism, tension and fragmentation between identity and loyalty frequently occur, and political allegiance to the state collides with the cultural construct of Arabism, a feature highly relevant to the invasion of Kuwait (and, for that matter, all wars and conflicts in the Middle East). Even more significant is how Arabism defines itself always in relation to Others – Zionism and the West – and in what sense this is part and parcel of the crisis. The reflective perspective thus discusses how Arabism is not only a discourse, but a living reality that is always invoked and even intensified in times of crisis between Arabs and others, for the sake of self-definition.

THE REFLECTIVE PERSPECTIVE: A THEORETICAL OUTLINE

Displaying the incompleteness of the two previous approaches in so far as the Iraqi invasion of Kuwait is concerned prompts the following question: why do certain ideas and symbols merit powerful semiology and evoke strong affective responses on the collective level, whereas others appear to operate only at the individual cognitive level? Questions such as this inspire social scientists to theorize about the substantive foundations whereby people understand and reflect on their world. In understanding the nature and the phenomenon of war and the circumstances that generate violent conflicts in this context, it is necessary to explore how the Iraqi leadership conceives its world, and how it understands the transformation from pan-Arabism (mediaeval/primordial) to the modern notion of sovereign states and political rule (Ruggie, 1993). It is by understanding whether political elites are able or unable to comprehend the modern notion of political rule that we will be able to explain how they adapt to the norms and rules of the international society. Thereafter, we can grasp the 'key intervening variable, not only for predicting war, but also understanding the whole phenomenon of war' (Vasquez, 1993: 145–6). The Iraqi decision to invade Kuwait is assumed to be an outcome of a myriad of competing factors. While decision-making is an overt process, it possesses deep roots leading to world views, values and perceptions. The combination of these factors and their interaction makes policy choices complex and demanding, for they are derived from societal and cultural practices accumulated by historical experiences. When states interact with each other in the international arena, it is the societal experience and cultural values that determine 'the actions of a state toward the external environment and the condition under which the actions are formulated' (Holsti, 1972: 21).

The reflective approach emphasizes 'the importance of the "intersubjective meanings" of international institutional activity'.[2] The central attribute of this approach is that Arabism as a social structure is analytically treated as ontologically primary, since Arabism (and Islam) through the Arabic language generates and shapes the Iraqi polity, Saddam Hussein, and not vice versa. As such, Arabism (and Islam) is the starting point for the analysis of the Iraqi invasion of Kuwait. This invasion cannot be analysed in isolation from the presence of various institutions that influenced and generated the mechanisms whereby the invasion occurred. As a discursive regime, Arabism is taken to be a *habitus* of shared meaning, ideas, world views and the core of cultural identities.[3] Thus, the emphasis is on 'the role of impersonal social forces as well as the impact of cultural practices, norms, and values that are not derived from calculation of interests' (Keohane, 1988: 381). In order to illuminate dimensions that might help us to understand why actors choose one type of decision instead of another, we have to consider and examine what is meaningful to them.[4]

The rational perception of the world, Hollis and Lukes (1982: 6ff.) argue, is often shattered by experience. There is a telling argument that conceptual variations and differentiations are relative to cultural contexts. Therefore, adopting or invoking a relativist approach in a *situational* sense – implying that a meaningful explanation can be drawn from the case's particular circumstances – is seen to be a necessary methodological procedure (Stake, 1995). Such a frame of reference links the particular to the general themes, and leads from the basic and concrete to the abstract, which it seems natural to designate as a way of reasoning and a type of thinking. A certain frame of reference that provides networks of images on which to convey an idea or a conviction about the world to one person, need not convey the same idea to another. For example, 'Westerners rely on categories of space, time, causation, number, and personhood, for instance, which are not undisputed among themselves and which differ in certain ways from those elsewhere' (Hollis and Lukes, 1982: 7).

In this vein, Edward Said (1993: 195ff.) notes that there is a prevailing Western frame of reference and structure of attitude that draws on the culture, places and peoples of the Third World which then unwittingly become taken-for-granted objects in the process of the production of knowledge. They are presented as cases in order to clarify and illustrate theories developed in the West that are not sensitive to diversity, and do not recognize 'the native's point of view', to use Geertz's well-known formula. Be that as it may, there are specific rational actions and proceedings that cannot be understood through universal frameworks, but ought to be placed within a particular cultural context (Geertz, 1973; Shweder, 1986). These incorporate the preconceived ideas implied in the way people gauge and understand their world – hence, people's mode of identification (e.g., metaphors, idioms and symbolism), lies in their capacity to evaluate and distinguish in order to identify their world of objects and facts, simply because 'the version of reality we construct is a product of both the universal and the nonuniversal rational processes ...' (Shweder, 1986: 181).

The Arab world cannot be understood apart from this historical transformation, for it contains so many valuable experiences for any given political analysis: demarcation of state boundaries by the colonial powers; the Zionist movement and the rise of the state of Israel; the frequent intrusion of the superpowers on the side of regional actors;

and the nature of its political and economic relations with the West. By the same token, while the international system and outside powers stipulate the setting and often function as catalysts for conflict by virtue of their presence in the area, it is crucial to place the underlying factors that can lead to conflict within their explicit and precise regional framework. It follows that critical and insightful understanding, as well as scientific evaluation based on and derived from these particular circumstances, are necessary to enable one to understand the social and political processes in the Arab world. Of even more importance, as Halliday (1995: 37) remarks, is the uniqueness of the social and cultural condition of diversity within the Arab world. The Arabs live in different states (with populations ranging from under 1 million to one state with over 60 million), and the regional and geographical settings vary widely (from the Atlas mountains of the *Maghreb* to the Nile valleys, to greater Syria and Iraq to the steppe of the Arabian Peninsula). Despite all these differences, Arabs share a strong bond of Arabism. This bond is articulated through their common language and culture, the shared feelings of a collective identity, a striking self-image of who they are, and a single vision of destiny (Brown, 1993; Hjärpe, 1994). These are features which are quite often ignored in the bulk of research and scientific examinations on the Arab world and the Middle East in general. Indeed, it is within this tension and fragmentation that the need to analyse the Iraqi invasion of Kuwait and the Gulf crisis lies.

What ought to be highlighted is 'the importance of human reflection for the nature of institutions and ultimately for the character of world politics' (Keohane, 1988: 381). Therefore, there is a good case for acknowledging that 'the relationship between cultural constructs, such as civilisation, and historically conceived supranational communities provides one starting point for explicitly "systemic" conception of international systems based on culture' (Pasic, 1996: 102). Indeed, the international system, Pasic further argues, is arranged and separated within the dichotomies of premodern cultural domain and civilizations – even though the modern state system is disguised by a secular conception of organizing principles – simply because the historical experience has indicated that cultural domains and civilizations are the underlying principles for the modern international system. The Enlightenment and Western rationality inserted 'a harsh wedge between cosmology and history' (Anderson, 1991: 36). In the Muslim discourse such a 'wedge' has not materialized, nor has there been the

equivalent of the Enlightenment exegesis that deals critically with and
helps to demythologize the heroic perceptions and image of Islam in
the way the Enlightenment dealt with the biblical era and the Christian
tradition (Djäit, 1985: 53). Hisham Sharabi (1970) argues that the
great reformation movement has been a total failure,[5] and that Islam
has been gradually but firmly transformed from a meaningful belief
into a way of belonging, a symbol of identity and, even more
ostensibly, a means of forming and cementing all-Arab and all-Muslim
solidarity. Islam, too, was transformed into a mechanism for
deprivation, not only of the basic economic and material necessities,
but, most importantly, of the basic individual and political freedoms
that generate protests at the grass-roots level, something that could
explain the success of fundamentalist movements.

Therefore, Islam and Arabism are important in the analysis of
political phenomena, simply because they function as a modality of
prepolitical awareness for the formation and assertion of identity in
the absence of modern institutions with historicopolitical – that is,
non-cosmological and secular – dimensions. The focus on the role of
Islam and Arabism falls into two parts. First, the role of Islam in the
formation of identity (e.g., Arabism) is assumed to be a part of the
perceptions and images of the decision-makers. As a world view and
normative belief, Islam and Arabism are assumed to play a role in the
manipulation and mobilization of the grass-roots and, thus, to have
affected the invasion of Kuwait, even if the Iraqi leadership had
rationally calculated the losses and gains.[6] Indeed, and with some
degree of irony, Islam and Arabism can be fitted into a framework of
realpolitik. Yet the focus here is on the way Islam and Arabism
influenced Iraq's decision, and how the case was presented to and
legitimized by the people – Arabs and Iraqis. As historical experience
has demonstrated time and again, Islam and Arabism have had a decisive
impact on the process of foreign policy-making, especially in times
of crisis.[7] Second, Islam and Arabism influence the policy-making of
Iraq (and other Arab states) as sociohistorical communities – 'history
encoded into rules' as March and Olsen (1989: 741) put it. In invoking
this approach and noting how it is connected with Iraq's decision to
invade, it is important to retain a certain emphasis on the role of history
(i.e. how actors use and are influenced by history, or rather what they
perceive as history), when formulating foreign policy objectives and

making strategic choices. History is an invention in which imagination and ingenuity play a vital role.[8]

We must take into account how Arabism influences people's views of politics through their self-image, generating a set of values and conceptions of political authority, perceptions of loyalty, and how it affects the attitude of people toward the modern state system of territorial sovereignty (Harik, 1990). On the eve of the Gulf crisis, Saddam Hussein's blistering attacks on the legitimacy of the Gulf rulers as not being devout and genuine Muslims/Arabs rather than as political leaders of rival states won a large audience in the Arab world, something that will be accounted for below. A broad spectrum of Arabs had been sympathetic to the Iraqi president's line and his accusations that the Gulf rulers had frittered away the Arab nation's vast resources while contributing little to the economic development of their poorer brethren. This state of affairs carries weight in a world where political legitimacy emanates from transstate sources – Arabism and Islam; hence, the idea of political practice is seen to consist of the art of recognizing the way people think and the positions they adopt when trying to make sense of politics. It is in this context that the sense of the word 'political' was transformed from a stance to be *held* into a *lived* reality.[9] In the same way, it shows the importance of 'the constraints posed by language, culture, and history on all aspects of individual's abilities to define and act on "objective interests"' (Goldstein and Keohane, 1993: 7).

ISLAM AND ARABISM: THE GENEALOGY OF A DISCURSIVE REGIME

What is Islam? Following the Weberian and interpretive approach of Marshal Hodgson (1974: 56–60),[10] the term 'Islam' refers to a tradition with three distinct yet related components.

First, 'Islam' implies a religious dogma and a system of doctrines proclaimed by Muslims to be the ultimate truth. It is based on the belief that Muhammad is the last prophet in a line that started with Abraham and that the Qur'an is the final and complete version of all earlier scriptures (i.e., the Old and New Testaments) revealed by Allah – unequalled before and since. These beliefs became the basis of a system of devotional observances associated with the practices of Islam as a religion. Islam is the immediate instrument and the eyes of Allah[11] for ruling His creatures. Islam is the embodiment and personification of Allah. The *ittisaliyah* (intimate connectedness) between Allah and the individual believer takes place, of course, without a mediator. There is no need whatsoever for such an intermediary between human beings and their Maker, who has known them since before birth, and is closer to them than are their blood cells. Yet, human beings alone are accountable for their deeds and, by implication, will encounter the final *hukm*, the verdict of Allah – the All-seeing, the All-hearing, the All-knowing Judge. Humans have no choice but to surrender to the Merciful, 'from Him to Him', says the Qur'an.[12] This surrender is proof of outright humility and hope, and is the very essence of the true faith of Islam, the absolute submission of oneself to Allah (De Santillana, 1961: 286–7; Rodinson, 1971: 83–5; Hjärpe, 1985).

Islam lays great emphasis on the problem of order and disorder within the politico-religious moral community (*umma*) and the personal qualities of individuals are related to their efforts to preserve the harmony of society as their duty before Allah. The chain of Abrahamic prophethood down to Muhammad had been sent and delegated by Allah to seek to materialize the moral order on earth as revealed by God. In Islam, Muhammad, as the seal of all prophets, enacts and performs as the exemplar of an ideal human on earth (Holton and Turner, 1989: 87; Rodinson, 1971: 70–4; Weber, 1968: 623–7; Watt, 1974). Theologically, the construction and reconstruction of the ideal *umma* is the absolute objective of Islam, an objective that has never been fulfilled, however. Islam as a religious practice and theological creed has remained virtually the same since its inception. However, this research is not directly concerned with this theological aspect of Islam.

Second, Hodgson (1974: 57–8) introduced the term 'Islamdom' in analogy with Christendom. It refers to a historical polity and a society of Muslims that constitutes the abode of Islam, *Dar-il-islam*. Moreover, it is a political/moral community, an *umma*, which was transformed into an imperial order. It then disintegrated into rival Islamic states which since World War I have become the modern states of the Arab world and the Middle East. Islamdom as a historical community has been characterized as a highly unstable and transitory body politic. The problem of authority – who rules and how – has never been resolved within its framework. The concept of Islamdom can be taken to be synonymous with a 'civilization' that includes Muslims (Arabs, Persian, Turckic, Berber, etc.) and their religion as the dominant force. Islamdom, in addition, constituted a labyrinthian, multifarious myriad of sociocultural interactive relationships out of several other groups of peoples such as Jews, Christians and Hindus, by virtue of affiliative relationships.[13] It is a *Gesellschaft* where Islam is seen 'not as dogma but as a cultural system with own world views and civilisational modes' (Said, 1983: 20; Ghazoul, 1992: 169).

This 'civilisational mode' might conveniently be regarded as an 'imagined community'[14] that stems from the social group's eagerness (through modern semiological technology) to identify themselves with its frame of reference in the group's daily life. The idea and the character of 'relationship' is essential in understanding the quality of association and belongingness such a social group yields, since it prompts the necessity to move well beyond the approaches that assume human behaviour can be analogized with mechanical and organic systems. To elaborate, the concept of 'imagined community' would correspond to the all-pervading and, indeed, vitally important sense of *twasül* (continuity) or *ittisaliyah*, that highlights a want or a passion for people's *ittisal* (connection) to form an intimate 'relation' with the symbols and the great personalities of Islam throughout history.[15] This intimate *ittisal* has always been extraordinarily emphasized both in Muslims' thinking and their social and political institutions throughout history. On the face of it, when depicting the origins of the structure of a human community, Islamic and other primordial societies have always given priority to an intimate, concrete and situational connectedness between the members of the community, and this connectedness was a central sociological feature in premodern societies. Nevertheless, unlike many others, as William Graham (1993: 501) suggests, Muslims have kept such traditions alive. These are manifested in various forms,

at different times, and in different sectors of their collective life, they have always done so in ways that are characteristic, identifiable, and central. Indeed, it is possible to discern a basic, recurrent pattern that is used to express their *ittisaliyah*, and hence their traditionalism.

Third, Islamdom was the channel which bore a myriad of interactive social and cultural entities producing what Hodgson dubbed the 'Islamicate'. This leads us to the following point.

The discourse of Arabic political culture

For Hodgson (1974: 59–60), the Islamicate is a highly eclectic culture and pattern of social interactions shared by both Muslims and non-Muslims insofar as they are integrated within the institutional habitat and practices of Islamdom. The Islamicate as a cultural tradition changed in emphasis from one area to the other without losing the essential continuity of the whole. The Islamicate, too, is a discourse of culture which persisted, took a definite form and a salient expression in the course of time, and to which people became attached as a result of its role in the formation of their identity. This research is confined to the Arabic domain of Islamdom. It is assumed that there are connections between Arab peoples all over the Arab states (it varies from a general sympathy to strong expectations and roles conferred upon them) and their individual leaders' (e.g., Abdul Nassir's and Saddam Hussein's) political ambitions, as long as the particular leader uses the '*a priori* codes' or 'sign of wealth'[16] with which all Arabs identify themselves and, moreover, appears to offer a stern challenge to the enemies of the Arab nation. Studies in foreign policy have asserted the impact that an invented and reinvented national history and a collective myth have on the decision-making process (Lewis, 1975; Jervis, 1976; Vertzberger, 1989: 296–341).[17] They affect how the ruling elites perceive the interests of the state and further perpetuate history and the collective myth through the production and reproduction of culture, the educational system and the socialization of citizens via state propaganda (Van Evera, 1984). Islam and Arabism are still the most effective forms of consensus in the Arab world, and form the basis of group identity and loyalty among the people. The Islamic reformism of Mohammad Abdu and Jamal ad-Din al-Afaghani of the nineteenth century and the pan-Arabism of al-Husari, al-Arsuzi, Aflaq, al-Bitar and al-Bazzaz and many others in the twentieth century, both sought a renaissance of Islam and its glorious past. Islam, as it is traditionally conceived, and the symbols in terms of which it gives meaning, still provide the motives which urge people to action (Yassin, 1981b: 175–86).[18]

In this respect, Kedourie (1980: 55) argues, Islam is taken by all modern Arab nationalists from al-Husari to al-Bazzaz to be the core of Arabism and the prime expression of the Arab national genius. The

Ba'athist doctrine, as pronounced by its most intelligible articulator the Syrian Greek Orthodox Michel Aflaq, 'held that Muhammad the Prophet of Islam was at the same time *ipso facto* the founder of the Arab nation, and was to be venerated as such by every Arab nationalist, whether Muslim or not' (ibid.). In a lecture in 1943, which developed later into the most influential book of all Arab nationalist thought, *Fí Sábil al-Ba'ath* ('In the Path of the Ba'ath'), Aflaq (1958: 43–4, quoted in Kedourie, ibid.) put forward a vision of Arabism that is inextricably entwined with Islam; he argued that Islam 'represented the ascent of Arabism towards unity, power, and progress'. In poetic and emotional language that drew on the structure of a highly refined and Qur'anic Arabic, Aflaq (1958: 158, cited in Kedourie, ibid.) insisted that Arabism

does not indicate spatial properties and betrays no passage of time ... is the fount of theories, and is not born of thought but is wet-nurse of thought. The national self, the historical subject, is itself a criticism of pure intellection and a reaffirmation of life.

Islam/Arabism in this way 'affects both what [people] do and whom [people] are, both our behaviour and our identity',[19] and hence is presumed to be *ipso facto* a discourse[20] – a comprehensive world view and philosophy of human life and the universe – embracing the value preferences and sociocultural principles that underlie people's conceptions of themselves and the world around them. World views are 'embedded in the symbolism of a culture and deeply affect modes of thought and discourse ... entwined with people's conceptions of their identities, evoking deep emotions and loyalties' (Goldstein and Keohane, 1993: 8). Islam as a religion, its symbols and sentiments, constitute the sociohistorical basis for and explanations of Arabs' identity and their political discourse.

This assumption is consensually linked to the shared experience of the various Arab societies, a common religion, the culture and language of Arabs, things that are primordial, original, 'magnified, mirrored and roseate' in the present (Lambton, 1988: 2). It is, moreover, a discourse of culture that can be understood as the realization and outcome of the extended connectedness between primordial groups that enable the inclusion of larger and larger groups through a basically spontaneous process of assimilation.[21] Although Islam is essentially a universalistic religion, there are intimate ties between Arabism and Islam – Islam was revealed to a man with an Arabic lineage and that the Qur'an is written in Arabic. This language remains the *lingua franca* for all Muslims all over the world, especially in their prayers. Indeed, Arabic culture is a crucial part of the authoritative structure of Islam, and Arabs perceive themselves as a people with a high culture that has made a significant contribution to human civilizations. As has been eloquently put by Al-Khalil (1989: 199):

In the person of the Prophet Muhammad, all Muslim Arabs are confronted with a member of their ethnic group and the prophet of their religion acting out the role of political leader. The will of God and Caesar was manifest in one real person, who was both the founder of the religion and the head of its first state.

The character of the Prophet Muhammad has been the exemplar which Muslims, especially political leaders, cherish and recognize as a teacher, a soldier, a statesman, and a founder and great organizer of a human community cemented with faith that grew, thanks to his religion, to be a vast empire (Rodinson, 1970). Even though political actions in the Arab world are derived from self-interest (as in the West), Arab leaders conceive of and even represent their actions as being based on, and associated with, their Islamic faith.

Thus far we can argue that there are clear associations between belief (i.e., religion) and social and political processes in the societies of the modern Arab world. Within the framework of the religious dogma's encounter with worldly affairs, it is important to understand the significance of the impact it exerts on collectivity and, by implication, on how the dogma accommodates and fits into the social, economic and political schemes of the group of people concerned. Max Weber was the first, and perhaps the greatest, social thinker to grasp the affinity between religious belief and people's day-to-day social behaviour and, more importantly, how this human and civilizational evolution come about. Weber's (1930/1992) powerful thesis on 'Protestant ethics'[22] and his other studies on the role of religions in public life are germane in this context. Any peoples in a certain cultural sphere, their identities, beliefs and the ways they behave and reflect their societal values (to themselves, with and towards others) are a reflection of their shared social meanings and the arena in which they practise their collective societal values.

Taking this as a point of departure for contemplating the rise of modern capitalism, Weber (1930/1992: 35–46, 128, 147, 178) recognized and emphasized the self-discipline of the individual, or what came to be known as the 'Protestant work ethic'. Beside the fact that the eagerness to work principle is otherworldly inspired, it is by the same token the *modus vivendi* which begets or creates conformity of conduct, always bearing in mind that for the believers the life in this world is merely a means of paving the way for the otherworldly eternal one, by way of salvation. This very process of searching for 'otherworldliness' is associated with – and involves a reconciliation with and an acceptance of living in – a regulated, routinized and ultimately rational and functional human condition. The essence of this *modus vivendi* – the Protestant ethic – can be traced to the practice of individuals to conform to generic social rules elicited from religious faith and the quest and struggle for salvation, so that the goal of salvation induces obedience that, in turn, generates salvation in a cyclical pattern. Salvation and obedience, moreover, engender arrangements and mechanisms of 'social control' which are the result of the individual's inner demeanour (Weber, 1930/1992: 120, 122, 130; Schroeder, 1992: 96–110; Pasquino, 1993: 38–9).

What is relevant to the modern Islamic condition and the role of faith in the discourse of politics is Weber's view of the direct link between the sacred and profane, especially his assumption that the greater the distance, the discrepancies and the tension between the domain of religious faith – the sacred – on the one hand, and the realities of the world – the profane – on the other, the more vivid and realized the vital role of religion becomes in political and sociocultural transformations. It provides the tension between religious dogma and (sacred) practice and worldly affairs that ultimately paves the way towards the reformation of religion into a logical, rational body of belief, adaptable to people's day-to-day needs. Therefore, Weber (1930/1992: 207–11) proposed three significant manifestations in religious domains where the interconnectedness between the sacred and the profane becomes vivid and coherent. First, the nature and degree of discarding and renouncing the world as a devaluated domain and the unworthiness of human life (Holton and Turner, 1989: 68; Schroeder, 1992: 148). This aspect is the equivalent of the idea of martyrdom, *shihadah*, in Islam, which is totally irrational, bearing in mind the ability of '*homo sapiens* … to reason and act upon the result of deliberation' (see n. 6). Second, the willingness to include others apart from oneself in the domain of religion by means of conversion – the whole question and principle of openness. Third, the nature of

the social institution, or the 'imagined moral community' (i.e., the
umma), whether it is organized according to the communal/filiative
Gemeinschaft or as an associated/affiliative *Gesellschaft*. It is by virtue
of this classification that Weber (1965: 207–22, 1968: 341ff.) sets out
to understand how religions intercommunicate with the social world
of flesh and blood (Turner, 1974: 124; Holton and Turner, 1989: 77).

As a classical discipline of the social sciences anthropology has been
concerned with the problem of meaning, the interpretation of
symbolism and the inquiry into the fundamental features of human
societies via the analysis of culture (Harris, 1987). To some extent,
therefore, anthropology can be seen as a hermeneutic inquiry into
belief systems, rituals and cultural practices. This view is common
among anthropologists who see the meaning of a particular social role,
myth, ritual or event as being the product of the relations and contrasts
with other roles, myths, rituals, and events (i.e., Arabism vis-a-vis
Zionism) (Gilsenan, 1982: 19ff.). Thus, the concept of culture is taken
here to be the symbolic and historically transmitted ideational frame
of reference of shared and common meanings (Geertz, 1973: 89;
Shweder and Le Vine, 1984; Kratochwil, 1996: 209), which means
that we cannot disassociate the discourse of Arabic culture from the
Iraqi invasion of Kuwait (and the political process in a general sense),
because it is interwoven in the social practices of the people.

Therefore, the role of culture is approached in two related aspects.[23]
First, it is a historically constituted domain of significant and comprehensive ideas about human life and practices – Arabism. Second,
Arabism is a discursive regime in which symbolic power delivers and
attains the highest conceivable quintessence in the political process and
the way states and leaders behave toward others. The 'cultural capital'
of this historically constituted regime is a wealth that can only be
possessed (or held) by those who have acquired the symbolic means
to make it relevant and fit it into their daily needs and concerns
(Bourdieu, 1991: 73, 75–6; 229–31; Foucault, 1978, 1980). It is,
moreover, an approach sensitive and responsive to the richness and
multifarious ramifications of local meanings and ideas, and the notion
of the 'social' in general. The literature on intersubjective meanings
and cultural studies approaches political processes by analysing the
relationship between symbolic, institutional and interactional power
relations. In such studies, scholars are concerned with the ways in
which symbols become 'cultural capital', which is employed for the

purpose of domination.[24] The implication of this approach ɪ
Arabism is not taken to be a single, rigidly bound set of strucᵤ
determining or interacting with other structures, but as a concept ɪ
identifies varying relations of practices, representations, symboʊ
concepts and world views within the same society and betweeᵤ
different societies. Within these domains, all human relations have
been significantly moulded and have evolved over time into something
recognizable to pundits and participants alike (Gilsenan, 1982: 19).

In this vein, an insightful approach and a genuine attempt
consciously to understand Islam's role and meaning in a modern society
is provided by Michael Gilsenan's *Recognising Islam*. Gilsenan (1982:
11) initiated his project with these simple but penetrating remarks:

I have come to write about ... class opposition, groups and individuals using
the same signs and codes but seeing events in quite different ways, concealed
significance in social life, complex relations to wider historical changes in
power relations and the economy. Finally, and not least, it draws attention
to the dagger of stereotypical images of another society and another religion
... it is inextricably bound up with many dimensions of social life in way that
are frequently not at all what they initially appear to be.

Since the time of the great (and aborted) social and political transformations of the late nineteenth and early twentieth centuries that
had as their main objective to place the Islam in the modern world
(Sharabi, 1970), the role of Islam in the public life of the Arab world
has been topical. Gilsenan's comparative approach to the diversified
forms and configurations of the domain of religion is located
conveniently within a broad range of the social transformation in the
political and economic processes of the society. These are circumstances
that through natural evolution or forceful integration have incorporated
Arab societies into the modern global capitalist system without
sacrificing the meaningful interconnectedness with their special past,
a past that is special because of the absence of reliable political
modalities, solid public institution and vibrant civil societies. This
dimension is still of great significance in the domestic political process
and foreign behaviour of the Arab states.

As with Weber and Geertz, for Gilsenan the social meanings of
the 'hidden layers', 'concealed motion' and of the religion of Islam
(through the medium of the Arabic language) retain a special import
in understanding the social, economic and political developments

ultural evolution.[25] These are processes that usually occur
...gh the efforts of the urban and commercial classes in Arab cities.
... is the terrain or the field of common views that combine the
...roccan philosopher al-Jabiri, the Algerian politician Ghozali, the
...unisian historian Djäit, the Egyptian poet Afifi Mattar, the Palestinian
...evolutionary al-Qaddumi, the Syrian professor of literature Abu
Deeb, the Jordanian political scientist Abu Jaber, the Saudi novelist
Munif, Islamist groups all over the Arab/Muslim world, as well as
ordinary people in the streets of the Arab cities. This is the reality
that Saddam Hussein (and for that matter any Arab leader in his
situation), reading his political statements, might have been counting
on during the Gulf crisis.

How does the cultural discourse exert influence on and frame
people's ideas and visions of politics? Of course, the outright answer
can be found in the resonance and motivating power of symbols and
'*a priori* codes' (Bourdieu, 1991), with the helping hand of the modern
technology of semiology. Saddam Hussein made four major speeches
(on 24 February, 1 April, 28 May and 17 July 1990) in which he
sought to attract support from a pan-Arab audience. Most of these
speeches were broadcast live all over the Arab world – people saw the
prominence of the Iraqi president and the hope he gave them to
deliver a strong signal to the enemies of the Arabs. Saddam Hussein
chose his words carefully, included the United States and the West,
as well as Israel, and made effective use of the vibrant rhetoric of the
Qur'an and Islamic idioms.

Indeed, given the considerable advances in the field of mass communication, symbols have proved to be one the essential constituents
of social relations. 'Symbolic forms', Thompson (1990: 58) notes, 'are
not merely representations which serve to articulate or obscure social
relations or interests which are constituted primarily at a pre-symbolic
level: rather, symbolic forms are continuously and creatively implicated
in the constitution of social relations as such'. For example, in analysing
the discourse of affinity between conformity of conduct (religious
faith) and the attribute of *Herrschaft* (i.e., body politic), Weber (1968:
53) moved beyond the inner and 'ascetic' dimension of obedience to
the government, by asserting that '[d]iscipline is the probability that
by virtue of habituation a command will prompt an automatic
obedience in stereotyped forms, on the part of a given group of
persons'. Hence, as far as the middle classes in Arab societies are

concerned, the social transformations have to be assessed within the scope of changing forms and substances in the meanings of Islam as a religion. The picture that has surfaced is rich, multifaceted and complex; Islam is above all interconnected with the social and political domains by virtue of its significance to these social groups. As Gilsenan (1982: 265) concludes, '[d]ifferent and sometimes mutually exclusive apprehensions and practices of Islam are emerging that separate societies and classes as much as they unite them'.

The Arab-Islamic cultural domain is thus treated as part and parcel of people's social life and, by implication, as an important variable in the political process, especially in the absence of public institutions that reflect and embody the collective action of society, and also bearing in mind the weak ties that people have to the modern state compared with their link to the superstructure of Arabism. However, this is not an outright handicap for the leader who seeks political hegemony and the status of leader of the Arab nation, even though he might lack the basic legitimacy and the simple acceptance of his own people in the state he rules. In the case of the Saddam Hussein during the spring of 1990, the paradox lies in the fact that his pan-Arab political record had been a poor one. His experience of the war with Iran showed that his pan-Arab appeals did not attract positive responses from all over the Arab world. Indeed, the Arab world had been split on the question of whether or not to support Iraq. Some countries (e.g., Libya, Syria) were openly supportive of Iran, while others had supported Iraq (e.g., Egypt and the Gulf states), although only on the basis of power politics.

However, when Iraq switched its attention to the Gulf states, and especially to Kuwait, a new language emerged along with a new set of enemies that unified the main social constellations throughout the Arab world. The Iraqi president might have had purely egoistic objectives and could have been pursuing personal power, but the language he used and the meanings his symbols and idioms conveyed was apparently something many Arabs wanted to hear. It was, after all, the type of language that all Arab leaders use when they are in conflict with outsiders (Israel and the West). But Iraq was in conflict with Kuwait, not with the United States and Israel, and despite the fact that Iraq had no 'concrete' grievance against or conflict with the United States and Israel, Saddam Hussein concentrated on attacking them to guarantee pan-Arab support needed for his policy. In short, what Saddam Hussein used as an instrument to attract pan-Arab legitimacy and support and to introduce himself in his newfound role of the great Arab leader was the language and the idioms of Islam, something that was welcomed by his listeners and easily recognized by the pundits (Bourdieu, 1977: 188ff.; Gilsenan, 1982). This leads us to a discussion of why the Arabic language is not only peculiar, but also why its self-generative system of meanings has an impact on political processes. The Iraqi invasion of Kuwait was a case in point.

The Arabic language and Arabic identity and politics

One of the most prominent and unique expressions of any culture is its language. As Wilhelm von Humboldt once observed, 'every language reflects the spirit of its people. It provides a nation with its own unique vehicle for the creation and communication of its ideas' (cited in Brint, 1991: 71). Indeed, it is the written language into which human activities and the development of deeply rooted habits, traits and peculiarities are channelled, the devotion of words to a space that augments and maximizes the potential capacity of language, sometimes beyond human imagination (Gusdorf, 1965; Ong, 1982). If this can apply to any language then it applies with particular significance to Arabic. Arabs acquire a sense of psychological wholeness, sociocultural unity, by virtue of the Arabic language and, indeed, from the intensity with which their common language is intimately interconnected with the Islamic faith. The political language is replete with metaphors that reveal the identity of Arabhood. It is the language that always stresses the fraternity of Arabism and the larger family, is the language used in all walks of Arab politics, by presidents, monarchs, revolutionaries, conservatives, reactionaries, state and non-state actors alike, be they anti-Western or pro-Western (Luciani and Salamé, 1988).[26]

Stefan Jonsson's (1995: 143) idea of the pendulum swinging between culture and language is apt at this juncture. 'Every culture, including its language and symbols', he argues, 'is a dynamic whole of the historical tension and fragment. Therefore, the human identity is the sum of all those positions it takes in the language symbolic order.' The intimate interconnectedness between the Arabic language and the glorious Arab past is illustrative of this idea. The Arabic language brings the past to life by virtue of its symbolism, as in Bourdieu's (1991) placement of the interactional relations of power within the societal 'habitus',[27] and in his analysis of the historical development of a legitimized linguistic style of the discourse of public language within the mechanisms of power in the society. In fact, the historical transformation of the language and the impact it exerts on people is a common theme of both Bourdieu and Foucault (with the French language as an empirical case). They argue, each in his own way, that the development of a 'neutralized' linguistic style is deeply embedded in, and reflective of, large-scale mechanisms of power in the society that are related, in one way or another, with the political processes and the social make-up. The function of language in Foucault's (1970: 294–300, 336ff., 1972: 107–10) discourse is the performative aspect of language, (i.e., what language does rather than what it denotes or connotes).

The Arabic language, moreover, reflects the world in an intimate and immediate context. It differs from many modern Western languages with their sometimes distanced textuality that reflects a plethora of highly impersonal mass institutions in which the individual senses that his/her performance consists only of marginal functions conducted in anonymity. For example, the standard opening to any meeting, whatever its topic, whoever attends it, wherever – even whenever – it take place in the Arab world is couched in the following language:

Brother heads of states of the ACC ... brother King Hussein ... brother President Mubarak ... brother Ali Abdallah Salih ... We meet in the Arab city of Amman ... which headed by our noble and brave brother His Majesty King Hussein ... In this part of Arabdom [Amman], where we are enjoying kind, brotherly hospitality among our kinfolk and brothers in blood, Arabism and common destiny, we have to come to carry out a brotherly Arabism role under a formula that has been willed by Allah and accepted by the righteous sons of this nation [28]

What is interesting here is that Saddam Hussein, or any other Arab leader, is obliged to use such language. On 20 July 1990, in responding to the psychological and media warfare conducted by the Ba'athist government of Iraq in order to get Kuwait's concession on the matter of debts and oil quotas, the Kuwaiti government used exactly the same discourse of language: 'out of line with the spirit of the existing fraternal relations between Kuwait and Iraq, and conflict with the most fundamental bases on which we wish to govern our Arab relations'.[29] The Kuwaiti government did not refer to the norms and framework of international law or the United Nations Charter as is usually the case when conflicts arise between states. This phenomenon emerges most clearly in the way Arabs settle conflicts between each other. For example, Arabism (and Islam) invariably refrains from settling conflicts or establishing peace between adversaries by resorting to the arbitration of impersonal and rational institutions. Instead, what is preferred is an intimate personal deliberation and what is usually called an aesthetic approach that sustains a harmonious order, and it was assumed that what was intended to be an Arab solution to an Arab affair in the crisis that arose between Iraq and Kuwait would be found within this framework. The assessment of a particular problem and the solution to it do not necessarily require reason and pin-point hard-logic explanations, but should be based on such factors as detached awareness, instinct, wisdom and spontaneity. Mutual deliberations and transstate negotiations are performed within the form of poems, stories or aphorisms. After the traditional brotherly kissing and hugging, Arab leaders are usually seen walking hand in hand at state visits or other Arab League summits. Even though hard bargaining sometimes followed by concessions always take place, their mutual talks and negotiations occur without any written record of the meeting, or other formalities that make the atmosphere distant.

Such a procedure, while it is almost a norm in inter-Arab politics, has it own positive and negative dimensions. As a norm in defusing conflicts and when mediating between leaders and states it has been very effective, save in the single case of the Gulf crisis. There are many examples: the reconciliation between King Faysal of Saudi Arabi and President Abdul Nassir of Egypt in 1967 during the Arab League summit in Khartoum; between Abdul Nassir and King Hussein of Jordan after the defeat of 1967; between the King Hussein and Yassir Arafat after their bloody war in Jordan in 1970; between Mubarak and Hafez al-Assad of Syria in 1988; between Mubarak and Khaddafi of Libya in 1989; and finally between Mubarak and Colonel Omar al-Basheer, the President of Sudan, after a bitter personal and political quarrel, at the summit in Cairo in July 1996. After the traditional Arabic greeting with hugs and kisses, leaders appeared hand in hand during the Arab League summit. Ironically, the exception was during the Gulf crisis. When President Mubarak of Egypt sought to mediate with Saddam Hussein and Kuwait on 28 August 1990, they behaved the way any two Arab leaders usually do. The two presidents walked hand in hand, and no written records was ever kept of the flimsy and ambiguous promises that were made. Afterwards, both Mubarak and Saddam Hussein had entirely different versions of their meeting, and since there was no official and mutually recognized account, it was difficult to decide which version could be verified.

In general terms, however, Arabism's use of language as a weapon is mainly in conflicts between Arab states and as a pretext for the interference of one state in the affairs of others. Prominent examples of this are Nassir and Saddam Hussein, appealing over the heads of governments to the Arab peoples. However, the roots of such sentiments lie too deep in history and conscience for ordinary people to be turned into the docile instruments of political leaders. Appealing to such deeply rooted and powerful ideas and sentiments is not a problem-free enterprise for two reasons: first, they become slogans caught up in the ambiguous discourse of power and the assertion of a certain leader's hegemony in Arab mainstream politics;[30] second, using such an appealing language more strongly and effectively than other Arab rivals are able to do may only intensify the level of conflict among the Arab regimes. Examples include Saddam Hussein vis-a-vis the conservative camp of Egypt and the Gulf states during the Gulf crisis, and Abdul Nassir against the pro-Western regimes during the 1950s and 1960s. At the same time this paradoxical situation always fuels and intensifies conflicts within the Arab regional setting as much as between the Arab world and all outsiders. It gives an unmistakable touch of legitimacy to leaders' actions against outside powers, whether they are entirely justified or completely erratic and gratuitous.[31]

There is an intimate affinity between the triangle of language, identity (Arabism) and politics. Public figures such as Abdul Nassir, Michel Aflaq, Hafez al-Assad and Saddam Hussein, to mention only a few, embrace a highly refined, attractive, simple and vibrant radical language that has enormous appeal, but when translated into other languages is then reduced – see Gibb (1963: 11–13) and al-Wardi (1994), for example. Unlike other languages, the reader of Arabic (and Hebrew) has to understand what is to be read before reading it. The visible text contains only consonants – the reader has to know the correct vowel in order to make sense of it. Arabic is an essentially oral language which, due to its connection with Islam, contains powerful psychological symbolism. This is one of the reasons that make it so difficult to translate into other languages. A great many Arabic words and metaphors are essentially culturally bound and their psychological impact is revealed only in the context of Arab and Islamic culture.

On the other hand, while the same language was used to tyrannize the downtrodden grass-roots in Arab cities, it also became a symbol of pride and a reason for resisting the *imagined* and the *real* enemies of the Arab nation. Consequently, these grass-roots form a powerful force that helps to mobilize all the social forces in support of the decisions and actions taken by political leaders, and confer legitimacy on such leaders. All the differences in ideological, ethnic, religious and even social background are to be set aside (for the time being) so that the common enemy can be combated. The Iraqi leadership put the invasion of Kuwait within this framework. As an articulated modern ideology of states (e.g., Nassirism in Egypt and Ba'athism in Iraq and Syria) Arabism has unavoidably been transformed into empty slogans repeated over and over again by the mighty propaganda machines of the ruling elites. The Arab grass-roots are often so bewildered by all the empty theatrical rhetoric, and so terrified by the limitless oppression of the state structures, that they have virtually no option but to remain, at best, indifferent – to which is added a political reality of which myth-making and submissiveness in public life are typical characteristics. Since there were no means by which civil society could contribute or influence the social or the political process, this become a state of normalcy in public life (Tylor, 1988: 117–20), and even the glorious past became phantomized and fabricated into a present-day device by a cynical leader who, in a ceaseless thirst for power, would do whatever it took to obtain and hold on to it. He did so by revitalizing the glorious past, *ihyaa* (or renaissance, *Ba'ath*, as the word virtually denotes), and disguised it as universalism and as the outstretched hand in what Anderson (1991) calls the 'horizontal comradeship' of anti-Zionism, anti-Western imperialism, fellowship and brotherhood among Arabs throughout the Middle East.

What really matters here is how this self-same leader could attract such support. Affection and sentiments work well, despite that fact that none of these societies are coherently associated or connected to each other by concrete day-to-day ties of organized political, economic and social activities, nor by any coordination between civil society constellations for solidarity with others in the face of outside threats. Reading through the literature on the politics of integration, political coordination or economic cooperation (e.g., Korany and Dessouki, 1984; Salamé and Luciani, 1988; Luciani, 1990), one is astonished at the remoteness of the prospect of integration, let alone the longed-for objective of Arab political unity. On the one hand, the impressive show of solidarity in Algeria, Morocco, Sudan, Tunisia and Yemen with the Iraqi Ba'ath during the Gulf crisis is a sober reminder of the need to examine the real '*a priori* codes' of this phenomenon. In his analysis of cultural politics and the political dimensions of the production of culture, Bourdieu (1991) associates social stratifications in society with the way they interact with (and within) various social institutions. Bourdieu contends that, as far as the common sense of everyday life is concerned, the understanding of material objects is spontaneous and immediate. The capacity to perceive (like that of imagining in Anderson's sense) is also taken to vary from one individual to another, since understanding daily life usually takes place through a prism of *a priori* codes that evolve into an attribute of a cultivated capacity for those who become familiar with them. The *a priori* codes in this context consist of the richness of religious symbols, idioms and metaphors in the powerful Arabic language, where the Islamic past come to serve the present. To this end the villages, cities, construction sites and roads are renamed – even the weapons, and especially the Scud missiles, were named al-Hussein, al-Qa'aqaa, al-Abbas, and so on.

Drawing on semiotics, Bourdieu suggests that this whole process of comprehension is enigmatic. In this vein, Benedict Anderson (1991: 47,72) who examines the use of images and the treatment of literary cultural artifacts, the influence of technology on ideas, and the way that organizing and establishing the process of print capitalism gave a new fixity to language, is relevant here. Accordingly, perceptiveness in reality is a variant of cultural deciphering. Bourdieu (ibid.: 205–15) asserts that the entitlement and the ability to decipher is unequally distributed within society, and this is a dimension akin to Marx's notion on the materialist angle. The powerful and prestigious status positions of public institutions in the society then require highly qualified and experienced individuals who have usually mastered these *a priori* codes, since for these individuals such codes constitute the source of the cultural wealth of any society. Similarly, such cultural capital is only and ultimately enjoyed by those who have the possession and control of the technology of semiology and utilize it to fit into the unconscious mastery of the mechanism of normalization. The magical power of signs is attributed to words and the images they invoke.

For example, under the Ba'athist rule in Iraq, Saddam Hussein fought a long, bitter and destructive war against Iran under the banner of defending modern secular values against religious fanaticism. Yet in his speeches during the Gulf crisis he resorted to vehement, emotional and admonitory language vibrant with religious metaphors so that 'the names of Ali, Mu'awiya, Al-Hussein, Al-Abbas, and Yazid are as contemporary as this morning's newspaper, more so than yesterday's' (Lewis, 1993: 159). It was the Iraqi leader's most effective weapon. In his 'The Mother of all Battles' speech of January 1991, Saddam Hussein declared,

Glorious Iraqis, O holy warrior Iraqis, O Arabs, O believers wherever you are, we and our steadfastness are holding. Here is the great Iraqi people, your brothers and sons of your Arab nation and the great faithful part of the human family ... And here is the infidel tyrant whose planes and missiles are falling out of the skies at the blows of the brave men ... *Allah* willing ... We in Iraq will be faithful and obedient servants of God, struggling for his sake to raise the banner of truth and justice, the banner of *Allah-u-Akbar*. Accursed be the lowly. (Quoted in Bengio, 1992: 189ff.)

As experience of all modern wars and conflicts between Arabs and outsiders, between Arab and Israeli and finally the Gulf crisis has shown, the normative power of pan-Arab identity manifested in the language as a political variable is central to an understanding, not only of how 'the contemporary importance of old rules [and] how one set of ideas rather than another came to be institutionalized' (Goldstein and Keohane, 1993: 21), but also of why Arab leaders and states behave the way they do, to the extent that there is an almost self-generative political discourse in the Arab world that is marked by ambivalence regarding the notion of sovereign states and the cherishing of Arabism. Below, I shall discuss the connection between the Arabic political discourse and the invasion of Kuwait, a connection consisting of feelings, aspirations, emotions, ideas, or, in other words, of the 'seamless web of significance', of 'hidden layers' or 'concealed motion'.

THE ARABIC POLITICAL DISCOURSE AND THE INVASION OF KUWAIT

Two aspects of the Arabic political discourse require careful consideration in so far as the invasion of Kuwait is concerned. First is the prevalence of the political allegiances and loyalty to the idea of Arabism vis-a-vis the territorial sovereignty of modern Arab states. Here the imperative of identification of Arabism with Islam as its essential ingredient and the language as its powerful manifestation still shadow and obscure the notion of sovereign territorial states in the Arab world. Second is the discourse of Arabism in constructing what it maintains are its opposites or Others (i.e., Zionism, the United States and a diverse array of Western societies). Then, the perceptions, tensions and the resentment in the relationships between the rich, the 'Gulfis', and poor Arabs need to be discussed within the context of Arabism. In the context of the second aspect, a review will be presented of how various categories of people reacted to Iraq's and Saddam Hussein's behaviour toward Kuwait, Israel and the United States in order to illustrate their striking conformity with the discursive formation of Arabism on this issue. This is why, when analysing the invasion of Kuwait and the Gulf crisis, factors such as economic needs, territorial disputes and the pursuit of hegemonic power by persons or states ought to be placed within, or at least seen through, 'the seamless web of significance of Arabism' in order to obtain a fair explanation.

The institution of Arabism vis-a-vis the system of sovereign states

The following section examines the widely held 'belief that Arab nationhood will be translated into Arab statehood, and that the present division of the Arab nation into several states is both artificial and temporary' (Korany and Dessouki, 1984: 27). In a similar vein, Hermassi (1987: 75–6, cited in Bayomi, 1995: 13) succinctly articulates the point:

There is loyalty, but not to the state, there is consensus, but not around it. In this case, authority is severed from the law and power from moral authority. The orders of state are implemented. Projects are achieved. The individual state provides the country with infrastructure, education, employment, organisation, etc. All these achievements do not, however, bring loyalty to,

or consensus around, the state. This is especially the case if its propaganda is
a constant reminder that this is only a stage towards the achievement of the
greater Arab state.

In order to understand the basis of the tension and fragmentation
between territorial sovereignty and the historically constructed
common identity, let me briefly sketch the grammar of the 'political'
in the Arab context. In full agreement with Aristotle, *Durr-al-Mukhtar*
contended that: 'Man is by nature a political animal, because he cannot
live by himself as other animals do, but requires the help and society
of fellow-creature.'[32] But the Augustinian and Hobbesian pessimism
and suspicion concerning human beings are, unfortunately, empirically
grounded. Although human beings are essentially and innately social
they do not always behave as they are expected to. 'Men are the
enemies of each other' says the Qur'an (xx: 121). If human beings are
left ungoverned and uncontrolled the instincts of violence, egoism
and greed will prevail, and in such a situation it would be meaningless
for them to live. The Rule and the Law of Allah are the instruments
whereby the evil nature of humans can be controlled. To insure that
the Rule and the Law become viable instruments they need to have
protectors, advocates and sustainers, and the existence of these
guardians and sustainers is of the utmost importance. Since Islam is
the basis and the substance, and the sovereign is the vital instrument
that upholds it, it follows that any sovereign is better than none; what
has no basis becomes chaotic and what has no protector will be eroded
and go to waste (De Santillana, 1961; Kedourie, 1980: 37, 38ff.).

In the Arabic discourse of culture, politics, *siyasa*, signifies the
thoughtful walk with others and the capacity to rule by *hikma*, reason.
Siyasa, too, is the governance of the disorderly state of nature through
the cultivated and devoted believer. The magisterial imposition of
power is the ultimate cultivated condition for an otherwise Hobbesian
nightmare of the cruel and brutish state of nature. So, *siyasa* is not the
domain whereby different claimants to power, or *mulk* and *sultan*,[33]
challenge and oppose each other and finally reach a consensus as to
who shall govern. On the basis of the need to uphold and safeguard
the *umma*, Arab/Muslim thought on politics was adapted to the
tradition of absolutism and the notion of authority of other ancient
Middle Eastern regimes such as the Byzantine and Persian empires.
Thus, the authoritarian political tradition dates back to the early Islamic
history. The 'syndrome of leadership', or 'rulership', to use Al-Khalil's

(1989: 110ff.) term, which permeated and spread throughout the Arab world is a repetition of this political tradition. Its basic component is: the ruler is he who wields power as long as he wields it. Thus, the duty of obedience is granted to any holder of effective power. The rationale was to avoid, at any cost, anarchy as it is reflected in the following dicta 'tyranny is better than anarchy', and 'sixty years of tyranny are better than an hour of civil strife' (Lewis, 1973: 269ff.; 1988: 43–70). Thus, for the sake of the stability and cohesion of the community sovereignty resided with the holder of power, and this power was hardly ever accountable before the populace. The Islamic system of Caliphate as *imagined* by Muslim theorists had never materialized. In the main, the Caliphate had a purely decorative function. The military chieftains were the *de facto* authorities that exerted real power within various Islamic empires, and the rival states within the abode of Islam were an extension of the traditions of oriental despotism with the patrimonial authority as its most significant attribute (Wittfogel, 1963). These highly unstable political entities never permitted the emergence of mature and legitimate political rule with a lawful delegation of power, nor did they produce structures whereby individuals could have peaceful recourse to obtain justice and political rectitude in the event of the abuse of public authority. The outcome of this tradition of political rule is a submissive individual instead of an active one who adopts an active role as a citizen in the community. Throughout the history of Islam there has never been a mechanism whereby people can be protected from arbitrary rulers (Lewis, 1973: 289–302, 1988; Ayubi, 1991).

The notions of *mulk*, or authority, had characterized the difference between statesmanship and the exercise of *siyasa*, which consisted of three related components, namely, *din*, religion, *hikma*, reason, and *alla-mahsoub*, caprice.[34] *Siyasa*, does not, however, provide the basis for authority, but is rather the *modus operandi* for politics and a precondition for the absolute practice and operation of public life. The premise of *siyasa* in Arab/Muslim thought consists of an evaluative discourse and of an *exempla* that illustrate a moral obligation to hold the community away from division and conflict. Muslim writings on politics are really more guidelines or handbooks for governance than abstract theories that create visions and a new outlook in order to understand and apply politics in the same way Rousseau, John Locke and others did in the European discourses of the seventeenth, eighteenth and nineteenth centuries and later (Ayubi, 1991; Al-Azmeh, 1993: 91). The other type of discourse on *siyasa* is the notion that it is the instrument whereby Allah's words would have worldly regulation. The *siyasa shar'iyya*, as this is called, is derived from *shar'a*, the Islamic body of belief. This discourse has absolute power as a taken-for-granted condition, and as such, it amounts to another *modus operandi* of authority, especially in regard to the question of political legitimacy, as in the cases of Iran, Saudi Arabia and Sudan (Al-Azmeh, 1993: 92–3).

This evolution occurs without alteration in the elite's conception of political rule. Modern Arab regimes operate within the same framework, but with far greater control over their populations due to modern technology that has reinforced their means of surveillance and coercion. In the era of independence, state control has been widely used to promote the power of traditional social groups and formations – families, sects, tribes and cliques with access to power (Ibrahim, 1992: 15). Far from being affected by the force of social criticism that swept many other states in the Arab world after the defeat of June 1967, the Iraqi political establishment, like all other political elites in the Arab world, remained ingrained in an apologetic historiography of Arab glory.[35]

The Arab leaders' notion of sovereignty and the way they deal with territorial disputes has to be seen in this context. Saddam Hussein's invasion and annexation of Kuwait highlighted what Martin Wight (1977) stressed as an essential component in the practising of sovereignty by states, namely, their respect for the norm of reciprocity. States have mutually to recognize and respect one another's claims of sovereignty. Wight argued further:

> it would be impossible to have a society of sovereign states unless each state, while claiming sovereignty for itself, recognises that every other state had the right to claim and enjoy its own sovereignty as well. This reciprocity was inherent in the Western conception of sovereignty. (Ibid.: 135, quoted in Keohane, 1988: 385)

Saddam Hussein, however, adopted, or adapted to, an 'Ottoman style of dealing with territorial disputes' (Ibn Abdul-Aziz, 1995: 191). Within only three months Kuwait was described in the terms of three different legal definitions by Saddam Hussein: in July 1990 it was a foreign state with an unfriendly government; on 2 August 1990, Saddam Hussein assigned a government and Kuwait was a foreign state with a friendly government; by October, Kuwait had always been the nineteenth province of Iraq. Shortly before all this, on 23 September 1989, as has been mentioned, the Amir of Kuwait had visited Baghdad on an official visit and had been given the 'Medal of Mesopotamia', or *Wesam al-Rafidain*, by Saddam Hussein, who praised his wisdom and generosity toward Iraq.[36]

Weber's (1947/1964: 154–7) definition of the state as the organization of domination remains the classical way Western social science has approached the state since the Enlightenment. He depicts the modern 'state' as 'a compulsory political association with continuous organisation [that] successfully upholds a claim to the *monopoly* of the *legitimate* use of physical force in the enforcement of its order ... continually within a given *territorial* area' (p. 154, emphasis in original). Indeed, the substance of the modern notion of the state, established and regulated on the Hobbesian logic of the covenant, rests fundamentally upon the concept of a pervading commitment and on a secular faith in the legitimacy of political authority. What are now known as the Hobbesian third-party solutions urge the delegation of power to the state (or *Leviathan*) in the quest for order at any cost in order to avoid the much-feared 'state of nature' (Putnam *et al.*, 1993: 157). When this is done, it often happens that the sphere of political legitimacy is taken away from the ruled (the initial authors of the covenant), and this has usually engendered the grave social, and political consequences that are discussed above (see pages 77–92).

As opposed to the Weberian and Hobbesian visions of the state, in Arabic political thought the term 'state', *dawla*, signifies a certain type of patrimonious (or patriarchal) institution that exercises power and authority delegated by an supernatural entity, Allah. The state was the means of upholding an order already given by Allah (i.e., the *umma*). But in the discourse of European Enlightenment and later, the state was the basis which led the whole idea of community to be realized, and this made it necessary to define and to relate all other social organization to the state (Giddens, 1985). However, the state was discussed within the Islamic political context only as an abstract locus of order and disorder and, more importantly, as a god-given *fait accompli*. In the writings of various medieval Muslim scholars such as Nizam al-Mulk (1018–1092), al-Mawardi (d. 1058), and Ibn Khaldun (1332–1406), *dawla* refers to the continuity over time of power exercised by a clique of successive sovereigns to the point at which a single sovereign exercises exclusive power. The conception of the state *as an organization of domination* over a given territory, in the Weberian sense, had not existed. Rather, *dawla* connotes essentially a body politic with three main components: a ruler, his troops and a bureaucracy that is exclusively linked to him, its main function being to safeguard the Allah-given order — *umma*. At this juncture, what must be stressed is that *dawla* is distinct from society at large and from what has come in modern times to be known as the civil society (Al-Azmeh, 1993: 90).[37] So, until their disappearance in the twentieth century different Islamic empires were mobile in Ruggie's (1993) sense, and the ruling elites within these empires could — if they had the military force — assume governance and legitimize it anywhere in the abode of Islam, because 'public territories formed a continuum with the private state' (Anderson, 1974: 32). One explanation might be that the title of sovereignty was defined in religious terms, unlike in Western Europe, where it was defined in territorial terms. In Islam, Lewis (1993: 168) argues:

territorial titles were used to belittle a rival, not to aggrandise oneself. In the conflict and also in the correspondence between competing Muslim great powers in the sixteenth and seventeenth centuries, the sultan of Turkey and the shah of Persia called each other by these titles, but never themselves. Each was concerned to reduce his rival to the level of a local potentate. Each in his own titulature was the Supreme Lord of the Muslims.

From the time of the Fourth Caliph Ali (656–661) who moved to Koufa in Iraq until the establishment of the third Saudi state in 1932, the Arabian Peninsula stood outside the mainstream of Middle Eastern and world history. During the course of the Arab conquests a new era arose in the history of the Middle Eastern and of the Islamic civilization as well, but Arabia was left isolated and drained of much of its population (Lapidus, 1990). The same applies to Mesopotamia after the decline of the Abbasid empires and Hulagu's invasion in 1258. During the centuries that followed until the colonial era the two regions were relegated to a marginal role in Middle Eastern history. Until the twentieth century they lacked central authorities and a central social organization based on fixed and clearly marked territories (Corm, 1992). There was little need for accurately defined borders because, it was, so to speak, *Ardd-u-Allah* (Allah's land), or *umma*. As the tribes and sand dunes were constantly moving these areas were technically *terra nullius* (i.e., they belonged to nobody), and in the absence of a multilateral agreement considerable conflicts could have developed in the rudimentary and uninhabited frontier regions (Kratochwil, 1986).[38]

It was only when the Europeans arrived that their notion of territorial sovereignty was introduced and fixed and defined within the framework of the Syckos-Picout Treaty of 1916, in which Britain and France agreed on their spheres of influence in the Middle East. They found that the drawing of borders was usually extremely frustrating, and often unsuccessful, as a glance at the map of the *Mashreq* demonstrates (Harik, 1990; Corm, 1992). The boundaries are rarely congruent with people's social and economic structures, and their arbitrary nature bequeathed to these states a complex and heterogeneous mixture of ethnic and social groups that became an obstacle in the process of nation building. Moreover, to cover up their failure to establish mutually accepted territorial units, the colonial powers introduced trucial areas, neutral zones, mutual control and other verbal compromises which, after the discovery of oil, proved to be sources from which violent conflicts arose (Anderson, 1987).

There is telling historical episode in the memoirs of Major Harold Dickson, *Kuwait and her Neighbours* (1956). Dickson was assistant to Sir Percy Cox, the British colonial administrator in Arabia, and during 1930s he was the British political agent in Kuwait. In November 1922, Cox decided to fix the boundaries of Iraq and Najid, providing the territorial heart of modern Saudi Arabia, and Kuwait became the victim of the creation of these two great regional powers, something that shaped the continuing tension between the al-Sabah and al-Saud families. As the political agent of His Majesty in Iraq (at the time it was a British protectorate), Cox was the only authority entitled to decide a matter of life and death for nations – defining their boundaries. By the same token, Najid was a British invention and Ibn Saud was patronized by Britain. As such, Cox invited the representatives of Iraq – the minister of communication, Sabih Beg – and Najid – Ibn Saud. The representative of Kuwait, however, was Major J. C. More, as British political agent there was in charge of Kuwait's foreign affairs. All gathered in a British army tent at Uqair in the Arabian desert (Draper, 1992: 46ff.; Schofield, 1993: 56–9).

Dickson recorded that Sir Percy Cox waited until 27 November, which followed five days of disagreement, claims and counterclaims, primarily from Sabih Beg and Ibn Saud. (Sabih Beg, for example, claimed that the Iraqi territory should include Ryiadh in the heart of Arabia, while Ibn Saud was adamant that his future kingdom promised to him by the British had to include the Euphrates to compensate for the dry desert of Arabia.) Thereafter, Dickson recorded that

> On the sixth day Sir Percy entered the lists. He told both sides that at the rate they were going, nothing would be settled for a year. At a private meeting at which only he, Ibn Saud and I were present, he lost all patience over what he called the childish attitude of Ibn Saud in his tribal boundary idea ... It was astonishing to see the Sultan of Najid being reprimanded like a naughty schoolboy by H. M. High Commissioner, and being told sharply that he, Sir Percy Cox, would himself decide on the type and general line of the frontier. This ended the impasse.
>
> Ibn Saud almost broke down, and pathetically remarked that Sir Percy was his father and brother, who had made him and raised him from nothing to the position he held, and that he would surrender half his kingdom, nay the whole, if Sir Percy ordered. (Cited in Draper, ibid.: 46)

After an emotional and heated quarrel with Ibn Saud, Cox was ready to give birth to three countries at one blow:

> At a general meeting of the conference, Sir Percy took a red pencil and very carefully drew in on the map of Arabia a boundary line from the Persian Gulf to Jabal Anaizan, close to the transjordan frontier. This gave Iraq a large area of her territory claimed by Najid. Obviously, to placate Ibn Saud, he ruthlessly deprived Kuwait of nearly two-thirds of her territory and gave it to Najid, his argument being that the power of Ibn Sabah was much less in the desert that [than] it had been when the Anglo-Turkish Agreement [1913] had been drawn up. South and west of Kuwait proper, he drew out two zones which he declared should be neutral and known as the Kuwait Neutral Zone and the Iraq Neutral Zone. (Cited in Draper, 1992: 46)

Dickson, moreover, narrated this emotional encounter between Cox and Ibn Saud:

> Ibn Saud asked to see Sir Percy Cox alone. Sir Percy took me with him. Ibn Saud was by himself, standing in the centre of his great reception tent. He seemed terribly upset.
>
> 'My friend,' he moaned, 'you have deprived me of half my kingdom. Better take it all and let me go into retirement.'
>
> Still standing, this great strong man, magnificent in his grief, suddenly burst into sobs. Deeply disturbed, Sir Percy seized his hand and began to weep also. Tears were rolling down his cheeks. No one but the three of us were present, and I relate exactly what I saw.

The emotional storm did not last long. Still holding Ibn Saud's hand Sir Percy said: 'My friend, I know exactly how you feel, and for this reason I gave you two-third of Kuwait's territory.[39] I don't know how Ibn Sabah will take the blow.' (Cited in Draper, ibid.: 46).

When Cox informed Ibn Sabah about what happened, Dickson reports it as follows:

Both Major More and myself, I only in a secretarial capacity, were present when Sir Percy broke the news to the ruler of Kuwait that he had been obliged to give away to Ibn Saud nearly two-thirds of the kingdom claimed by Shaykh Ahmad. Shaykh Ahmad pathetically asked why he had done this without even consulting him. Sir Percy replied that, on this unfortunate occasion, the sword had been mightier than the pen, and that had he not conceded the territory, Ibn Saud would certainly have soon picked a quarrel and taken it, if not more, by force of arms. As it was he [Sir Percy] had placated Shaykh Ahmad's powerful neighbour and brought about a friendly feeling for Kuwait. (Cited in Draper, ibid.: 46–7)

Finally, the ruler of Kuwait,

Shaykh Ahmad then asked if Great Britain had not entered the war in defence of the rights of small nations. Sir Percy admitted that this was correct. 'If some day,' said Shaykh Ahmad, 'Ibn Saud dies and I grow stronger like my grandfather, Mubarak, will the British Government object if I denounce the unjust frontier line and recover my lost territories?' 'No!' laughed Sir Percy. 'And may God bless your efforts.' Thus faced with a fait accompli Shaykh Ahmad agreed to add his signature to the agreement. (Cited in Draper, ibid.: 47)

Thus, the definition, and demarcation of sovereign territorial units, and mutually exclusive and recognized state formations did not emerge in the *Mashreq* until after the disintegration of the Ottoman empire. Ibrahim (1992: 4) argues that 'the idea of the nation or territorial state with fixed borders was a new concept for ... Arabia and the Gulf. The majority of the nomadic people identified themselves with a particular tribe or a system of tribal alliances.' Political elites in the Arab world (e.g., Nassirist Egypt; Khaddafi's Libya; Ba'athist Iraq and Syria) often find themselves better served by pan-Arabism. The emphasis on a transstate identity represents efforts to inspire loyalty based on ethnic and religious allegiances which ultimately undermine the territorial loyalty so essential for the modern state (Anderson, 1987: 13; Harik, 1990; Barnett, 1993).

The narrative and perception of identity and authority in the work of modern pan-Arabists is an extension of premodern Muslim historiography. Writing the history of Islam, and of caliphs, sultans, dynasties and inventing the history of the Arab nation means presenting this history as an extension to a glorious Islamic history, but never as a history of countries or nations in the abstract, sovereign or modern sense (Anderson, 1991; Lewis, 1975, 1993: 168). Political loyalties and submission to states within fixed, defined and mutually accepted territorial borders are alien concepts to the tribes in Libya, Mesopotamia and Arabia. Ruggie (1993: 150) argues that 'the spatial extension of the mediaeval system of rule was structured by a non-exclusive form of territoriality. In which authority was both personalized and parcelized within and across territorial formations and for which inclusive bases of legitimation prevailed.' The social and political allegiances are personally bestowed, and only to their tribes and tribal leaders, not to an imagined abstract state as is implied in the European state system (Kelly, 1964: 18). Thus, all the ingredients of what Kratochwil (1986: 33; see also Nardin, 1983) terms as the 'negative community' as far as the Arab world is concerned, are in place. The negative community denotes a situation in which there is an agreement on common practices and rights, but not on a common purpose:

Thus, a 'negative community' – one not united by a common purpose or a vision of the good life, but only by common practices and the mutual recognition of rights – comes into existence. Boundaries become lines (although their exact demarcation must wait until better means of geodesy develop) instead of remaining zonal frontiers.

Arabism and the genuine feeling of being one people with a common destiny is a historically brewed and firmly conceived amalgam of sentiments and traditions dating back to the high point of the Arabs' role in the establishment and expansion of the Islamic faith.[40] We are now approaching the end of the twentieth century and 'the Arab world still paradoxically constitutes a single area of psychological, emotional and intellectual resonance transcending state frontiers', as Walid Khalidi (1991: 4) has written, but:

the failure of the Arab political order, as it has evolved since the end of World War II both in the Mashriq and Maghrib, to be approximate in any of its constituent sovereign states to minimal levels of genuine power sharing or accountability in government, much less to self-governing parliamentary institutions operating within democratic forms and constraints.

Furthermore, when Iraq invaded and annexed Kuwait, the Kuwaiti, Saudi and other governments who condemned the Iraqi action did not do so on the basis of international law or the United Nations Charter. Instead, they referred to analogies drawn from Islamic history, the Prophet's preachings and practices, and quotations from the Qur'an to enforce their own view of the invasion and annexation. In the first place, in ejecting the al-Sabah family as a first step towards liberating the Arab land and resources from Zionism and Western imperialism, Iraq had to put forward the Iraqi views through many of the Islamic *fatwas* proposed by pro-Iraqi Islamic theologians. Second, Saudi Arabia had to justify the invitation of an 'infidel' army on the holy land of Islam, with the help of other anti-Iraqi Islamic theologians who asserted that the Prophet had asked for the helping hand from 'infidels' as a measure to safeguard the community. What is interesting to note is that despite the fact that Iraq's action was considered to be naked aggression by any law in the modern world, the Kuwaiti government (i.e., the victim) and its other allies in the Arab world were on the defensive in putting their case, essentially because of their association with the United States and, by implication, Zionism.

To conclude, '[t]erritoriality, like propriety, is not a simple concept, but comprises a variety of social arrangements that have to be examined in greater detail' (Kratochwil, 1986: 28). Territorial disputes, it has been noted, have been the prime motivations behind the majority of wars in human history. This is what makes territorial issues so essential in understanding how decision makers deal with them. Territories are not only matters of geostrategic concerns, they are also attached to people's historical memories and, in many cases, embody powerful symbols of a collective human identity. Foreign policy decision-making, power politics and the invocation of war must be seen through the way neighbours settle their territorial disputes, for it is a reflection of the political culture and the framework within which all states learn to operate (Walzer, 1976; Vasquez, 1992: 151–2). For reasons beyond the scope of the present research, the Arab political discourse was unable to establish and develop societal and political institutions that would function as a common forum for cooperation and mutual interaction within and between states. Most importantly, such mechanisms would be able to assimilate and ultimately control the outbreak of conflicts between two or more members of the Arab state system, on the one hand, and with outside powers, on the other. Therefore, the arena is quite often open and enables outside Western powers to step in. The history of foreign involvement has many serious implications, from the European colonial arrangements to economic imperialism to the exploitation of the Arabs. Indeed, Zionism and the Jewish state, with what these imply in the Arabs' discursive formation, embody both evils, and so Arabism can be seen as the set of normative ideas 'that specify criteria for distinguishing right from wrong and just from unjust ... they translate fundamental doctrines into guidance for contemporary human action' (Goldstein and Keohane, 1993: 9). This leads us to the following point.

Arabism and 'others' – Zionism and the West

The perception of Otherness, Herder once observed, usually renders people more ethnocentric since there is no shared sense of humanity to which they can jointly appeal. As mentioned earlier, the Iraqi president had concentrated almost exclusively on Zionism and the United States in both his speeches and Iraqi government statements before the invasion of Kuwait. This was a natural and basic premise if Saddam Hussein was to be guaranteed the unequivocal support of the Arab intelligentsia, the middle classes and the grass–roots. The prevalence of Arabism's vision of Zionism as its absolute opposite is unmissable and relentless in textbooks, educational systems and the media throughout the Arab world. It takes sometimes frenetic forms in its denunciation of the existence of Israel as a state and of the apparent success of Zionism as a political and ideological movement (Yassin, 1981a). Indeed, modern Arab writers, novelists, playwrights, syndicated writers and political commentators all adopt the same style in their passionate portrayal of Israel as a construction born of conspiracies or plots by imperialism and its cherished offspring, Zionism.[41]

The defeat in the Six–Day War in 1967 was a blow to the Arab's image of Israel. This victory requires an explanation beyond the normal processes of rational thought (al-'Azm, 1968; Lewis, 1986: 186–91; Yassin, 1981a: 21–6). In their endeavour to demonstrate and prove the conspiracy connection, some writers go so far as to implicitly or explicitly rely on the ignorant bigotry of Canon Rohling and the

Protocols of the Elders of Zion, the masterpiece of anti-Semitic fabrication (Lewis, 1986: 199). In the end, the literature of anti-Semitism that emanated from Europe provided such an explanation. The Jew of the Arab tradition, associated with plots and schemes, was malevolent but timorous, and all his efforts would be unavailing against the might of Arabism and Islam, 'for Allah is a better schemer'. One example among too many to review here is provided by Hazem Hashem (1986), *Al-Muaamara al-Israeeliyya ala al-Aql al-Misri* ('The Israeli Conspiracy on the Egyptian Mind'), who depicts the cosmic struggle which must now ensue between the forces of good (i.e., the Arabs, from leftists to fundamentalists), and evil, the masters of all plotters who seek world domination (i.e., Zionists and their Western lackeys), these being personified by the Israelis. He sees the enemy in both individual Israelis (who seek a dialogue with their Egyptian counterparts) and in Israel as a Zionist state. Some prominent voices within the cultural elites in the Arab world still share these views and refer to Egypt's peace and the Oslo Accords with Israel as betrayal and surrender.[42]

It is interesting to note that Arab intellectuals and regimes quite often denounce and accuse one another of being Zionists. In this context of accusation this extended meaning of the term has come to imply many things. During the war between Iraq and Iran, Saddam Hussein and the late Ayatollah Khomeini, both die-hard enemies of Zionism, denounced one another as Zionists. In the course of the Gulf crisis Iraq and the pro-Iraqi camp denounced the Kuwaiti and other Gulf rulers, as well as other allied Arab states, as being Zionists or a 'spearhead' in the body of the Arab nation. On 2 August 1990, for example, the first Iraqi communiqué announcing the invasion of Kuwait read as follows: 'Allah helped the liberals from among the honest ranks to undermine the traitorous regime in Kuwait who is involved in Zionist and foreign conspiracies.' Against this background, reviewing a notion of the 'enemy' becomes necessary in order to understand the context in which ethnocentrism, emanating from the inability of people to share a common sense of humanity, is the most important source of imagined or real enmity.

The conception of 'enemy'[43] is deeply rooted within historical and cultural reservoirs, and is particularly evocative in the context of the encounter between two societies or cultures involved in an abnormal conflict. This motif is fairly recognizable in the discourse of Arabism's conception of Zionism and of the West as its backbone, with the West gradually becoming the puppet of international Zionism. This conflict is abnormal in the sense that it resembles a titanic clash where the fight is to the end,[44] simply because it is not a conflict of divergence on economic or other spheres of material interests, but one of identity and self-image. It is also conflict that involves an almost total refusal to accept the basis for a common human condition – equality in being human beings (Said, 1980; Yassin, 1981a: 99–120; Lewis, 1986; Brown, 1993; Shachar, 1996). On the face of it, part of a nation's self-image is to make enemies. As Norton (1988: 56) puts it:

[I]n choosing what they will reject, nations determine what they stand for and what they will become. The recognition that polities are defined in difference should teach them to choose their enemies (sometimes with care). Their enmities define them. Nations constrain themselves, as they constrain their citizens to be other than the enemy, yet they oblige themselves, and their citizens, to oppose the enemy ... Yet nations are rarely mindful of their enmities.

This 'outgroup', cast or society (or any collective term used to denote the 'Other' and the way it is defined and represented) becomes the essential component for setting the stage for conflicts and wars, through indoctrination and in motivating and mobilizing one's own people against the Other. The whole idea of 'Otherness', Harle (1993: 28) maintains, is usually an absolute precondition for the perception of one's own identity, in other words 'no cultural *thema* without *anathema*'.[45] As in other cases, one cannot comprehend the large without a knowledge of the small; people are unable to recognize who they are without fully perceiving who they are not. Indeed, the conception of 'Otherness' is usually the background of and the framework for posing and articulating one's own references to one's own awareness and interests, and the role of culture is preordained and authoritative in this process. The norms that culture gives birth to, and the language that denotes them in its meanings, metaphors and symbols, evolve over time into a 'metalanguage of a cultural typology in which other cultures appear not merely as other, but as contrary' (Al-Azmeh, 1993: 128). For many Arabs the extensive and universal encounter between good and evil in times of great crisis with outsiders (the Gulf crisis is a good example) inevitably acquires not only cultural attributes but also extends to political and even military domains. What is of most importance in this context is the powerful Islamist discourse that has dominated civil society throughout the Arab world from the beginning of the 1970s, and has intensified as a consequence of the Iranian revolution (Lewis, 1993). This powerful discourse that dominates the educational system and cultural production in major countries like Egypt, Jordan, Saudi Arabia (including the other Gulf states) and Sudan views all forms of contacts and interrelationships with the West as an intellectual intrusion, even as an invasion, *ghazu fikri*. This attitude applies also to the introduction of modern, antagonistic Western social science into the Islamic institutions of learning.

The case of the renowned scholar of Islamic studies, Nasr Hamed Abu Zaid of Cairo University, demonstrates the power of the Islamist discourse. Abu Zaid wrote some major, yet controversial, works using modern hermeneutic methods to interpret Islam. He argued that the Prophet Muhammad dealt with people in events which could be seen as having a magical dimension, and that as such texts depicting Muhammad's words and deeds must be interpreted symbolically. Fundamentalists, however, argue that such interpretations seriously question the Qur'an as a given truth of God. Abu Zaid had to fight for his convictions and freedom of speech, and later, following harrassment, left his job and moved from Egypt to Holland, where he now works. His opponents even attempted – and failed – to enforce a divorce between Abu Zaid and his wife, on the basis that no Muslim woman should be married to a man who (supposedly) confesses to blasphemy. The literature of both fundamentalism and pan-Arabism conforms to the same perception of the West and Zionism. The Islamist discourse, moreover, is concerned with the tempting attractions of American and Western consumerism. By denouncing the United States as the 'Great Satan', the late Ayatollah Khomeini was asserting a firmly held concept of Western and American culture as merely seductive and empty consumerism. There is also the term *a'aada-u-Allah*, 'enemies of Allah', which often appears in the literature and the discourse of Muslim fundamentalist groups (Lewis, 1993).[46] Indeed, this state of affairs strengthens the assumption of 'the supposed antipathy of Islam and the West, and the received wisdom appeared to acquire a new vitality during the Gulf crisis' (Piscatori, 1991: 13).

While Muslim fundamentalists, on the one hand, and liberals, nationalists and radical leftist groups, on the other, have been in bitter conflict for the dominance of civil societies throughout the Arab world, both sides are in full agreement with regard to Israel, the United

States and the West. Both perceive the West as evil and as pursuing inconsistent and hypocritical policies toward the Arabs that are motivated by genuine hatred and contempt for them. In the Arab world there has always been fertile soil in which to plant all manner of perceptions or misconceptions regarding Zionism, the United States and the West. Such a discourse can only take place in the absence of systematic knowledge in the form of university courses or research centres that thoroughly study the society, culture and politics of the Arab world's unanimously defined 'enemy'.[47] Understandably, as is most often the case, when responding to an intellectual, political or cultural challenge such a discourse evolves in a defensive, reactive and even paranoid manner, and this in turn produces a rhetoric of blame and defensiveness (Yassin, 1981a: 29–35).

Having said that the Arab world is not only bound by its common language and culture – indeed that it 'still paradoxically constitutes a single area of psychological, emotional and intellectual resonance transcending state frontiers' (Khalidi, 1991: 7) – so Arabhood – the idea of belonging to one nation with a common language, culture, history – is knitted and woven into the fabric of education and the mechanism of producing culture. However, honouring and com- memorating the uniqueness of Arabhood has come about 'usually and invidiously at the expense of others' (Said, 1993: xxvi). On the face of it, there are temptations for both Islamists and pan-Arabists in their journeys to the glorious past to retreat defensively to that lost and unrenewable time when the *umma* was 'magnificent' and so reclaim a glimpse of a bygone age. In a sense, the high point of history often provide adequate compensation for today's misery and subjection, a handy way of forgetting the miserable conditions of the present and of a hazardous and more-or-less unknown future. Nevertheless, this journey back into one's own history, as Stuart Hall (in Hall *et al.* 1992: 395) argues, 'hides and even disguises a genuine striving to set in motion and reactivate one's own "people" against "others" who threaten their identity, and to gird their loins for a new march forwards'. Indeed, it fabricates identities and emphasizes the appeal of always escaping to historical glories. It also produces an inability or unwillingness to face modern life as it is.

It is here that the significance of Arabism in the analysis of the Gulf crisis and the political discourse of the leaders and states in the Arab world resides. The prevalence of Arabism's symbols and representations is the clue to comprehending the popularity of the Ba'ath and Saddam Hussein before and during the Gulf crisis. Despite its 'fragile and artificial identity' the Ba'ath regime Iraq (and Syria) were easily able to exploit the generally held and trusted perceptions and resentment against the West for the abominable history of its association with the Arab world (Greenfeld and Chirot, 1994: 116). This resentment, while it has been used to justify the repeated and abortive endeavours by the Arabs to live in peace and in charge of their own economic and political destinies, has also tended to 'contribute more bitterness to the ... Arabs when there was already far too much of that around ... there was less and less objective reason for that bitterness by comparison with any other period in the long and thorny history of the Arabs and the West' (Makiya, 1993: 318). Such a process is always used to mobilize people to legitimize the otherwise illegitimate political structures, and the activity of frequently fabricating outside die-hard enemies fits into this framework.

The Iraqi leadership's judgment or misjudgment of the United States' and Israel's intentions are deeply rooted in and conditioned by this discursive formation of Arabism. This attitude is strengthened by the long-standing image and perception of the United States as an imperialistic power that supports Israel at all costs against the Arabs, and works through their agents – the rich rulers of the Gulf – against the interest of all Arabs (Stein, 1992). It is a powerful image that runs parallel to Edward Said's (1978) analysis of Orientalism, in which he describes a Christian Europe that has projected its fears about itself on to Islam and the Orient. There is a similar perception, which some call 'Occidentalism', by which the same projection of fear of the West and Zionism is used in a more prosaic way by leaders to legitimize their even sometimes erratic international behaviour. Saddam Hussein, Ibrahim (1992: 12) argues, justified and legitimized his decision by invoking the principles of Arabism and appealing to sentiments that are widespread in the Arab world. Such common feelings and the consciousness of Arabism and the intimate cultural bonds that Arabs have to one another 'are in fact conditioned by a concrete situation which is the product of social factors informed by thousands of years of history' (Rodinson, 1979: 45). For the Arab nationalists, leftists, Islamists and other social constellations with a direct impact on politics within the Arab world, the situation during the spring of 1990 was explosive. Indeed, it was a pan of boiling oil waiting for someone to throw a lighted match on it. The Arab setting was pregnant with 'the entire range of discontents that emanate from developing, inefficient, over-bureaucratised, and undemocratic societies crystallised in the illogical but no less real hope for some release' (Piscatori, 1991: 11). The Iraqi regime did not bother about preparing its historical, territorial and economic case against Kuwait; there were no preparations whatsoever, and no divergence concerning the way the two countries drew their maps. As was mentioned earlier, all the maps in Iraq showed a clear border between Iraq and Kuwait.

The vital aim was to convince as many Arabs as possible that the Iraqi president was able to deliver the longed-for goal of all-Arab self-definition, and so challenge once and for all the hegemony of the United States and Israel and help the Palestinians to regain their land. The Iraqi narrative had been focusing on these issues to the point where Kuwait was almost invisible, though Kuwait and the Gulf had already been described as having squandered the Arab nation's wealth and as being part of conspiracy against Iraq as the most reliable defender of the nation. As it was, Saddam Hussein's strategy worked by attracting unprecedented support for his leadership, and the pan-Arab response to Iraq and the Gulf crisis was such that they reacted in striking conformity and all were quite clear about whom they were reacting against. Ironically, it was this same strategy that led to the crucial blunder that nullified the Iraqi strategy of invading Kuwait. For by admitting the US army, Saudi Arabia and the other major Arab states who had strongly opposed the Iraqi invasion of Kuwait paved the way for the United States' action to eject Iraq from Kuwait, with disastrous consequences and enormous costs for both Iraq and Kuwait.

The gulf Arabs as perceived by other Arabs
At this point, let us touch upon the issue of the 'Gulfis'. This is a dimension that in essence does not alter the substance of how Arabism views Others, since the Gulf Arabs are part and parcel of the domain of Arabism; however, there are vital differences between the Gulfis and other Arabs, and since the discovery of oil created the vast wealth the former suddenly gained, these differences have been used to focus attention on the increasing misery of the rest of Arabs. Saddam Hussein manipulated these differences to the full by contrasting the haves and the have-nots as part of this strategy to rally the majority of poor Arabs behind Iraq. Social scientists and historians of the Arab world need to

take more account of the question of identity as being one of the fundamental points of departure when trying to understand the genealogy of modern Arab societies and the discourse of politics (Barakat, 1984, 1993; al-Naqeeb, 1987; Sharabi, 1987, 1988). The Gulf crisis and the war that followed have urgently raised these issues in the most acute forms and this is especially true with regard to the disparity, real or imagined, between the Arab East, al-Mashriq al-Arabi, and the Gulf region. There is an overriding perception within the Arab world that the Gulf Arabs differ from the other Arabs of the Fertile Crescent and North Africa, or what Heikal (1992) called 'the Arabs of the north'. First and foremost, the Gulf Arabs' extravagant wealth, in comparison with that of other Arabs (and for that matter many other people on earth), is a dimension that naturally engenders resentment and envy among their poorer brethren. Another feature is the clear resilience of the tribal networks in social, economic and political life, and how tribal loyalties often decide the individual's place in the public scheme. A third and important difference in this context is that the Gulf Arabs have been reluctant to participate in the struggle to create a modern vision of Arabism along the lines of the Ba'athist and Nassirist ideologies of the 1960s and 1970s (Halliday, 1995). Kuwait, however, should be excluded from this latter category because of an active Arab nationalist movement led by Ahmad al-Khateeb, al-Saadun and other prominent Kuwaiti public figures. This movement has been institutionalized and active in Kuwaiti politics since the late 1950s. Serious and even puzzling as these matters may be, it is usually the case that they are problems of how one group perceives the other. Even so these differences are seen as an outcome of the social, economic and political experiences the Gulf societies have encountered throughout history, and they are important factors in inter-Arab politics.[48]

The media and newspapers in Egypt, Syria, Jordan and other North African countries told one story after another about how much money various rich Gulf Arabs lose in the gambling clubs in Europe and North America. On 24 August 1990, Dilip Hiro, in an article in the *New Statesman and Society*, narrated a typical story similar to those frequently printed by the media circulating in cities populated by poor Arabs:

Last week at the Carlton Club casino in Cannes, Shaykh Eyani, an advisor to Prince [Saud al-] Faysal [Foreign Minister]of Saudi Arabia, lost £8.8

million (about $17 million) at the roulette tables. He immediately wrote a check to settle two thirds of the debts. The story flatters every cheap caricature of the super-rich Arab princeling, and adds a new note of fiddling while the Gulf burns. But we need to recall one truth about the status quo Saddam Hussein threatens. The Shaykh is in the casino because the Western powers put him there, and kept him there. When the dust of battle clears, a restoration of 'business as usual' will mean more grotesque inequality, more resentment and, in time, another Saddam to voice the anger of Arab poor. (Hiro, 1991: 408)

We are not here talking about the encounters that usually take place between extravagantly rich individuals and hopelessly poor people, as in the case of rich North Americans versus Jamaicans or Haitians, or Japanese versus Filipinos, or West Europeans versus East Europeans and other Mediterraneans. In the Arab case, the grudge against the Gulfis, at least as far as the Arabs are concerned, is legitimate. Arabism maintains that the poor Nile farmer, the slum residents of Algiers, Amman, Cairo, Damascus and Gaza or the West Bank are all entitled to share the wealth of their common 'imagined community' – the Arab nation. Therefore, the Gulfis and the Kuwaitis were targeted by other outraged fellow Arabs, described as 'wastrels' and 'corrupt', and the Kuwaiti state was frequently called an 'imperialist creation', 'archaic' and 'historically illegitimate' by prominent figures within political as well as civil society constellations. The Saudi novelist Abdel-Rahman Munif is one of the most renowned personalities in modern Arab literature and is known for his famous trilogy *Sharaq al-Bahr al-Mutawasit* ('East of Mediterranean'), and *Mudun al-Malah* ('Cities of Salt'), in which he displays an impressive knowledge of Western (and particularly American) culture and society. This author was stripped of his Saudi citizenship for his writings that portray and satirize the Gulf Arabs' way of life and attitudes when travelling as tourists in Lebanon, Egypt and Europe. Munif (1991: 40) declared defiantly that 'Kuwait is not important' for the sake of the Arab nation.[49] Another author in the same mould is Moncif Marzouki, president of the Tunisian Human Rights League, who wrote,

In all the demonstrations that have shaken the Arab world, no slogan is shouted more violently than that which targets the monarchies and principalities of the Gulf. 90 percent of all Arabs profoundly hate these dictatorial and archaic regimes that have squandered Arab resources and honour and have always treated Arab citizens as despised party crashers. It is this deep aversion that explains the global and massive character of the pro-Iraqi demonstrations where Saddam is less acclaimed than Fahd is vituperated.[50]

Of course, the economic dimension is also of importance here, given the hardships and misery of daily life and the huge and persistently widening gap between the rich and the poor. Living conditions for the great majority of Arabs cannot get any worse. It is true that the endemic poverty of many Arab societies has always existed, and during the last ten years there has in fact been an overall improvement in living conditions. Yet public awareness of the gap has become clearer, thanks to the media with their frequent stories of Gulf Arabs gambling and squandering money everywhere they go. During the Gulf crisis Saddam Hussein worked tirelessly and with particular intensity to illuminate this gap and manipulate it to serve his own political ends.[51] This is of enormous interest since the majority of Arabs live in extreme poverty. Walid Khalidi (1991: 18–19) sheds light on this by arguing that

the main feature of [this] socioeconomic status quo was the incongruence between the geography of wealth and that of population distribution ... the fact that eight percent of the 200 million Arabs who lived in the oil countries owned more than fifty percent of the aggregate gross national product of the Arab world and that the per capita income of the native populations of the oil countries ranged between $15,000 to 20,000 while that of the vast majority of the 200 million Arabs was below $1,000 – for example, Egypt's 53 million ($690), Morocco's 25 million ($750), Sudan's 24 million ($310), Yemen's 9 million ($545).

... Kuwait represented this status quo and Saddam's action was seen as delivering a belated electric shock to it which, given the bankruptcy of inter-Arab institutions, might goad the system toward greater distributive justice.

This was a dimension that the Iraqi government and Saddam Hussein invested in heavily when speaking publicly or issuing any statements immediately before and during the Gulf crisis. Exploiting the possibility of his speeches being heard for the first time by a wide pan-Arab audience, Saddam Hussein condemned the Gulfis for their extravagance and for squandering the wealth of the Arab nation, *al-umma al-Arabiyya*. Consequently, Saddam Hussein's popularity rose as it was

fuelled by the distinct unpopularity of the Gulf monarchies. Ostentatiously wealthy and often arrogantly claiming that God had chosen them for special favour, the 'Gulfis' have incurred the envy, and more often the enmity, of poorer Arabs and Muslims ... the Gulf Arab regimes have become widely synonymous with corruption, insincerity, and licentious, un-Islamic conduct. (Piscatori, 1991: 13)

The Syrian poet Nizar Qabbani is a well-known figure in modern Arabic literature, primarily for his controversial political poems that usually contain severe criticism of the Arab political order – states, leaders and even ordinary people are sometimes a target for his anger. Qabbani was a staunch supporter of Iraq and Saddam Hussein (in the name of Arabism) during the war with Iran and his was a show of outright defiance against the Syrian government that very few would dare display. Almost 18 months before the invasion of Kuwait, Qabbani wrote yet another notorious and polemical poem entitled 'Abu Jahl Buys Fleet Street'[52] which uses within the framework of the haves and have-nots and, indeed, intensifies the resentment of the 'North' and poor Arabs and the stereotypes of the Gulfis, especially the Kuwaitis, for their long association with the West at the expense of the Arab cause. He wrote this poem despite the direct political engagement and economic support of the Gulf states through their petrodollars in the cause of Arab brotherhood and other Muslim activities throughout the Muslim world – in particular Kuwait, who at least until July of 1990 had donated the exceptionally large sum of 14 per cent of its GNP in an effort to help the poor Arab states (Piscatori, 1991: 13; Unwin, 1993).

For many Arabs – grass-roots, mainstream, as well as Islamist – the Gulf crisis has been one of those rare moments in modern Arab history (others include the Suez crisis, Yom Kippur) where they searched for self-definition. From the early days of 1990, Saddam Hussein understood and emphasized this. Even after the invasion of Kuwait, he said that the settlement of the crisis 'must be found within an Arab framework', and he sought to engender and provoke a sense of self-definition and a desire for Arab self-determination that had no need of American and other outside intrusion. However, this took place in the shadow of his vital blunder that violated all the principles of Arab brotherhood and of the fact that he was unable to generate broad Arab support for the Iraqi case against Kuwait, and certainly not for invading and annexing Kuwait with all that it implied politically, socially and economically for Iraq, Kuwait and for the Arab world. In the following, I shall review examples (classified in three different categories: grass-roots, mainstream, and Islamist) from all walks of life and across various social and political domains throughout the Arab world that highlight a discursive formation which, in a way, is peculiar to the Arab cultural sphere. It is a dimension through which the invasion of Kuwait must be understood and approached.

The grass-roots Arabs, Iraq and Saddam Hussein

When it come to rights and active participation there is a view that emanates from the realities of the political awareness of the grass-roots Arabs. The volatile Arab political atmosphere makes people vulnerable to any gust of opinion that gives them some recognition, however illusive. Even though he considers himself a true pan–Arabist, Mohammad Heikal (1992: 156) could not help but put it bluntly: "From a nation traditionally fond of story-telling, the Arabs have a tendency to embroider or over–simplify political rumours until something striking emerges. In the absence of reliable information, any story becomes accepted fact.' The time that preceded the invasion of Kuwait was one of those periods in modern Arab history that was characterized by an atmosphere of intense political psychology, with a flourishing '"counterculture" pitted against the *status quo* and all the pretences and inequities it represented' (Tylor, 1993: 88). How could the Iraqi invasion of Kuwait be understood as part and parcel of this *status quo*? The connection between Iraq's invasion of Kuwait and the political atmosphere have been simply and eloquently depicted by Fahmy Huwaidy, a renowned syndicated columnist in *Al-Ahram* and an influential Islamist figure who, under the heading 'Arab Irrationalism', wrote that

> there is a logical explanation for this phenomenon [the support for Saddam Hussein]; with the overwhelming frustrations, consciousness has been separated from truth. We have to admit that people lack hope and feel depressed and humiliated. As a result, they await a saviour so eagerly that they are capable of responding to a mirage.

Right or wrong, lawful or unlawful, logical or illogical, rational or irrational, this far from explains the behaviour of ordinary people in the streets of the Arab cities. The Iraqi president enjoyed the popular support he seemed to have been counting on – which in certain cities and states was overwhelming – and to be understood, the invasion of Kuwait has to be put within this framework. Khalidi (1991: 13) argues that, to probe into the question of the support Saddam has elicited is a legitimate and necessary exercise in the comprehension of powerful psycho-political perceptions and emotions that reverberate across the frontiers of the Arab countries. It is legitimate and necessary, because these perceptions and emotions are part of the reality.

Saddam Hussein's four major speeches (24 February, 1 April, 28 May and 17 July 1990) paved the way for the crisis and the war that followed. His attempts to emphasize and intensify Arab hostility against Zionism and United States was a relatively easy task, especially when there was already much of it around. The speeches centred on Israel and the miserable situation it created for the Palestinians in particular and for Arabs in general, and formed part of the strategy designed to attract the constellations of civil society in other Arab states behind his leadership. From the Arab League summit on 28 May, which was broadcast live all over the Arab world, people saw the prominence of the Iraqi president and the hope he gave them to deliver a strong signal for the enemy of the Arabs. As the crisis dragged on, Saddam Hussein resorted mostly to the vibrant rhetoric of the Qur'an and the pan-Arab/Islamic idioms. On 24 February Saddam declared that:

[d]espite the difficulty of finding a closer vantage point from which to view the lights of Jerusalem, we see the city from Baghdad through our faithful, penetrating eyes, which have plenty of room for Jerusalem – which, as you well know, has been the scene of great Arab sacrifices and glories, making its name evoke only good memories. We can see Jerusalem from anywhere, no matter how far from that city, because Jerusalem brings out the good things in our hearts. So, the line of sight is between us and that city, and in fact between that city and any Arab, Muslim, or Christian among sons of Arabism. This makes Jerusalem very close. Thus, the signs on the path of liberating Jerusalem are clear and remain unobliterated by the vicissitudes of time, Allah willing. (Cited in Bengio, 1992: 38–9)

On 1 April he warned that:

[the Americans] will be deluded if they imagine that they can give Israel cover in order to come and strike at some industrial metalworks. By Allah, we will make fire eat up half of Israel if it tried anything against Iraq ... O Allah, stop the excessiveness of the reckless and unjust people. We will say no more than what our forefathers have said: Give us a strong back, not a light weight. With Allah's grace the Iraqis will cling to the rays of sun and light wherever there is sun. (Ibid.: 60–1)

On 28 May 28 he said:

When we rely on Allah – and we do rely on Allah – and depend on deep fraternal dialogue conducted in an encouraging brightness in our hearts; and when we recall – without forgetting – the stand point of our nation, which we know very well; … when we fear nobody but *Allah* as we moved toward unity; …[then we] can restore every lost right – especially our right to dear Palestine, which is waiting impatiently to see Arab flags, especially the Palestinian flag, flying over it and over the domes of holy Jerusalem. (Ibid.: 90–2)

On 7 August he said:

O great Iraqi people, O masses of Arab nation. O Arab leaders, whenever you support the principles of truth and the interests of the Arabs, and whenever you overcome obscurity and selfishness and reject the foreigner's pressure, ways, and plots, this has been our decision. It is a rightful, just, and fair decision. It is a decision for the present time and for the future. At the same time, after Iraq acted on 2 August along with all its sons to carry out this honourable national duty, this decision made for the Arab nation as a whole in view of the power, capability, faith, and aspirations it implies … After seeking Allah's forgiveness and help, we will demolish blasphemy with faith. A new dawn has broken in the lives of the Arabs, so that they may add it to what few days they have rejoiced in together, and so that it can act as a beam to dissipate darkness. The dawn has broken to stay, and the bats will have to go back to their caves. Allah is omnipotent and omnipresent, … Allah will curse the accursed, and every one will pay for his actions. And the faithful will be rewarded. Say *Nothing will happen to us except what Allah has decreed for us, He is our protector, and in Allah let the believers put their trust* [Qur'anic verse]. *Allah-u-Akbar; Allah-u-Akba*r; *Allah-u-Akbar;* let the lowly be accursed, and Allah's mercy be upon you. (Ibid.: 122–4).

As mentioned above, the main target of the conflict – Kuwait – was almost invisible. There were a very few scattered references to it in the Iraqi presidents' political speeches during the Gulf crisis and in the main they described Kuwait as being active within the American and Zionism's grand scheme against Iraq. At this juncture, an Iraqi citizen expressed what many other grass-roots Arabs thought in the following words: 'Nassir made promises, but could not deliver. But, when Saddam speaks, he acts.'[53] The PLO chairman, Yassir Arafat, expressed in similar terms what the Iraqi citizen had said when he remarked that 'the most important thing to be said is that the [28 May 1990] Arab summit conference under the chairmanship of brother

President Saddam Hussein has given a new Pan-Arab resurgence to our Arab nation through Iraqi ability [to deliver]' (quoted in Telhami, 1993: 188–9).

In the Arab world there are times when politicians and statesmen take positions in line with the popular view, however illogical and volatile it may seem. The condemnation of and attacks on Iraq and the personality of Saddam Hussein in Israel, Europe and the United States, especially by the pro-Israel lobby, generated sympathies the Iraqi leader needed at that point. The depiction of Saddam Hussein as 'butcher, a torturer, a manipulator'[54] by the Republican Senator Alfonso D'Amato of New York, one of the main pro-Israel figures in the Congress, is one of many examples. These attacks had the effect of diverting the sympathy of the Arab and Muslim world to Iraq and Saddam Hussein. For Iraq's Arab supporters, fears of a military strike against Iraq had been aroused by the inflammatory demonization of the Iraqi president. In fact, the Arab League summit in Baghdad on 28 May, attended by all the Gulf states including Kuwait, had concluded with a strong show of support and brotherly solidarity with Iraq against 'the vicious Western campaign' to deny the Arabs and Iraq the possibilities to defend themselves from potential Israeli aggression. Moreover, on 18 June the International Islamic Popular Conference condemned 'the savage campaign of misleading propaganda launched by imperialist circles in the United States and Britain' and appealed to all Muslims all over the world to see it as a duty and an obligation 'to use their resources and capabilities to confront any potential Zionist aggression against Iraq' (cited in Neff, 1991: 37).

Immediately preceding, and even throughout the Gulf crisis, Saddam Hussein – like Gamal Abdul Nassir in the 1950s and 1960s – appeared to many Arabs to be in line with the vision and discourse of Arabism and to have articulated the much-longed-for sense of resistance and fearlessness to combat the intruders and enemies of the Arab nation. The first priority, moreover, was to restore the impaired and injured Arab pride and dignity. In short, Saddam Hussein was perceived as revitalizing the legend of Salah Eddin in Arab history, though this was certainly reaction to the despair that characterized the political atmosphere in the Arab world. As Khalidi (1991: 20) writes,

all Arabs ... had become sick and tired of the pusillanimity of the Arab leaders everywhere in the face of the sabre-rattling of the Begins, the Shamirs, the Eytans, and the Sharons of Israel. Nor are there many people who think that

Israel would come to the negotiating table unless it perceived some degree of mutual deterrence [with] the Arab world. The quest for such a deterrence has eluded the Arab world since 1948, particularly in the face of the American commitment to maintain Israel's strategic preponderance over any combination of Arab countries.

In the Arab world, conducting a demonstration for whatever reason can lead to severe punishment unless it is officially sanctioned by the government, but during the rapid and intense events that preceded the Gulf crisis the great majority of demonstrations were spontaneous expressions by people who were prepared either to support Iraq and Saddam Hussein, or else to protest against Western intervention in the area. The massive public demonstrations in the Arab streets in Algeria, Jordan, Palestine and elsewhere were not, however, necessarily a show of support for Saddam Hussein, nor for the Iraqi (otherwise outlawed) invasion and annexation of Kuwait. It is worth noting here that the strongest support for the Iraqi president was most evident in countries that had been historically and traditionally connected with pro-Western interest, such as Jordan, Morocco and Tunisia. The survival of King Hussein and the Hashemite family and the protection of the state of Jordan from the most serious outside attacks (e.g., the Syrian case in 1970, in a show of solidarity with the PLO who fought the Jordanian forces loyal to the King), and against internal uprisings (too many to count here) had been thanks to the West – Great Britain and the United States – and Israel. Since independence in Tunisia, Bourghaiba, and even his successor Ben Ali, have maintained very close relations with France and the United States; this is also true of Morocco.

These demonstrations reflected rather the keen desire to destroy the *status quo*. For millions of Arabs in Algeria, Egypt, Lebanon, Morocco, Sudan, Syria, Tunisia and Yemen, the *status quo* is essentially something that destroys, damages and even belittles the Arab quest for self-definition and the longed-for objective of real independence, along with the capacity to define and decide over their own affairs. On 12 August 1990, there were demonstrations in support of Iraq and Saddam Hussein in the Jordanian cities of Amman and Mafraq, in Yemen's capital Sanaa, and in the south Lebanese city of Sidon, while on 25 January 1991, in Nouakchott, the capital city of Mauritania, about 20,000 people demonstrated against Western involvement in the Gulf. Even in a country like Syria, where demonstrations are considered sinful by the repressive government of President Assad, there were public riots.[55] But during the Gulf crisis the government was not able to stop all the expression of public anger at Syria joining the anti-Iraq international coalition in cooperation with the United States and, by implication, Israel. On 21 January 1991, in an unusual, highly publicized conference for Arab intellectuals in Damascus, the attendants issued: *Bayan min al-muthaqqafin al-Arab fi Suriya difa'an an sha'bina al-Arabi fi al-Iraq* ('A communiqué from Arab intellectuals in Syria in defence of our people in Iraq'), in order to 'express their opposition to the Gulf war and affirm their faith in collective Arab action and in the necessity of "Arab power"' (Abu Khalil, 1992: 27–8, n. 28). In Egypt, too, the government delayed the start of a new academic year in the national universities to avoid the organized and often powerful protest that students usually delivered against the government, which was an active participant in the anti-Iraq policy. But two months later, in late October 1990, when the government allowed the students to return, there were an estimated 30,000 demonstrators occupying the university campuses daily throughout Egypt (Baker, 1994: 477). On 24 February 1991 20,000 anti-war demonstrators in Cairo shouted the slogan 'No God but Allah, George Bush the enemy of Allah'. On the same day around 100,000 people demonstrated outside the presidential palace in the capital Sanaa, condemning Egypt and Syria for their contribution in the war against Iraq, and the day after saw about 80,000 students, mainly from Cairo University, demonstrating against the West and the United States' involvement in the region. The students clashed with the police and dozens of them were injured as a result. On 3 February 1991, despite its contribution to the International Alliance against Iraq, the Moroccan government authorized about 300,000 demonstrators in the streets of Casablanca and Rabat to put on a massive show of support for Iraq and demand the immediate withdrawal of Western forces from Arab land.

The mainstream Arabs, Iraq and Saddam Hussein

There is general agreement on what Israel and Zionism are; indeed, there is in this respect great unanimity and conformity within the Arab political discourse that unites all sides – presidents, monarchies, leftists, the conservative right, pan-Arabists, Islamists, radical anti-imperialists and even liberal cosmopolitans. During the Gulf crisis, Makiya (1993: 325) argues, Arab intellectuals went out of their way to extend their responsibilities in siding wholeheartedly with Saddam Hussein, despite the terrifying political and human rights records of his rule over Iraq. This support was not based on the fact that moral issues were at stake, but vested exclusively on the fact that he was in conflict with Israel, which has always been the 'unfathomable entity in Arab eyes' (ibid.: 314) along with its apologist and protector, the United States. The end of the Cold War accelerated the disappearance of totalitarian communist regimes in Eastern Europe, and it is worth noting the tragic fate of Nikolai Ceausescu in Romania.[56] However, the prospects for a similar development were exaggerated in so far as the Arab world was concerned at the time. Despite the US administration's clarification on the issue of the *Voice of America* editorial (see page 5) that, as Senator Bob Dole assured Saddam Hussein in their meeting in Mousol, Iraq, in April 1990, it was a mistake by the editor of VOA for which he was removed from this post, there had been deep Iraqi suspicion in regard to American ill-intentions. Generally speaking, the end of the Cold War was perceived by many people in the world as a relief from the shadow of wars and conflicts, but in the Arab world it was conceived in quite a different way since it was closely related to the fact that mainstream Arabs feared that having the United States as a sole world power would imply Israeli hegemony in the region of the Middle East. Saddam Hussein was one of the major proponents of such a view in the Arab world, and on 28 February 1990, at the Arab Cooperation Council meeting in Amman, Jordan, he remarked:

Given the relative erosion of the role of the Arab–Zionist conflict, and given that the influence of the Zionist lobby on US policies is as powerful as ever, the Arabs must take into account that there is a real possibility that Israel might embark on new stupidities within the five-year span I have mentioned. This might take place as result of direct or tacit US encouragement. (cited in Bengio, 1992: 42)

In contrast to what many specialists within the Middle East believe (e.g., Brown, 1992; Dunn, 1992; Stein, 1992; Telhami, 1993), anti-Americanism has always been the rule, not the exception, and it is intensified in times of crisis and political despair as during the spring and summer of 1990. In addition to this was the right-wing government of Prime Minister Shamir with its harsh attitude to the peace issue, and there had been an influx of Soviet Jews which had dramatically changed the demographic balance in the region. At this juncture, even those Arabs who wanted a pragmatic and moderate approach in dealing with the United States and Israel were disillusioned. The example of Ashraf Ghorbal is a case in point. After the government of President Anwar al-Sadat expelled the Soviet experts from Egypt in 1972 in dramatic circumstances, Egypt adopted a policy of rapprochement with the West and the United States. As the Egyptian ambassador to the United States from 1974, Ghorbal was a strong pro-American voice and, indeed, was Sadat's man in the US. During the 1980s, however, Ghorbal's view shifted completely, and (through his outspoken press interviews and public speeches) went along with pan-Arabists, radical leftists, and even Muslim fundamentalists in their view of the West, of the United States and, of course, of Israel. In the spring of 1990, Ghorbal was quoted as saying, 'Arabs are sick of their governments emphatically begging the US to plead with Israel to please let them have peace.'[57] Telhami (1993: 188) also quotes the spokesperson of the Muslim Brotherhood in Jordan's Parliament as saying, in an identical tone, that 'US hostility and arrogance must motivate our Arab and Islamic nation to put an end to the course of begging and capitulation that it is immersed in.' When the United States decided to discontinue the dialogue with the PLO as a reaction to the raid by one of its factions on the Israeli coast in May 1990, a reaction the PLO did not condemn, this only intensified the anti-Americanism in the region. Even the Kuwaiti newspaper *Al-Qabas* reacted by urging the Arabs 'to adopt serious and objective stands against the United States which persist in a position hostile to the Arab causes' (quoted in ibid.: 188).

The foreign minister (and later prime minister) of Algeria, Sid Ahmad Ghozali, declared with great enthusiasm that Iraq and Saddam Hussein 'incarnate ... the spirit of resistance to those who wish to humble the Arabs'.[58] He was reflecting the mainstream Algerian street view of Iraq and Saddam Hussein. Another example is that of the otherwise disciplined and pro-Western King Hussein Bin Talal of Jordan, who had reacted angrily to the political and media campaigns waged in April 1990 by the United States, Great Britain and Israel. The King accused the West of planning a 'vicious and harsh' campaign against Iraq.[59] Soon after he declared that the Iraqi president 'was an innocent victim of an outrageous plot [by the West]',[60] and on 4 August 1990 referred to the Iraqi President Saddam Hussein as 'a patriotic man who believes in his [Arab] nation and its future and in establishing ties with others on the basis of mutual respect'.[61] Yet another sign of the King's indignation came on 6 February 1991 when he delivered a speech to 'the Arab and Islamic nation', containing the following words:

> When Arab and Islamic territory is presented as a base for the armies of the allies to destroy the Iraq of Arabism and Islam ... I say ... any Arab Muslim can imagine the size of the crime committed against his religion and nation ... As for our people in Iraq ... to those kinsfolk, we extend all love ... while they are defending us all and raising high a banner saying God is great, the banner of Arabism and Islam. (Quoted in Brumberg, 1991: 208, n. 41)

Farooq al-Qaddumi, the 'foreign minister' of the PLO, provided strong support to Iraq and Saddam Hussein by stating on 24 August 1990: 'We stand alongside Iraq to defeat all these colonialist armies trying to harm it; their destiny will be nothing but failure and defeat, Allah willing.' The official PLO stand was expressed in a message sent by its chairman Yassir Arafat to Saddam Hussein, which expressed Palestinian solidarity with the kinfolk of Iraq.[62] As a professor of political science, Kamal Abu Jaber is one of few prominent Arabs intellectuals who has studied Israeli political life and institutions within an academic framework, something for which he has been severely criticized by pan-Arabists in Jordan and elsewhere. As a Christian Arab, Abu Jaber was also at one time the Jordanian foreign minister who signed the peace treaty with Israel in 1994. Even though Abu Jaber knew that Iraq and Saddam Hussein were going to be crushed and defeated militarily, in his eyes Saddam Hussein 'will remain a hero for the next 1,000 years. School children will sing songs about him and mothers will call their sons Saddam.'[63] He was correct in so far as the last prediction was concerned; there were many press reports about families, not only in the Arab world but also as far away as Indonesia and Great Britain, where Pakistani immigrants named their newborn babies 'Saddam'. This name incidentally is quite uncommon as an Arab or Muslim name, as it means 'the one who confronts', or 'the defier'.

The chairman of the Tunisian Human Rights League, Moncif Marzouki, denounced the West and Western media for being the 'soldiers of psychological war against Iraq and the Arabs. The Western media's groundless lies and tales of the destruction of the Iraqi Army is today the laughing stock of all.' The Iraqi army's courageous show of force was striking evidence that led the West to recognize the

determination, the defiance and insolence of the Iraqi soldier was a classic instance of the human being confronting the machine ... In the Gulf war, it is not only Western information and technology which have failed, but above all the credibility of the famous values of the West. The dogma [of human rights], because that is what it is, is sinking all along the southern shores of the Mediterranean ... Seen from the southern shores of the Mediterranean, the Gulf war is shaping up as a prelude to the divorce between the West and the Arab world ... Paradoxically, only insofar as we Arab democrats succeed in uncoupling and disassociating the democratic project and values of human rights from Western centrism will we be able to salvage something from the rising tide of all 'isms'. (cited in Makiya, 1993: 247, 347)

The Moroccan philosopher Muhammad Abid al-Jabiri is one of the most distinguished and rationalist intellectuals in the modern Arab world, and an authority on the history and culture of the French and European Enlightenment as well as of Islam and the Arabs. In the London-based Arabic daily *al-Quds al-Arabi* he wrote five articles under the heading '*Man howa Saddam Hussein? khebrat al-madi wa affaq al-mustaqbal*' ('Who is Saddam Hussein? The experience of the past and the horizon of the future'), in which he portrayed Saddam Hussein as the exemplar of the Arab leader who sought to accomplish the 'national project for liberation, modernisation and unity, including the achievement of self-determination of the Palestinian people' (cited in Makiya, 1993: 349, n. 22). The Egyptian Dr Sherif Hetata, a left-wing writer who as an activist was imprisoned for his political opposition to the government of President Sadat during the 1970s, is the husband of the well-known Arab feminist, medical physician and radical political activist Nawal Al-Sa'dawi. Immediately after the Egyptian government announced in September 1990 that it would send troops to defend Saudi Arabia, Hetata wrote somewhat pointedly that:

When the crisis erupted many people in Egypt found it difficult to accept that Egypt should choose to be on the side of Israel and the West against Iraq, that the Egyptian army should fight side by side with the allied forces. They knew that the war had not really been launched to liberate Kuwait, or uphold international law, or establish a new international order where peace and justice would prevail, but to keep control of the Middle East, especially the Gulf oil reserves, and to ensure oil money stayed in the banks. They knew ... the destruction ... of an Iraq that which could be a threat to American interests in the Gulf and to the heavily militarized state of Israel which has been so effective in helping to thwart many legitimate Arab aspiration ... Nevertheless, for a writer like myself it is difficult to see these aspects and forget that the return road of Kuwaiti Sheikhs and American oil derricks to Kuwait has once more been paved with Arab lives and Arab blood. (Hetata, 1991: 241, 247)

Hisham Djäit is one of Tunisia's well-known pan-Arab intellectuals. He is a professor of history in the University of Tunis, and a scholar of Islamic history. He was a graduate of the Sorbonne and obtained high academic qualifications in France. As an expert, Professor Djäit was interviewed in the French newspaper *L'Express*, in which he asserted that Saddam Hussein had obviously and certainly retained the 'the edge' over other Arab regimes who had cooperated with the United States in its attempt to maintain a rotten *status quo* – an American order instituted with the earnest help of Saudi and other Gulf money. For the secular Djäit, the Iraqi leader's endeavours to resort to his real identity (Islam/Arabism) and the use of Islamic idioms and metaphors:

corresponds to a reappropriation of self, to the restoration of a deep identity ... Iraq and Saddam Hussein bring hope to the Arab world. For 20 years, the Arab world has been stuck in a frigid, depressing, virtually rotten order, a Saudi–American order whose horizon does not go beyond petrodollars ... I need not remind you, Europeans, that your nations were born out of wars. In annexing Kuwait, Saddam Hussein has entered into the dynamics of history ... He was undertaking the beginning of the unification of the Arab world. Sometimes legitimacy is more important than legality ... War has the merit of clarifying things. With respect to your contradictions and with respect to ours. We have everything to gain from this clarification. We have nothing to lose from this war, even if it ended in defeat. Because thanks to Saddam Hussein, it is taking place on the level of realities – oil, military force, etc. – and no longer on the level of symbols.[64]

The Lebanese Dr Clovis Maksoud was the Arab League representative in Washington for almost two decades until he resigned on 11 September 1990 in protest against the Western and American military build-up in the Gulf. Later Maksoud (1991: 176) wrote that:

[w]e have seen the attack on Iraq, brilliantly performed in military terms, but brilliance divested of policy vision. We have seen how this military success, that has generated a fascination with technological performance, has also brought home to the Arabs their sense of vulnerability. This inflicts deep

wounds on the collective Arab psyche; the threat of famine and epidemic among the Iraqi population and the pathetic transfer of population compound the sense of shame that such a disaster was not diverted through Arab collective efforts.

After the destructive war of January–February 1991 between Iraq and the international coalition and its ruinous consequences for Iraq and the retreat from Kuwait, the General Secretariat of the Union of Palestinian Lawyers announced a show of support for Iraq, glorifying Iraq and Saddam Hussein in Jordan's largest newspaper, the daily, *al-Dustour*. A whole page showed a picture of Saddam, with the following text beneath it: 'Support and Congratulations on Victory to His Excellency the President, Saddam Hussein, May God Preserve Him.' It went on to extol the 'legendary steadfastness' of Saddam Hussein, the Leader of the Arab Nation 'in the face of the conspiracy of the evil invaders'.[65]

Saddam Hussein was often associated with Hitler, first by the American president George Bush and also by other Western politicians and media, for whom such an association came to be taken for granted. The issue provoked debate within the Arab world only after an article by Hans Magnus Enzensberger[66] in which he made the comparison. Even though Enzensberger's focal point was that Hitler's and Saddam Hussein's compulsion for nihilism and their striking incapacity to differentiate between their personal calamity and that of their own peoples, Arab intellectuals were either very reserved or angry with Enzensberger, who, for many of them, is an otherwise much respected German writer. Indeed, the background of the Hitler association with Middle East politics and politicians dates back to the late 1930s. When Nazi Germany arose in Europe to challenge the die-hard enemy of the Arab liberation movements in Egypt, Palestine and Iraq, all these movements saw Hitler as a natural ally. This was according to the age-old dictum, the enemy of my enemy is my friend. The association of Sheikh Amin al-Husseini (the uncle of Yassir Arafat and the father of Faysal al-Husseini, a prominent Palestinian figure in Jerusalem) with Germany was well known, but like everybody else in the Middle East (and even in Europe) he was completely ignorant of the evil nature of Nazism. The regime of Rashid Aali al-Keelani in Iraq, who fought the British and was defeated in 1941, also had close relations with Germany (Shalabi, 1982). The extreme nationalist militias in Egypt during the 1940s (e.g., *misr al-fatah*, Young Egypt, Muslim

Brotherhood) were organized according to Nazi and fascist models, and in their narratives they even called Hitler al-Haaj Mohammad Hitler, regarding him as a saviour from Britain, the much-hated colonial power at the time (Shalabi, 1982: 327–33; Salem, 1989: 658ff.).[67]

Consequently, those Arab intellectuals who opposed Iraq's invasion of Kuwait and were very critical of the Iraqi president from the beginning, such as the distinguished Egyptian intellectuals Saad Eddin Ibrahim and Fouad Zakariya,[68] might have been made apprehensive about making such comparisons. Also relevant here is the case of the Arab poet and literary critic, Ali Ahmed Said Isber, who writes under the pen-name 'Adonis' and is a heavyweight within modern Arab culture. (One of the most distinguished Arab intellectuals in modern times, Adonis has also been nominated for the Nobel Prize for Literature.) After a long and unusual silence during the hectic and, for many Arabs, confusing time of the Gulf crisis, Adonis wrote an article entitled 'The prayer and the sword: or savage democracy',[69] in which he argued that the Gulf crisis and the West's reaction to it asserted once again the negative Western attitudes and prejudices about the Arabs, and that such attitudes made cosmopolitan Arabs such as himself reconsider anew the discourse of the relationship between Arabs and the West. Adonis was mainly concerned with Enzensberger's article and dismissed the analogy of Saddam with Hitler as 'exaggerated to the point of mystification'. While he acknowledged that it was true that the Iraqi president is a malicious and distasteful tyrant, and, moreover, has killed many of his own people ruthlessly, he argued that he is not in any way comparable with Hitler. Adonis insisted: 'Your Hitler certainly was the incarnation of all evils, but our Saddam Hussein is a run-of-the-mill despot.'[70]

Mohammad Afifi Mattar, a pan-Arab nationalist and renowned Egyptian literary figure as a poet and translator of, among many things, the Swedish poet Edith Södergran's works into Arabic, was briefly jailed by the Egyptian authorities in September 1990, accused of being an Iraqi spy. Afifi Mattar's staunch support for Iraq and the Iraqi president emanated from the fact that, by invading and annexing Kuwait, Saddam Hussein was putting things in the right order, and ensuring that the Arab nation would become a close reality not a distant imagination. He argued that Saddam Hussein showed his steadfastness and delivered a firm response to Zionists and American threats

by being the first Arab commander to inflict pain on the Jews and strike
fear into their own society (an allusion to the Scud missiles). Even if
Iraq was defeated, Mattar thought, it had restored the stigmatized
dignity and pride of the Arabs.[71]
Ahmed H. Elorf, a literary critic writing in the Tunisian newspaper
al-Cha'ab, portrayed the damage done to some civilian compounds in
the Israeli city of Tel Aviv as a result of an Iraqi Scud missile, and added
that he cheered with an almost Neronian[72] excitement: 'Oh, this
noble destruction is beautiful.'[73] What was widely known during the
Gulf crisis as 'Scud mania' reflected for some Arabs, and particularly
the Palestinians, a feeling of strength and a capacity to combat the
powerful Israel. By the same token, Elorf was articulating the
Palestinians' anger and revolt against the *status quo* they feel to have
suffered from most due to the extreme right-wing policy of the Likud
government of Prime Minister Yitzhak Shamir. The Palestinians'
support for the Iraqi president was of special intensity. For them,
Saddam Hussein was the first Arab leader to actualize the threat of
burning the Zionist state after the Iraqi Scud missile attacks on Israel,
which included strikes on the cities of Tel Aviv and Haifa. The encouragement with which the Iraqi Scud missiles were greeted by some
Palestinians led the Israeli peace activist Yossi Sarid to react angrily.
He wrote in the Israeli newspaper *Ha'artz*:

Now they are up on the roofs and like lunatics they yell 'Allahu Akbar' [God
is great] and applaud the terrorist missiles raining down on our heads ... After
the war, when 'Allah' is less 'Akbar,' don't call me ... In the shelter, I don't
have a phone ... and in my gas mask, my breath comes with difficulty and
my words are muffled. (Quoted in Sifry and Cerf, 1991: 438)

Rami G. Khouri, a Palestinian/Jordanian political commentator,
once an editor of the *Jordan Times* and an influential figure in both
the Jordanian public and media domains, has written:

Even though most Arabs didn't support the invasion of Kuwait, Saddam
Hussein's fearlessness in standing up to our enemies Israel and America appeals
to the new spirit of the Arab world – a spirit that says we'd rather die on our
feet than live grovelling on the ground ... Saddam Hussein ... has lived by
the gun all of his life. Yet this unlikely, autocratic man has become the
medium of a new Arab fearlessness that aims to cast off oppression and
subjugation both from abroad and at home. (Khouri, 1991: 403)

Jonathan Kuttab, a Christian lawyer and human rights activist from East Jerusalem, considered the Iraqi president as not only a symbol of resistance and steadfastness against Zionism and American imperialism, but as the conveyer and sustainer of a new Arab 'liberation theology'. With enormous nostalgia, Kuttab depicted Saddam Hussein as 'something revolutionary and wonderful that is expressed in the traditional slogan "Allahu Akbar"', which I understand as the faith in a great God: Greater than sophisticated airplanes … and all the might of the twenty-eight states that attacked Iraq.'[74] Jonathan's brother, well-known Palestinian journalist Daoud Kuttab, in conversation with the American journalist Scott MacLeod of *Time* magazine, emphasized the powerful effect of this 'liberation theology' on Palestinians and other Arabs through the firm and serious threats that Saddam Hussein has made and promised to fulfil, such as to 'burn half of Israel'. Daoud added that '[t]hroughout the *Intifada*, Palestinians watched as Israelis managed to carry on their everyday lives, going apparently undisturbed to the beach or to concerts. Then this guy six hundred miles away makes statements, and all of a sudden we see Israelis rushing out to get gas masks.'[75]

The Muslim fundamentalists, Iraq and Saddam Hussein
The name of Salah Eddin, as an example of bravery and chivalry, evokes powerful nostalgia, emotional memories and a sense of pride in the Arab consciousness (although he was an ethnic Kurd). Modern Arab leaders such as Nassir, Assad, Khaddafi and Saddam Hussein, to mention only a few, have always associated themselves and their polities with Salah Eddin, and modern Iraq has been especially evocative of this by virtue of its mythical intimacy with the figure of Salah Eddin. Several roads and villages and even a large province in northern Iraq were renamed as *muhafazat* Salah Eddin (previously *Ninawi*); both Saddam Hussein and Salah Eddin were born within the same province approximately 800 years apart. Saddam Hussein's stirring representation of Salah Eddin as a rhetorical focus against the West constitutes a semiotic message with which the great moments in early Arab history are rejuvenated and exploited. Such an amalgamation and consolidation of the present with the multivocal characters of mythic and symbolic historical persons, Norton (1988: 106) argues, provides an incentive to the arousal of feelings and affections. Thus, the Iraqi president's evocation of Salah Eddin encompassed a covert appeal to

Islamic fundamentalism within the vivid image of the Muslim triumph over the West's Crusaders at the Horn of Hettin above Tiberias in the year AD 1178.

This exploitation of and association with Salah Eddin led otherwise independent and even hostile constellations, such as Islamic fundamentalist groups, to rally behind the president. For some of them Saddam Hussein presented in Salah Eddin a model of legitimate rule to which he would thereafter be expected to conform. In this way he was persuaded to display and use symbols indicating Muslim religiosity – by adding *Allah-u-Akbar* on the Iraqi flag during the Gulf crisis, by giving the Iraqi missiles typical early Muslim names, by exhibiting himself at prayer in the *Ka'aba* in Mecca – in addition to those actions symbolizing the idea of Arabness that is necessarily in sharp contrast with the West.[76] The example of Sheikh Asaad al-Tamimi, the leader of the Islamic *Jihad-al-Bait al-Muqaddas* organization in Jordan, is an interesting one. In spite of the fact that the entire polity and society in Jordan sided unequivocally with Iraq during the Iraq–Iran war as an obligation to Arabhood, Sheikh Asaad and his organization were among the very few in Jordan who deviated and strongly supported Iran and the Imam Khomeini as an exemplar of the Muslim leader. But the position of the *Jihad-al-Bait al-Muqaddas* shifted completely during the Gulf crisis. Under the heading 'Islamic Leader Says Saddam Sent by *Allah* to Help Palestinians and Rule Iraq', Baghdad radio interviewed Sheikh Asaad, who perceived Saddam Hussein's use of Islamic language, idioms and metaphors as the embodiment of 'a high point in the Islamic awakening'. The Sheikh asserted that '[t]his is a battle between faith and atheism … the side of faith is led by Saddam … those who fight beside America today are doomed, for they have betrayed their nation and faith'.[77] Sheikh Asaad sought to revive the Islamic Caliphate, with Saddam Hussein as a Caliph of the glorious Arabic period (between AD 632 and around AD 850).[78] Based on the Islamic concept of *tawba* (to regret previous wrongdoing and be obliged to follow the Islamic path), Saddam Hussein's heroic stand against the evils of Zionism and the West had qualified him for such an honour. Sheikh Asaad al-Tamimi was put on the spot by the Western media, because of his claims that he had an army of followers who could spread terror and violence all over Europe and the United States. Sheikh Abd al-Mun'im Abu Zant, another prominent Jordanian parliamentarian from the powerful Islamic fundamentalist group the

Muslim Brotherhood, warned that '[t]his battle [the international coalition led by the United States against Iraq] is not between Iraq and America but between Islam and the Crusaders ... It is not between Saddam and Bush but between the infidel leaders and the Prophet of Islam.'[79]

Mainstream Islamic fundamentalism throughout the Arab as well as the Muslim world was opposed to Western interferences in the crisis, even if it did not openly support Saddam Hussein and Iraq or condemn the invasion of Kuwait. In Egypt, the Muslim Brotherhood, the largest active Islamist organization anywhere in the Arab world, also adopted such an approach. The invasion of Kuwait was denounced as *baghi* (a Qur'anic term combining injustice, outrage and atrocity). Many such organizations were financed by Gulf states and so all in one way or another had close relations with them. However, they were very apprehensive of Western objectives and aims in the region.[80] The same view was expressed by Sheikh Madani Abbasi of the Algerian Islamic Salvation Front (FIS), who gradually changed his position as the crisis dragged on and opposed any Western presence in Islam's Holy Land. Despite the FIS's financial dependence on Saudi Arabia, Sheikh Madani travelled to Baghdad as a show of support for Saddam Hussein and declared there that 'any aggression against Iraq will be confronted by Muslims everywhere'.[81] The second man in the FIS, Ali Belhadj, dressed in a military uniform, propagated for a jihad (a holy war) against the Western invaders and urged the Algerian government to give military aid to its Arab brothers in Iraq (Malley, 1996: 245). Eventually this powerful popular support compelled countries like Tunisia, Morocco and Pakistan, which had been strongly opposed to Iraq, gradually to change their positions and distance themselves from those Arab governments who were associated with the International Coalition against Iraq (Malley, 1996: 196–7). The Algerian government had severely criticized the Western (in particular the American) presence in the Gulf, whatever its rationale, and voted against the proposal from Saudi Arabian and other Gulf states that the United States should be asked to help eject Iraq from Kuwait. There were many Arab countries, such as Algeria, Jordan, Libya, Mauritania, PLO, Sudan, Tunisia and Yemen, who opposed any foreign intervention in Arab internal affairs, and even in countries such as Egypt, Lebanon, Morocco and Syria there were many who had a genuine fear of Western intervention in addition to those powerful

elements who favoured indirect support to Iraq (Khalidi, 1991).
However, the Islamic movements in Jordan and Palestine were among
the most enthusiastic supporters of Iraq and the person of Saddam
Hussein, despite the fact that, like all other Islamic fundamentalist
groups within the Muslim world, they were on the payroll of the Gulf
states and that the Iraqi leaders, together with the Syrian president,
Hafez al-Assad, and the late President Anwar al-Sadat of Egypt, are
regarded as some of the worst enemies of Muslim fundamentalist
groups due to their respective regimes' harsh treatment and oppression
of Islamists.

The Egyptian government made almost draconian efforts to contain
and control the organizations and cadres of Islamic fundamentalist
groups, most notably *al-Gamaa al-Islamiyya*, in order to avoid demonstrations against Western involvement in the Arab affair and in support
of Iraq. The government's objective was achieved as a result of the
assassination of Rifaat el-Mahgoub, the speaker of Egypt's People's
Assembly, by members of *al-Gamaa*. Even Amnesty International
reported, on 17 October 1990, on the mass arrests and the illegal
detention and torture of Islamists in Cairo, a measure that had
weakened the momentum of demonstrations by Muslim fundamentalists in support of Iraq in Egypt (Bennis and Moushabeck, 1991:
368; Hetata, 1991). Moreover, the Egyptian Labour Party (who held
a combination of Muslim fundamentalist and an ambiguous stream of
Fabian socialist views) dispatched a delegation headed by the party
leader Ibrahim Shukry and the influential yet controversial Islamist
publicist Adel Hussein, the editor-in-chief of the party daily newspaper
al-Sha'ab, to Baghdad to meet the Iraqi president. Their purpose was
to express their support and solidarity with their Iraqi kinfolk. The
party spokesman in Egypt considered Saddam Hussein as a champion
of Arabism.[82] *Al-Sha'ab* was considered (or accused by the Egyptian
government) to be 'an Iraqi publication in Egypt'. During the intensive
bombing campaign of Baghdad it carried the headline: 'Muslim! Your
brothers are being annihilated. Hurry to aid Iraq in its heroic steadfastness.' It took only hours for all the copies of this particular issue
to be sold, and the Egyptian government had no time even to stop
it.[83] Both Shukry and Adel Hussein, among many other members of
the Muslim Brotherhood from Egypt, Jordan, Syria, Sudan and
Tunisia, and even Islamists from Afghanistan, Bangladesh and Malaysia,
attended a meeting in Lahore, Pakistan, on the initiative of the *Jamaati-*

i-Islami, Pakistan's largest fundamentalist movement. They all condemned the West for making 'a war ... against Islam and its civilisation ... an alliance of Crusaders and Zionists' which was attempting to humiliate Muslims, occupy their land and steal their wealth. The conference sent a delegation led by Hassan al-Turabi, leader of Sudan's Islamic Front to the Pakistani president, demanding the withdrawal of the Pakistani troops from the International Coalition and urging support for Iraq 'in its steadfastness ... against the "infidel's aggression"' (Ahmad, 1991: 184, n. 35).

The pro-Iran Islamic fundamentalist group in Lebanon, *Hizbullah*, saw the Western and American intrusion in the Arab world as a greater peril than the Iraqi takeover of Kuwait, and vowed to fight the forces of the 'Great Satan' to eject them out of the region (Baram, 1991: 38, 39, 50, n. 8). In a different dimension, and yet taking a similar stand, the Palestinian Islamic Resistance Movement, known as *Hamas*, in the occupied territories of the West Bank and Gaza Strip, issued several communiqués as a reaction to the Iraqi invasion of Kuwait. While *Hamas* had, surprisingly, a supportive position toward Kuwait, mainly because of the financial assistance it obtained both from the Kuwaiti government and from Palestinians working there, the support waned and Hamas eventually responded to the grass-roots Palestinians few days after the invasion of Kuwait by switching sides in support of Saddam Hussein and Iraq (Baker, 1994: 475–6).

The watershed of Palestinian support for Iraq as an antithesis to their treatment by the Israelis came when 19 Palestinians were killed on the Temple Mount by Israeli police and soldiers in October 1990. Popular feeling in support of Saddam Hussein intensified. Harsh criticism began to be levelled by the mainstream Arab politicians, intellectuals, Muslim activists and ordinary people at the endemic 'double standard' of the United States' policy in the Middle East of outright support for Israel. The Iraqi strategy to use the grass-roots to pressure governments is in fact an old strategy which was most effectively used by Nassir. Several important constellations of civil society in the Arab world, such as the Islamist groups and other liberal-oriented public figures, refrained from criticizing Saddam Hussein or Iraq. They were instead rather concerned, given their historical experience of the foreign presence in the Arab world. However, *Hamas* gave unequivocal support to Iraq and its president in the face of the hateful Christian plot [by the West] against our religion, our civilisation and our land, this plot inspired and headed by the United States which commands all the forces hostile to Islam and the Muslims ... the chief of the false gods, [George Bush] the leader of the forces of evil ... America has exploited the entry [*dukhul*][84] of Iraqi forces into Kuwait and has used it to occupy the region directly, whereas before it had occupied [the Arab world] and had controlled its riches through the intermediary of its collaborators in the region.[85]

Viewed in this way, Arabs in all walks of life have been voicing their views with striking unanimity, which is why the discourse of Arabism was the soil wherein the Iraqi president sowed the seeds of his pursuit of power in the Arab world. When invading Kuwait, Iraq might have been in real need of economic assistance, or territorial access to the Gulf, or it may have simply initiated an over-reactive self-defence action against the conspiracy of the United States, Israel and the backing of the Gulf states,[86] but it is the identity of Arabism, Islamic idioms and the language that remain essential if one is to understand the grammar of the invasion of Kuwait. If we aspire to a genuine understanding of the nature of modern Arab society and the behaviour of states, then the question of Arabism ought to be integrated thoroughly into the study of the social and political process of the modern states in the Arab world, and of how they behave towards the outside world. This is a question which this research has attempted to explore, through the context of the invasion of Kuwait. The invasion was indeed a landmark in modern Arab history, and the Arab world will never again be the same.

EPILOGUE

The emphasis in this book has been more on historical experience, sociocultural realities and political practices than on the methodological clarity claimed by realist notions of representation and truth and protected by a continued adherence to common-sense empiricism needed to pinpoint who is responsible for what. The difficulty in formulating any adequate sociocultural approach to the political behaviour of international powers – or indeed of any social organizations – lies in estimating the ultimate importance of factors which elude the objective calculus of statistics and conventional empirical data. Can we understand political organizations in terms of the ways in which people are taught to believe and participate in them? As a question of multiple dimensions, the invasion of Kuwait was approached not only through the *reality* that engendered it, but also through the *discourse* that envisioned it. For this reason, commonplace social meanings, whether they are seen as 'thick description', 'experiential understanding', 'hidden layers' or 'concealed motion', are essential to the analysis of human behaviour, not only in the sense of ordinary people making sense of their world, but also in the sense that decision-making reflects the world around them. By the same token, how people conceive of themselves and others, whether objectively or not, are the perceptions that always provide the basis for the judgements made by decision-makers and other social actors. For example, the Kuwaitis no doubt found it difficult to understand what the invasion and annexation of their country had to do with the Arabs' battle of destiny against Zionism and imperialism, since they had always been among those Gulf Arabs who had previously financed the Arabs' efforts to combat Israel and United States' policy in the region. Alternatively, and in a different vein, we cannot study thoroughly the history of Zionism, Israel and plight of the Jews in pre-1945 Europe by using Saddam Hussein's narratives during the Gulf crisis as a point of departure, just as we cannot study Arab history or the plight of the Palestine from the praxis of Zionism.

Indeed, questions that have sociocultural and historical dimensions challenge us to investigate the international system not only as an objective historical process, but also as a range of subjective idioms in which the agents involved in the production of the system seek to exercise their agency. This is a process that has to be conducted both at the level of social and cultural meanings and at the level of their acceptance or rejection of one another's political and social practices. As Arabs and Israelis usually do, both Saddam Hussein and George Bush talked about each other and their respective political systems in scornful terms, but the irony is that by making such propaganda attacks on each other, they were both at the same time reflecting deeply held ideas prevalent in their own society about the other's society. It is important, therefore, to pay attention to the question of identity and beliefs in future research on foreign policy behaviour and on wars and conflicts between states, not only because these issues can transform private affairs into public concerns, but also because they prepare the path for war by sanctioning and endorsing violent campaigns by people who stand to benefit from them.

The Iraqi official explanation for the invasion of Kuwait is that it was a defensive measure against Zionism and imperialism and was necessary for the common good of the Arab nation.[1] Whatever the underlying reasons behind the invasion of Kuwait were, it has been a significant event in modern Arab history, and the crisis that followed was also significant in world politics. It was the first time in modern history that an Arab state invaded and annexed another Arab state, even though each had recognized the other's sovereignty in a number of regional and international institutions. What is more important, however, is that there was no Iraqi preparation for a merger with Kuwait, such as strengthening the irredentist claims over Kuwait in political or cultural terms. None of the maps printed by the various Iraqi governments since 1922, official documents, school books or media ever indicated that Kuwait had been part of Iraq. Prior to the invasion in August 1990, the Iraqi media's PR offensive had not mentioned any claims on Kuwait. Instead, attention had been focused almost entirely on the hypocritical policy of the United States against the Arabs and on Israel's expansionist policy in the land of the Arabs. On the other hand, Kuwait and other Gulf states entered Iraq's official narratives and Saddam Hussein's speeches at a later stage as part of the vast conspiracy orchestrated by America and Zionism and designed to destroy Iraq.

The political, social and economic processes in the modern Arab world must always be approached in relation to the question of its historical experience, its interrelationship with the West and the rise of the State of Israel, and the identity of Arabism reflected in these two aspects if we are to able to account fully for the evolution of these processes. Owing to the reasons and the historical background touched upon in this book, these discursive variables are associated with and ingrained in the political and social processes in ways that are unique to the Arab world. Therefore, any separation of these will nullify any attempt to understand why Arab leaders and states behave the way they, as rulers, do. Some would argue that for the sake of methodological clarity we need to sort out the variables in order to pinpoint who is responsible for what. Certainly, such a functional approach, helpful as it may be, will in the context of inter-Arab politics neglect many variables that are worth considering, even at the expense of methodological straightforwardness. Bearing in mind the complexities and intricacies of the Gulf crisis, we have approached the Iraqi decision to invade Kuwait from three different, yet related perspectives.

I

First, in devising, amending or pursuing foreign policy options, decision-makers would consider possible alternatives, selecting those most likely to advance particular goals at the least possible cost. Indeed, it is indisputable that the Iraqi president acted and reacted in regard to Kuwait within realism's approach to the practices of statecraft by political leaders. The focus has been on the Iraqi president as the prime object of analysis and therefore the invasion of Kuwait can be seen as a classical action emanating from asymmetrical power relationships between, on the one hand, a weak but enormously rich state and, on the other, an overwhelmingly powerful yet poor neighbour which bore a grudge. Foreign policy-making here refers to a particular decision undertaken in pursuit of specific objectives. For example, if we follow the realist premise then the case would be put as follows: according to the Iraqi leadership's proclaimed intention the invasion of Kuwait was chosen in order to mitigate the economic pressure, to have proper territorial access to the Gulf and to punish the al-Sabah family for their boldness and indifference to Iraqi needs. The decision to invade Kuwait was formulated by a decision-maker, President Saddam Hussein of Iraq. In implementing a selected option, it is assumed that he might have reacted to an identified set of problems by analysing information, determining objectives, formulating options and evaluating the choices, and so have reached a conclusion.

The foreign policy of a state is the result of a combination of the societal values, political, economic and strategic concerns within which decisions are formulated and implemented. We should assess the decision-making process in connection with a proper understanding of its main objective, since decision-making is the process of selecting an option for implementation. Obviously there were power-based motives behind Saddam Hussein's decision, but like any Arab leader in his place he put his case in the guise of Arabism and Islam. Matters became more complicated because of the nature of inter-Arab politics, and because leaders usually claim that they are acting on behalf of all Arabs, while many Arabs outside the leaders' particular state assign the same role to him to reaffirm and maintain the Arab's quest for self-definition by repelling the Arab nation's real or imagined enemies. The 'seamless web of significance' of Arab politics around this power-seeking and goal-maximizing autocrat needs to be examined in order properly to assess the invasion of Kuwait. Korany (1983: 468–9) argues that psychological reductionism and the modern version of 'the great man' theory of history that attributes all facets of political life to the leader's character, perception, words and deeds are not helpful in accounting for the foreign policy behaviour of the states. This approach, however, might have an appeal in the case of Iraq. Apart from the phenomenon of Saddam Hussein's leadership, there is a total lack of reliable information, documentation or archives, and an absence of political and societal institutions that might exert influence on the state's foreign policy. The relevance of psychological variables cannot be disputed here, though the relativity of their degree of influence and the demonstration of their causal impact should be put in their proper context.

By the same token, the foreign policy behaviour of states is not merely a result of one individual at the top of the political system. There are discursive regimes of images, beliefs and world views, and institutions that embody these variables which shape and limit the conduct of states. Decision-makers are:

conscious of a common political culture and of an attendant set of values, and conscious of their role and responsibility – publicly monitored – to pursue the national interest. Their political fortunes – even their survival – depend to a great extent on how they are popularly perceived to have discharged this responsibility. (Robinson, 1994: 417–18)

The social and political realities of the Arab world, make the realist approach fall short in accounting for how human collectivities envisioned on grounds other than the modern sovereign state behave within the international system. Iraq might have been driven by purely *realpolitik* motives, but the way the Iraqi leadership set out to justifying and carry out the invasion of Kuwait render it necessary to go beyond the realist premises in order to put all the pieces in their correct places. Realism, Keohane (1988: 391) argues, does not take into account the impact of the social processes of reflection or learning on the preferences of individuals or on the organizations that they direct. The approaches to individual interests that are based on abstract and material argument fail to account for sociocultural construction of the individual's values.[2] Unlike models of technical rationality, cultural studies recognizes the differentiations that account for anomalies. The concepts of security and powers are often socially and culturally situated in that they evoke symbols and metaphors associated with identity and differences. The key problem with realism as a functionalist enterprise is that it evades the question of common or shared identity central to the concept of society. Such constructs are not acknowledged by realists as a guideline for a normative theory of action. In our case, while accepting some of the realist claims on human behaviour, it is equally important to recognize the legitimacy and utility of these constructs for the analysis of political behaviour (Kratochwil, 1996; Cox, 1986).

The growth of a multilateral and highly interdependent and stratified global system provides a whole set of new dimensions for the international behaviour of a state. Foreign policy decisions are affected by the history and nature of the political and societal situation in which actors find themselves embedded; the values, beliefs and personalities of the decision-makers are causally linked with these domestic dynamics and with the external setting through interactions, pressures and manipulations by intended and unintended forces. The outbreak of the Gulf crisis as the Iraqi forces poured into Kuwait cannot be fully explained and understood in terms of a distracted and misperceived decision-maker who acted out of frustration in the face of the indifference of an opponent. Nor can disputes between two states that have sharply different views on how to solve their differences be simplified or reduced to fit neatly within a certain theoretical framework. This reductionism always overlooks the association and overlapping of various factors and the richness of intersubjective domains in helping to illuminate the paradoxes, intricacies and complexities of any human and social phenomena. Related to this point is a question that needs to be sorted out and clarified: how and why do certain violent initiatives and endeavours command popular support? The positivistic and actor-oriented approaches omit and overlook pivotal aspects of conceptual interconnectedness and historicity within the realm of symbolism that nourish and offer crucial clues in understanding why 'private' concerns become a 'public' interest to be defended.[3] Such taken-for-granted assumptions of political behaviour are manifested in the abstraction of states and policy-making. Indeed, critics (e.g., Kratochwil, 1996; Cox, 1986) argue that realism confuses the role of the scientific paradigm to explain and understand human and social phenomena with that of being merely prescriptions for policy-makers, i.e., a problem-solving theory. As such, it takes the objects of analysis for granted, whereupon the actual situation is not only be created, but also reproduced. In this vein, Cox (1986) draws a clear distinction between a problem-solving and a critical perspective, in that the first takes the world as theorists find it. Waltz's interpretation of Rousseau's Stag Hunt parable (1959: 169, n. 24), the condition whereby decision-makers behave rationally and assume that others would also do the same, is the only conceivable pattern to avoid the security dilemma. Ironically, this is supposedly the outcome of the interrelationship between two egoists and profit-maximizing rational actors.

As for Iraqi–American relations, the question might be seen as rather puzzling. First, American Middle East policy has been always inconsistent and partial in order to benefit Israel, and this dimension has often led many Arab states to be suspicious of the United States. The US, on the other hand, never misses an opportunity to maintain such a perception, especially in its dealings with radical states such as Iraq. Second, no indications were given to Iraq to make it clear that the US intended to defend its vital interests in the Gulf region. There were no security arrangements, no defence treaties between Kuwait and the United States, and, despite the claims that the Gulf region is essential to its national interest, the way the US showed this vis-a-vis Iran was, to say the least ambiguous. It is my understanding that there were no natural (or rational) communications between Iraq and the US whereby the latter made it clear to the former that the cost of intruding into its sphere of interest would very much exceed the gains. Even if we suppose that there were deterrent efforts from the United States in the form of assurances or other political manifestations to convey to Iraq the consequences of any violence against Kuwait, Arabism's 'seamless web of significance' has always been too dense to allow any *realpolitik* to pass through its prism. Indeed, Arab leaders have always exploited this, intentionally or unintentionally, in their actions against Zionism, the United States and the West. The behaviour of Saddam Hussein during the crisis, when he refused to withdraw from Kuwait, is a case in point.

Therefore, to assign pivotal roles to personal attributes, or ahistorical and nonevaluative political culture traits, such as locating experiences in the Arabs' history as episodes in a chain of political misery without situating and differentiating these factors within a wider context, and in interaction with other factors, would be inadequate to understand why Iraq invaded Kuwait. For this reason we are urged to ask the following question: why does history so frequently tend to affect, and even manipulate, modern-day societies and politics in the Arab world in patterns rarely found elsewhere? As I see it, such a question cannot be only answered or investigated by theories of abstract actors in the style of Allison's rational actor model, let alone the genre of *homo Arabicus* so characteristic of mainstream literature on the Gulf crisis, unless it is integrated and put in context within a wider frame of reference; within, say, an actor-specific approach that is related to the discourse of politics and identity versus 'Otherness' in the broader perspective. In this context, the following points are relevant: how people understand or perceive their world and that of others who usually affect it (i.e., the Arabs' view of the West and Zionism); how

the Iraqis and the Arabs identify themselves socially, culturally and
politically; the manner in which they convey their identity.

II

From the second perspective, the invasion of Kuwait can be seen as
a natural and spontaneous (or rather gratuitous) action that the Ba'ath
polity was compelled to take in order to ease the pressure from within
and divert attention away from Iraq's internal economic, social and
political problems. Or, to put it simply, the Ba'ath projected its fears
away from itself on to little Kuwait. This is a classical theme that has
been empirically proven. However, while accepting the rationale of
this assumption there are other variables that shed further light and
help us to understand why the Ba'ath regime acted the way it did,
when in fact it did not need to invade Kuwait to achieve the political
and economic objectives thought by many pundits and observers to
be behind the operation. In discussing the likely institutional impact
of the Iraqi polity on the decision to invade Kuwait, we are faced
with the problem of the watertight overlapping nature of the Iraqi state
and the *imagined* institution of Arabism. The interconnection between
the Iraqi polity (with its unusually illustrious top decision-maker) and
Arabism compel us to move beyond the confines of the Iraqi polity
to examine its links and encounters with the wider context of the
Arabic political discourse. In other words, the invasion of Kuwait had
been brewed and engendered by the Iraqi polity (with Saddam Hussein
at its core), interchanged with the Arabic political discourse. If the
interrelationships between cultural practices and politics are to be
appreciated, we have to move beyond such reductionism and
understand the cultural grammar of the Iraqi polity – the internal
coherence of its social, cultural, and discursive practices. Power
becomes actual and accurately understood, primarily through the
execution of ideas already in people's minds. Eventually, important
questions such as how people conceive of their world and what they
judge to be their own role within it, would become more comprehensible (Street, 1994: 104).[4] It is my understanding, therefore, that
what was interesting in this context was not that fact that a political
tyranny had been in perpetual conflict with itself and with other states
and actors around.

In this context, the analysis departs from the family and the nearness of kin as the central variable in understanding not only Arab social life but also the public political institutions. The focus on the theoretical approach has been to discuss the nature and the anatomy of institutions in Iraq's public life in particular, as well as in the Arab world in general. Awareness of the peculiar ways Arab leaders and peoples alike perceive the public political institutions was necessary in order to understand the Ba'ath government's ambivalent and confused stance between the notion of an 'Iraqi state' and the idea of the 'Arab nation'. Indeed, even the political elites of states throughout the Arab world often find themselves better served by this ambivalence between loyalty to the nation-state and adherence to pan-Arabism. The nationalism of the ruling Ba'ath in Iraq and Syria, the international vocation of the Libyan regime, the Islamic republic in Iran and the Islamist Kingdom of Saudi Arabia, to mention only a few, are all attempts to inspire political loyalty on the basis of ethnicity and religion, which deny the primacy of the state as an object of fidelity and, therefore, of significance to the analysis of political behaviour.

Many of the scholars studying the modern Arab world tend to associate Arab nationalist ideologies (e.g., Ba'athism, Nassirism and Syrian socialism), which seek to revive and reclaim the glories of the Arab *umma,* with the European idea of nationalism and 'patriotism' or *wataniyah* (reflected in attempt by Arabs to adopt European terminology), and so they often confuse and overlook the essential differences between Arabism (i.e., Arab nationalism) and European nationalism. The idea of nation and nationalism – comprising an ethnic group of people defined by language, culture and real or imagined descent – which crystallized in Europe, gives a geographic imperative and a spatial dimension to a preconception of culture – tradition, habit, faith, pleasure, ritual – all dependent on enactment in a particular territory. Moreover, territory is the place which nourishes rituals and contains people like oneself, people with whom one can share without having to explain. Territory thus becomes synonymous with identity, and, in an even deeper sense, it also encompasses the morality of kinship and the aptitude and calibre, in Anderson's (1991) sense, to *imagine* kinship beyond its immediate concrete manifestation, the family, the clan and the sect. Thus, the idea of an Arab nation-state contradicts the idea of Arab *umma* and addresses the conflict between the universal claim of the *umma* and the 'local' call for nationalism in the sense of being Iraqi, Syrian, Egyptian and so on. Arabism is not a feature of the state; Arabism is the attribute of a people – the Arab people. The intensity and peculiarity of these interrelationships are of great importance in understanding the course of the Gulf crisis. No less important, in this context, is not the leader who might act and behave as if s/he were an accountable political figure, but rather the leader who is seen here as a socially, culturally and historically sanctioned family patriarch. Such a dimension would be evident in the light of the fact that Iraq did not need to invade Kuwait to obtain the financial leverage it needed, nor was it motivated by the quest to control the oil sources of the Gulf.

III

Third, the overriding objective of the reflective approach is to integrate the question of identity and culture to the analysis of the political behaviour of individuals and states. It also has another important objective – it endeavours to fill in the blank spaces left by both the realist and institutional approaches. In the study of the Arab world, the question of identity should appropriately be considered in order to understand the genealogy of modern Arab societies and, hence, the discourse of politics. The Gulf crisis and the war that followed have urgently raised anew these issues. There is an apparent connection between the behaviour of the individual state and pan-Arab legitimacy, with the latter more visible. In addition is the role conflict (self-enacted as well as confined by others) of the political leader as well as that of the polity (i.e., pan-Arab versus Iraqi). During the intensive weeks preceding the invasion of Kuwait, the grass-roots demonstrations from Morocco in the west to Jordan in the east and the show of support from intellectual, cultural and political establishments all over the Arab world have to be understood within this frame of reference. This situation requires the student of Arab politics to go beyond the traditional outline of the state in a strict sense, and to consider how societal institutions formed and shaped the political process.

Islam's association with the Arab identity is firmly implanted in peoples' daily life in a way that is easily recognized by observer and observed alike. To lean to Islam and Arabism in social and political affairs is not only natural, but happens spontaneously among ordinary people, political elites and leaders in the Arab world. An act is sometimes considered pragmatic without being perceived as egoistic. In the absence of concrete political modalities and solid public institutions (a given factor in liberal democracies), then the variables (i.e., religions and invented or real primordial identities) that function as prepolitical modalities in peoples' daily life become important substitutes. In addition to the question of religion and politics, it is the decisive role of the middle classes and of ordinary people, motivated by what they perceive as important for them (i.e., Islam and Arabism), to signal to an Arab leader (i.e., Saddam Hussein) that they support in one way or another his policy as long as it is directed against Zionism, imperialism and the United States, the antithesis of Islam and Arabism. In line with this the Iraqi leadership has always claimed that the invasion of Kuwait was a defensive measure against Zionism and American imperialism.

What the crisis in the Gulf revealed is that the means that the Iraqi president chose to employ in pursuing his policy objectives, the invasion of Kuwait with overwhelming military strength, and then in justifying it, by appealing to pan–Arab and Islamic sentiments, tend to be important symbolic objectives in themselves that were widely welcomed by the intended audience – the Arab grass-roots and certain constellations of radical pan–Arabists and Muslim fundamentalists that meet together on the broad field of anti-Western and Americanism. The Gulf crisis, like many other crises, was a clash of interests that were (and still are) sharply contested by the actors involved (Ibrahim, 1992: xi, 7–11). The unfolding and the escalation of the crisis often degrades the decision-making process, but this should not lead us to ignore the factors that lie beneath the processes and procedures that generate the act of force. In this context, the notion that competition, insecurity and potential violence are the only central components of the political process in the world arena need to be reviewed.

One premise of the reflective approach to world politics is that it becomes necessary to understand the internal social and cultural dynamics of the societies involved in world affairs. Such an approach, moreover, integrates the issues of identity and culture with the analysis of the foreign behaviour of states and highlights the significance of these problems in relations between states in the international arena. We have seen that to political leaders these issues are not matters that should be subject to compromise and are, therefore, potentially likely to lead to conflict and can motivate them to go to war. In the same way, it is important to recognize the fact that foreign policy decision-making is an endeavour conducted by a community whose social and cultural dynamics affect the decisions taken by its members. These dynamics produce a world view that is embodied in symbols which evoke both cognitive and affective responses from the members of the community. All such symbols direct attention to a limited part of the world with the result that models based on them can easily become all too narrow. The potential value of the social and cultural aspects of world politics in general has often been emphasized in recent years, but despite this the literature on foreign policy-making and international relations in general remains dominated by functionally oriented technical analyses and technological concerns.

A theory sensitive to culture, Kratochwil (1996) maintains, would illuminate the idea that the sameness of traditional societies has little to do with evolutionary pressures, but rather with the conscious favouring of the past over the present and future. The past reproduces itself through the actions of the actors looking at a history understood and recorded in paradigmatic terms. Conflicts and war are usually the product of societal circumstances, sustained and transformed by mechanisms within society itself. Therefore:

preparing for and justifying the use of force require the invocation of constitutive principles of body politic ... Such axioms of civil society ... constrain leaders through the state's institutions; mutual understandings of the nature of the state and its values translate into mutual understandings of the obligations of sovereign office. (Robinson, 1994: 411)

The Gulf crisis, moreover, revealed the total lack of stable and mature political institutions in Iraq that could have deterred Saddam Hussein from frequently threatening neighbouring states. The crisis, too, emphasized the absence of coherent regional security arrangements and institutional settings that are necessary to solve and reconcile conflicting long-term interests and so contain the autonomous conflict processes which frequently lead to war. This circumstance urges us to chart different paths by exploring the Iraqi political system and its interconnectedness with the transstate institution of Arabism, and how the sociocultural discursive regime of Arabism was instrumental in shaping, confining and influencing the Iraqi decision to invade Kuwait. These are all domains hitherto largely ignored in the analysis of the political process as well as foreign policy behaviour.

APPENDIX: WRITING TO UNDERSTAND OR MAPPING TO CONQUER: DE/CONSTRUCTING THE MYTH OF *HOMO ARABICUS*

The function of this book is not necessarily to map and conquer the world, as the bulk of Western (mostly American) writers on the Gulf crisis mentioned below sought to do, but to help to understand the intricacy of war. Human and social phenomena are too complex and demanding for any theory to completely grasp and gauge. The Gulf crisis covered an extremely wide range of social constellations, political institutions and individual activities, with numerous accusations, agitations, claims and counterclaims, of deeply rooted and firmly held ideas of the collective self-image and of prejudices about the 'Others'. It is these dimensions that were most noticeable in the public records, books, scientific works, press coverage and reports about this most memorable affair in modern Arab history. The paradox here, however, as Said (1993: 302) notes, is of 'the most covered and the least reported war in history'. While the world lived through the Gulf crisis, watched its main actors in the flesh, speaking live, and read about it everywhere, the reliable materials by which we can assess scientifically the course of events are sparse, especially as regards the materials and data specifically related to Iraq and the Arab world.

It is in the availability of differentiated, complex and extensive information that the problem lies. Most of the writings and public records tend to be polemical and partial, and serve special interests. The scientific works on the causes and motivations behind the Iraqi invasion are few in comparison with what has been written on the Gulf crisis in general. Most (if not all) the works are mainly concerned with analysing the personality and behaviour of Saddam Hussein. In this context, the Iraqi president was not only a catalyst; he was also a

prime mover of events and the principal factor behind the invasion.[1]
Despite the impressive range of books, articles and press reports on
the events that sparked and even exacerbated the Gulf crisis, there are
few works that contain thorough investigations or analyses from
political scientists and foreign policy experts on the decision to invade
Kuwait. Moreover, the bulk of the writings on the crisis are essentially
partial, narrowly focused and designed to serve particular interests,
whether from the Western, American or Arab side. Thus, with a few
exceptions, they are inadequate to provide constructive and in-depth
research as far as the Middle East, or the Arab world are concerned.

This impressive array of writing (most notably those that are
journalistic in character), is not concerned with historical and societal
conditions that form the basis of the modern Iraqi state, nor with the
interrelationships between Iraq and the regional settings. Nobody
discusses the discursive formations that mark the interlocking of Iraq
and its populations with other Arab states and their populations within
the Arab order, nor do they base their analyses on the historical
conditions that shaped the Arabs' behaviour towards other non-Arab
actors in the Middle East region and ultimately towards the world at
large. Despite the devastating blow that Edward Said directed to
Orientalism, it is still the dominant discourse on Middle Eastern studies
in most Western universities and the public view of Arabs and Islam.
For example, the mainstream literature on the Gulf crisis can be seen
more or less as excerpts of modern Orientalism. Orientalism's
construction of Arab/Muslim's Otherness – a seemingly incontestable
description of Arab society that almost no one would dispute – is of
an extremely religious and, by implication, irrational society. Hence,
Orientalism aimed to curtail, designate and even degrade the diversity
and complexity of the Arab/Muslim world by locating and identifying
it within neat typologies and conceptual frameworks that represent
the antithesis of Western modernity. Images become highly localized
and may communicate certain supposedly negative attitudes and
falsehoods about Arab culture (Hassan, 1995). The latter is powerfully
manifested by Said's *Orientalism* in his critique of Orientalists' attitude
towards of Arab/Islamic society, which again came to the fore and
acquired justification in the West through the media reporting on the
Gulf War.

The very same literature is characterized by a lack of skill and
knowledge of the Arabic language, a serious handicap indeed,[2] since

the writers usually depend on translations produced by politically influenced governments (Bill, 1996). In the case of the Gulf crisis, almost all the writings by non-Arabs in English that I came across in this research rely exclusively on translated materials from Arabic by the United States State Department Service (SDS), or on other Western media coverage and reporting.[3] These books rely and draw almost exclusively on translated interviews with political and diplomatic sources, and the impressionistic and subjective character of these interviews becomes problematic as a result of the journalistic tendency to refer to unnamed sources, such as the Western diplomat or businessman or Americans, Europeans, Arabs or Iraqis, who in conversation said, commented, expressed or rumoured, and so on. At the same time, they display, and vividly, the great disparity between brief visits to a certain country without either knowledge of the language, culture or history, or systematic and scientific field research.[4] Moreover, one finds all Arabic sources through the United States SDS services, and almost nothing in Arabic.[5] The Iraqi publicist Kanan Makia's[6] contribution to this wave of literature, which is marked by the dehumanization of Saddam Hussein, the Ba'ath Party and, by implication, the state of Iraq and Arabs as whole, was decisive for their logic and arguments. Al-Khalil's *Republic of Fear* became the well from which all the other superficial, impressionistic and hastily published books that followed the Gulf crisis uncritically draw; they are strikingly identical in their description of the causes of and motivations for the invasion of Kuwait and the crisis and, what is more, they all include a particular focus (sometimes to the point of obsession) on the psychology and personality of the Iraqi president.[7]

Karsh and Rautsi (1991) provide an impressive and detailed history of Saddam Hussein the political leader, 'professional survivor' and 'man for all seasons'. They draw on data from Israeli, British and American sources to build a psychological analysis and the sociopolitical circumstances of his rise to power as the undisputed leader figure and president of Iraq since 1979. All the data and materials seemed to be oriented towards portraying a tyrant of almost superhuman nature, who utilizes everything around him, including the Iraqi state entire wealth, for one exalted aim: to be the one and only unchallenged leader of Iraq and the Arab nation. The invasion of Kuwait, like that of Iran in September 1980, was approached from the point of view of this incredible man's complicated personality and intricate mentality.

These are both points of departure and the conclusion of others who wrote about the Gulf crisis and Saddam Hussein.[8]

Following the Saddam argument that Karsh and Rautsi (1991) put forward, many claims are worth noting here: 'Saddam Hussein may possess certain idiosyncrasies, but naiveté is not one of them' (p. 153) 'his readiness to lose face whenever his survival so required' (p. 156); 'Saddam Hussein has predicated his personal rule on the Ba'ath party. His logic, like that of his predecessors [Stalin and Hitler], has been strikingly simple: since the party possesses the organisational infra-structure and ideological basis for controlling people's actions and minds, it would control the masses and the state machinery while he would control the party' (p. 176); 'This deep dialectical combination of impotence and omnipotence, of a deep economic plight and fears of an Israeli attack, on the one hand, and the undistinguished air of self-importance, on the other hand, sealed the fate of Kuwait' (p. 211); 'This defiant response [Kuwait's attitudes and reactions to Iraqi demands of a huge sum in financial aid] was the last nail in the Kuwaiti coffin. Not only was it taken by Hussein as a vindication of his long-standing perception of Kuwait as a parasitic state thriving on Iraq's heavy sacrifices, it was also a personal affront made by a minor neighbour' (p. 213).

An identical point of view is put forward by Miller and Mylroie (1990), as follows: 'Iraq is run as a private preserve of Saddam and his inner clique' (p. 38); 'Saddam trusts no one. Those who have had long experience with him know that. ... Mubarak has called him a "psychopath." The Saudis have called him "psychotic"' (p. 40); 'Saddam understands that his ability to project power outside the country helps maintain his authority inside the country' (p. 54); 'Both of Saddam's misjudgments [the invasion of Iran and Kuwait], a decade apart ... in both cases he had also overestimated his strength. The misjudgments, moreover, reflect Saddam's appalling lack of knowledge of the world beyond Iraq ... Saddam Hussein has caused two major world crises in a decade in a relentless quest to wield power and win respect' (pp. 21–2).

Other similar views are presented by Simpson (1991): 'Many people have endured brutal upbringing and exhibited paranoid symptoms in the service of a cause [to rule Iraq alone]' (p. 22); 'The war against Iran was a personal memorial to Saddam Hussein. It showed exactly the same combination of opportunism and overconfidence he demonstrated ten years later [in invading Kuwait]' (p. 39); 'There was no pressure on Iraq to pay these debts, but while the Saudis were prepared to commute a good proportion of them to outright gifts, the Kuwaitis were not. Saddam did not forget this. He took such things personally' (p. 88); 'Saddam Hussein and his government approached the invasion [in a way that it] has all the hallmarks of something done on the spur of the moment, almost on a personal whim' (p. 87); 'Saddam Hussein tried to perpetrate upon the entire world. The dictator of a smallish country in serious financial trouble, he invaded a much smaller and much richer neighbour on a sudden whim ... It is hard to think of a bigger bluff since Hitler's men entered the Rhineland in 1936' (p. xiv); 'The history of the crisis becomes the history of Saddam's growing anger and frustration. The best political intelligence available indicates that there was no plan, no blueprint, that, as always, he moved from one position to the next on the basis of instinct and feeling, with no one to hold him back. Most international crises are the result of interacting forces and influences: this time the overriding force was Saddam Hussein's personality' (pp. 88–9).

Laurie Mylroie's article, 'Why Saddam Hussein invaded Kuwait' (1991: 124), departs from the 'misreading Saddam's goals' by the other actors involved such as the Kuwaitis, Saudis, Egyptians and the Americans. Since the 'Nature of Tyrants', which 'We' (i.e., the Americans) have to be aware of, since 'misreading Saddam ... entailed a failure to appreciate his goals and the tenacity with which he pursued them. Many of us saw the insecurity and brittleness of Saddam's rule, and that blinded us to his ambition'. Mylroie quotes works like those mentioned here in this category, as well as other Arab leaders, merely to confirm her initial conclusion that it was Saddam who worked it all out.

Bruce Jentelson (1994: 15–16, 139), seeks to uncover the questions of how and why the United States' active policy since 1982, under the two Republican presidents Ronald Reagan and George Bush, to 'bring Saddam and his country into "the family of nations" failed so profoundly'. Rich with documents and containing material of great relevance to the Gulf crisis (from the US perspective), Jentelson's book remains a by-product of US internal politics and partisan polemics.[9] The impressive array of data and the display of information on policy-making during the Gulf crisis is primarily from the American standpoint. However, all the material relating to Iraq and the Arab world consists of United States' government translations which, by implication, are not necessarily objective as far as the Iraqi state of affairs is concerned. Examples abound: 'Right from the start, Saddam ruled ruthlessly. He wanted nothing less than "absolute power and unconditional subservience," and unleashed the bloodiest purge yet, executing hundreds of party officials and military officers, some of whom were close friends and associates' (p. 39; see also Karsh and Rautsi, 1991: 4); 'Saddam's decision to go to war against Iran was partly a matter of being provoked, but mostly his own opportunism' (p. 41); 'Saddam also used the ACC first anniversary summit to issue demands on his fellow Arab states ... Saddam also proposed that other Arab states directly and indirectly provide Iraq with $30 billion in new economic aid' (p. 150); 'Saddam further demonstrated his regard of world opinion when on March 15, [1990] he executed a British journalist falsely accused of spying' (pp. 152–3); 'Saddam had strong tendencies toward paranoic views of enemies in general. This was his upbringing in Iraqi politics and part of how he sustained his own rule' (pp. 203–4); 'the Iraqi rhetoric from which the paranoic un–deterra-bility has been imputed could well have been quite simply international misrepresentation and fabrication' (p. 205); finally, 'there is nothing inherently undeterrable about such a pattern of behaviour. It is only normal among nation-states with aggressive aspirations – analytically speaking, quite rational behaviour. When convinced of the threat of resistance or retaliation from other powers, Iraq had not been inter-nationally aggressive. When not so convinced, it has. It indeed has a history of needing to be deterred – but of being deterrable' (p. 206).

Jerrold Post's (1993) work aimed at developing 'a comprehensive political psychology profile of Saddam Hussein in late August 1990 ... the profile became the object of widespread attention from electronic and print media because of the intense interest in the personality and political behaviour of Saddam. The profile was presented to the House Foreign Affairs Committee hearing on the Gulf crisis in December in 1990' (p. 63). It is worth noting in this context that Professor Post had no single source in Arabic, he had not conducted any personal interview with Saddam Hussein or any of his associates, and there is no mention of sources and material on Arab history, society and culture required in order to make such a com-prehensive political psychological profile. Thus, the well-known maxims about Saddam are only repeated time and again. This is particularly evident in the following excerpts: 'After a long, defiant, and self-justifying speech … one of Saddam Hussein's sycophantic subordinates proclaimed "Iraq is Saddam; Saddam is Iraq"' (p. 4); 'he is surrounded by sycophants who are cowed by Saddam's well-founded reputation for brutality … Saddam epitomizes Lasswell's *homo politicus* or power seeker who displaces a private need onto public object and rationalizes it as being in the public good' (p. 50); 'in his mind, the destiny of Saddam and Iraq are one and indistinguishable. His exalted self concept is fused with his [Ba'athist] political ideology' (pp. 51–2); 'While Saddam can be extremely patient and uses time as a weapon, his tendency to rely on his own instinct can lead him to "miss the moment"' (p. 64); 'Iraq's invasion of Kuwait produced a torrent of inflammatory rhetoric concerning the irrationality of its president, Saddam Hussein, who was characterised as "the madman of the Middle East". In fact, irrationality in the seat of power is inconsistent with sustained leadership. An examination of Saddam's life and career reveals a judicious political calculator who is by no means irrational but is dangerous in the extreme. While not a psychiatrically disturbed individual out of touch with psychological reality, he is often out of touch with political reality. Although he is a rational political calculator, it is because of his often flawed perception of political reality that he frequently miscalculates' (p. 49).[10]

To make such claims, the question related to empirical proof has to be solid and pronounced. But since within such a framework, and given the absence of experiential verification such as deep personal interviews, reliable first-hand material, memoirs and official documents etc., it is impossible to clarify the actual motivations behind the Iraqi president's action against Kuwait. A qualified scientific answer that can claim objectivity in answering intricate questions on the causes and motivations for warfare requires the researcher to account for much more than that offered by this hastily compiled problem-solving literature. What characterizes all these books is the lack of verifiable empirical data, the consequence of which is far more critical than is admitted. Generic assumptions about the nature of tyrants or Arab political culture or counterculture can never be a substitute (Bill, 1996; Said, 1981). Indeed, the personality and history of Saddam Hussein may have been the prime (if not the only) focus and concern, and the Iraqi president has been characterized by and accused of displaying so many, often contradictory, peculiarities and qualities that in the end they appear to be unrealistic. These works explain so many things that in the end they explain nothing. On the face of it, they are all ultimately ahistorical, since they concentrate primarily on Saddam Hussein (i.e., *homo Arabicus*) as possessing inherent, absolute, non-evaluative and even unchanging peculiarities. On the other hand, the core and the scope of these books *are* historical since they relate Iraq and its political leader and elite to the bygone days of the pre-classical eras of the Sumerians, the Babylonian king Nebuchadnezzar and Al-Hajaj of the Umayyads.[11]

All the otherwise interesting variables – such as the state, nation, societies, peoples and culture – or domestic constraints, outside pressures, the impact of history including the exposure to colonialism, are certainly relevant to the analysis of Iraq's political behaviour throughout the crisis. Instead, they all appear as 'blank spaces' characterized by ontological emptiness. The media coverage of the Gulf crisis was also faithful to this attitude of obsession with the *homo Arabicus*, Saddam Hussein, 'the personalization of Arab politics was convenient during the Gulf War', as Abu Khalil (1992: 26) writes, 'especially the impression created that only Saddam lived in Iraq and that it was, in essence, an uninhabited land'. All these are the consequences and evolution of multifarious factors, and a myriad of forces operating within many fields of human and social sciences in the West. There is always the danger of constructing, along the line of orientalism, a stereotyped *homo Arabicus*, or *homo Islamicus*. Unlike the normal *homo* Westerner, he is devoid of the capacity to act in accordance with, or react to rational or regular social stimuli (Abdel-Mallek, 1963: 108; Said, 1978, 1981).

The main thrust of the literature on the Gulf crisis compels the readers and, indeed, the researcher on the Arab world and the Middle East, to counter the effects and repercussions of an ahistorical perspective that essentially rests on cognitive and psychological observations about political manner and comportment. These works might differ in focus, in documentation, in the way they approach the invasion of Kuwait and the Gulf crisis, but, in substance, the underlying argument of almost all of them is repeated time and again. Generally, it tends to be an 'essentialist', unchanging, *sui generis* political and social construction that has usually been an attribute of Orientalism. Even more important, it represents a landmark in the analysis of the Arab world in that it stipulates a pattern whereby the presuppositions of the age-old views of and ideas concerning Islam and Arabism would perfectly implement research into an understanding of present-day Arab society and politics (Halliday, 1995: 37, 207). Throughout the last 1,500 years in the history of Islam and the Arabs, nothing has been changed, everything stands still[12] – apart from some ideas and ideologies introduced from the West. The historical development, social evolution, cultural diversity and activities of the political process in the 22 Arab states, all these things are reduced to 'a single, all-encompassing, and apparently enduring totality' (Halliday, 1995: 204). During the Gulf crisis, the literature and media coverage alike has linked the behaviour of Arab political leaders and people in general directly to Islamic theology (Rodinson, 1980; Abu Khalil, 1992: 24).

NOTES

CHAPTER 1: UNDERSTANDING THE IRAQI INVASION OF KUWAIT

1   See also the appeal written by Noam Chomsky, Edward Herman, Edward Said and Howard Zinn, in *ORDFRONT Magasin* (NR: 3/99) March 1999, Stockholm.

2   To use Clifford Geertz's (1973) phrase signifying the impact of the symbolic domain on the social and political actions of individuals.

3   See Edward Said's article 'Clinton's rampage' (1998), in *Al-Ahram Weekly*, 24 December 1998, Cairo.

4   To use Philip Marlow's phrase to depict the territories of natives 'who have a different complexion or slightly flatter noses than ourselves', in Joseph Conrad's *Heart of Darkness* (cited in Said, 1993: 213, n. 23).

5   For example, the otherwise moderate daily editorials of the Egyptian newspaper *Al-Ahram* (the semi-official newspaper of the pro-American Egyptian government) had reacted agonizingly to the way the prime minister of Israel, Benjamin Netanyahu, was received in the US Congress. The editorial on 21 July 1996 notes Congress's warm applause of what is considered (by international law and all UN resolutions on the Arab–Israeli conflict) to be an illegal claim by Mr Netanyahu that a united Jerusalem is the immortal capital of the Jewish state. Israel, it seems, has total control of the highest US political institution. See also foreign editor of the newspaper Ihsan Bakr's article 'Iraq and its moving sand' on 27 October 1996, in which even harsher views were expressed. Similar Arab reactions came about when Newt Gingrich, the Speaker of the US Congress, made the same illegal claims in the Israeli Knesset in May 1998.

6   The second is the government of Benjamin Netanyahu, formed in July 1996. The Tzomet Party, led by former chief of staff Rafael Itan, for example, urged (and still does) in its programme the eviction of the Palestinian population from their land in Gaza and the West Bank.

7   The UN Security Council had agreed on Resolution 242 in November 1967. It urges for a peaceful settlement between Arab states and Israel within secure and recognized borders. Israel would withdraw from territories it had occupied in June 1967, and a solution would be found for the Palestinian refugees. However, there have always been different interpretations in regard to this Resolution by Israel on one side and Arab states and the Palestinians on the other: whether Israel should withdraw from all or some of the lands; whether the Palestinians should be regarded as a nation or a mass of individual refugees.

8   The Iraqi decision to invade Kuwait took place in the relaxed international post-Cold War atmosphere, which coincided with the collapse of the Soviet satellite regimes in Eastern Europe and the fall of the Berlin Wall, powerful, symbolic events that ultimately accelerated the disintegration of the communist hegemony within the Soviet Union itself, and the gradual but definite Soviet retreat from the international and Middle East scenes. Unlike their earlier support for Iraq's claim on Kuwait in 1962, the Soviets were not willing this time to restrain the United States' response. Rather, they supported the United Nations and, by implication, the United States' position against Iraq. China – considered the UN's Third World representative – was also reluctant to support Iraq.

9   As was the case in 1962 when the then Iraqi president Abdul-Kareem Qassim (1958–63) claimed that Kuwait was historically an integral part of Iraq, Arab states like Saudi Arabia, Syria and even Nassir's Egypt, the vanguard of pan-Arabism, defended Kuwait's sovereignty side by side with the British, the symbol of imperialism and colonialism (Finnie, 1992: 130–1; Ibrahim, 1992: 15; Schofield, 1993: 100–4).

10 Since 1932, throughout the history of modern Iraq, there have been three well-known incidents of territorial claims to part or whole of Kuwait: first, by King Ghazi, who had been on a collision course with Britain and the pro-British Iraqi politicians

like Nuri al-Said, because of his outspoken claim on Kuwait in March 1938 (Finnie, 1992: 103–6); second, by President Abdul Kareem Qassim in 1962; and lately, by President Saddam Hussein's decision to invade on 2 August 1990, and the annexation on 8 August 1990.

11   As in the cases of the Ba'ath Party, Nassir and others. Nor is it a desperate imitation of the nationalism that appeared in Europe during the nineteenth century.

12   Unlike in the other world religions, Weber (1968: 625) argues, in Islam 'an essentially political character marked all the chief ordinances of Islam: the elimination of private feuds in the interest of increasing the group's striking power against external foes'. It is this dimension of political ordinance that makes Islam unique in resolutely bridging politics and the public order with religious life. The connection has two dimensions: the first is that of the world view; the second in terms of the impact of Islam on social and political life (Turner, 1974; Schroeder, 1992: 66ff.).

13   See for example Gilsenan (1982), like Weber (1965, 1968), Geertz (1973) and Hodgson (1974: 71–99).

14   Clifford Geertz's (1973: 8–125) phrase; he also borrows from Malinowski.

CHAPTER 2: THE REALIST PERSPECTIVE

1   Stanley Hoffman (1965) argues that despite many ideological quarrels between scholars within the research field of world politics, its dilemma has remained essentially the same from Machiavelli to our day. He further argues that '[w]hoever studies contemporary international relations cannot but hear … a kind of permanent dialogue between Rousseau and Kant … Kant draws the picture of a world dragged into peace by conflict and by greed … Rousseau tells us, however, that the very intercourse of nations breeds conflicts; that if it is not possible to end such intercourse, the only remedies are fragile mitigating devices' (Hoffmann, 1965: 86).

2   Even Kant, unlike some of his nineteenth-century liberal followers, was forced to recognize that pluralistic conflict could only be ended by a long-term radical transformation of the inter-

national system itself. Kant's speculations remain the most influential guide for those who, for one reason or another, find the realist account to be superficial. For the convinced realist, however, even Kant's highly qualified universalism remains entirely utopian, and the proper understanding of international politics is provided instead by those who recognize the pre-eminence of pluralism – Machiavelli (H. Williams, 1992: 68–97).

3   However, 'scientific' facts are never 'just facts', because they often framed with value judgments that can be intentionally introduced and exploited for any reason the actor might give. Such 'technical rationality' excludes a wide range of substantive cultural and social facts (Simon, 1983).

4   The rational actor model takes lineage from Morgenthau's assumption concerning the statesman's conception of the national interest, and from Thomas Schelling's assumption that leaders probe (through game theory) all the possibilities available to attain a credible deterrence strategy to preserve peace. In the worst-case scenario, if wars become inescapable they should be limited and controllable. The gist of the model is to associate foreign policy decisions with reasonable assessments (pp. 4–5, 10–11). The rational actor model, too, exhausts various sequences of events and plans of managing and containing nuclear war. Basically, however, the model is an articulation of the classical *homo economicus* in which a decision-maker has to be (if s/he is not already) conformed and arrange the most favourable alternatives in strictly confined circumstances. In the meantime, such an actor (or rather abstracted individual) is expected to minimize the likely losses and to maximize the gains that s/he comes across. Within this approach, the rational decision-makers are assumed to know quite well what they are doing when formulating and executing policy decisions (Allison, 1971: 29–30). Analytically, this line of argument leads students of international relations to consider decision-makers as undisputed, unrestricted individuals who are practically 'organisationally programmed automatons ...' (Steiner 1977: 419). Decision-makers are unrestricted in the sense that they are independent of a social and cultural context and, indeed, are able to produce and conceive their social context (Finnemore, 1996). Moreover, for the sake of accuracy, events are explained not teleologically in terms of goals and purposes, but scientifi-

cally in terms of causal determinants that are subject to investigation. Yet, in the overall analysis, Allison 'unwittingly introduces goals and purposes as "the essence of decision"' (Steiner, 1977: 419).

5 Saddam Hussein's speech on Revolution Day, 17 July 1990.

6 In the language of the Arabic political and social discourses the word 'nation' or *umma* refers only to the Arab or Muslim nation. Immediately after the Gulf War ended, the Syrian Kamal Abu Deeb, a poet, professor of Arabic literature at Columbia University in New York and renowned literary critic, published a piece with the title: *Sarkhah fi Matah* (Screaming in a Wasteland), to express his own agony and anger with a clear sense of defiance:

> We cannot be but with the nation ...
> The nation may be a gargantuan tyrant ... The nation may be a policeman whose dogs chase us everywhere inside its walls.
> The nation may be the cave of our disillusionment, or the slaughterhouse of our sweet dreams, or the grave of our freedom and honour.
> ... And the nation may be a thousand worse and even more terrible things.
> Still, we cannot but be with the nation.
> (Published in London in the Arabic literary monthly *an-Naqid*, No. 33 (March 1991) 4–5, and cited in Makia, 1993: 245)

7 Saddam Hussein's speech on Revolution Day, 17 July 1990. Examples abound: 'We wanted to tell our brothers in Bahrain and Kuwait that [Iranian] forces will be powerless to attack the sovereignty of any Arab land or people. As long as we are in a position to fight back, we shall do so. Iraq's geographical position may not enable it to place its Army to face the "Zionist entity", but it is certainly capable of positioning its forces against any threat aimed at Bahrain or Kuwaiti sovereignty, and at the Gulf in general': Saddam Hussein interviewed on Iraqi TV, November 1979. On another occasion he argued 'That if the *Arabs* have a certain weapon, they will use it ... We talked about using chemical weapons should Israel threaten us or threaten the *Arab nation* militarily, including using nuclear weapons that it owns ... when anyone threatens us with aggression, or tries to raise slogans of aggression, against Iraq or any part of the *Arab homeland*, then it would be natural for the Arabs to say to him: "if you attack us, we will retaliate against your aggression with the weapons we

have"': the Iraqi News Agency, 7 April 1990 (quoted in Karsh and Rautsi, 1991: 210–11), emphasis added. And finally, Saddam Hussein urged Arabs and Muslims to 'rise and defend Mecca, which is captured by the spears of the Americans and the Zionists': the Iraqi News Agency, 8 August 1990.

8   Although in reality the Ba'athist Iraq is one of those Arab regimes that benefited most from the financial and other forms of support from the ruling families of the littoral Arab Gulf states and the objective was not in any way to encourage or provoke a popular revolt to overthrow them. However the American military presence and the defiant behaviour they displayed after the war with Iran was threatening to pull these sheikdoms away from Iraq's regional sphere of influence. The absence of reliable collective security arrangements that included all actors in the region made these ruling groups insecure in their own societies without an outside protector.

9   'The Communiqué of the Iraqi Patriotic and Islamic Movement', cited in Baram (1991: 40).

10 This even applies to non-Arab Muslim communities, as was the case in the war between Iraq and Iran.

11 This is akin to what K. J. Holsti (1970: 245–6,) calls '"national role conception," and which refers to the conception that decision-makers have of themselves and the state they represent, such role conceptions influence and are influenced by interactions'.

12 In a conversation with the British MP Tony Benn in October 1990, Saddam Hussein is reported to have said: 'I would say something to you I wouldn't say publicly – that I didn't want to take over the whole of Kuwait. I just wanted the disputed areas – the 80 kilometres that he claimed the Kuwaitis had gained by moving the frontier north, and the Rumayla oil field, and access to the sea. But if I had just done that, the Americans would have come into Kuwait and attacked me from there.', interview with Tony Benn in the London–based Arabic magazine *al-Ghad*, 22/23, February 1992.

13 Studies on popular attitudes in the Arab world have clearly indicated that, from the 1950s, Arab citizens' loyalties have been divided between ethnic and/or religious, pan-Arabism and Islam (Ibrahim, 1980; Yassin, 1981b).

14   The Iraqi president swears by *Allah* to 'pluck out the eyes of those
     who attack *the Arab nation*', adding that 'we would rather die in
     dignity than live in humiliation, and vow to fight until death'
     (speech broadcast on Iraqi television, 7 August 1990, emphasis
     added).

15   Saddam Hussein's speech on Revolution Day, 17 July 1990.

16   Quoted in Lisa Anderson (1987: 5).

17   Rather than in the form of rationally put forward policy objectives
     that have to be executed for the good of an abstract state or
     institution that individuals do not personally encounter in daily
     life.

18   In the language of Arabic political and social discourses the word
     'nation' or *umma* refers only to the Arab as a collective linguistic
     and cultural unity. However, in prerevolutionary Egypt (before
     1952) the *Wafd* Party which dominated Egyptian politics between
     1919–52, together with other liberal constellations, with historical
     legitimacy, had frequently called Egypt by the name of *al-umma
     al-miseriyya*, the Egyptian nation, a name that was abandoned by
     the Nassirist discourse to the Arab nation.

19   The Iraqi News Agency, 4 August 1990.

20   *Le Figaro*, 4 March 1991 (quoted in Piscatori, 1991: 16).

21   Up until the failed attempt to unify the two countries under the
     leadership of the former Iraqi president Hassan al-Bakr in 1978.

22   As Abdullah Hourani, PLO Executive Committee member,
     maintained, the shift from Egypt and the focus on Iraq was a
     necessary measure because Egypt was heavily dependent on the
     United States, and as such it lacked the resolve to put pressure
     on the Americans in regard to the peace settlement (Bennis and
     Moushabeck, 1991: 363).

23   Before the invasion of Kuwait, the Ba'athist government of Iraq
     was reported to be the real owner behind at least 30 daily and
     weekly Arab-speaking newspapers and other publications in
     Europe, Egypt, Lebanon and elsewhere in the Arab world, and
     there many also editors and prominent media figures in the Gulf
     region and other Arab states, most notably Egypt, on its payroll.
     This is a well-known tradition in the Arab world, where regimes
     buy-off the media in other Arab states or in Europe.

24   This is akin to what, in the context of the utility of history in
     decision-making processes, Vertzberger (1986: 225, 227) termed

as the 'circumscribing role – the recognition of roles and status appropriate for the actor and the choice among these policy alternatives', whereby history itself has an impact upon the decision-maker's self-perception and his/her perception of how the others will act or be likely to react.

25 As Tariq Aziz stated in an interview with Milton Viorst of the *New Yorker* (June 1991).

26 As was once put by Morgenthau (1940: 279, and cited in Keohane, 1988: 385), 'to put their normal relations on a stable basis by providing for predictable and enforceable conduct with respect to these relations'. The key problem with the realist and other functionalist approaches is that they evade the question of common identity and belonging that is central to the concept of community (Goldstein and Keohane, 1993:6).

27 Even Edward Said (1991), a well-informed scholar of Middle Eastern history, culture and society, claims that Saddam Hussein 'was almost invited to invade Kuwait'. It is impossible to verify empirically such a claim, however. The theory that the United States deceived Iraq into Kuwait so that it could trap and destroy the mighty Iraqi army and thus eliminate the danger to Israel was and is still the most popular of all theories that probe the enigma of why Iraq invaded Kuwait. Indeed, on 22 March 1991, the Pakistani chief of staff, General Aslam Beg, openly accused the United States of having intentionally misled Iraq into Kuwait for the sake of Israel's security (Piscatori, 1991: 229).

28 On 24 July 1990, after meeting Saddam Hussein in order to mediate between Iraq and Kuwait, President Mubarak of Egypt urged the United States to keep a low profile and avoid any act of provocation that might entangle the atmosphere of reconciliation between 'two Arab brothers and neighbours' (Bennis and Moushabeck, 1991: 364). Even more significant, the Kuwaiti government (the factual recipient of the intended protection) declared that the dispute should be settled within the Arab framework and without any foreign interference (as was usually the case), and that if the United States did provoke Iraq, the process of defusing the crisis might be counterproductive. Thus, the United States had no choice but to react the way it did, given the pattern of its policy in the region and the demands from its friends in the Gulf.

29   Indeed, the Soviet Union's intrusion into the Middle East through the Egyptian–Czechoslovakian arms deal in 1955 was the beginning of an epoch of the Middle East as a highly militarized region (Sid-Ahmed, 1984).

30   Unlike Syria and Egypt, Iraq, due to the vast oil resources, has had a relatively independent relationship with the superpowers. Ever since 1972, after the nationalization of the oil industry and with the existence of vast oil resources, the Iraqi government has freely used oil in its relations with the superpowers in general.

31   The Iraqi–Soviet bilateral relationship was based on the Agreement of Mutual Assistance and Friendship signed in 1971, and renewed in 1978. However, there are reasons that might explain the background to the Soviet's regional position and what might have motivated them not to support Iraq. First, since 1980 the relationship had experienced strains due to the independent position adopted by the Iraqi leadership toward the Soviets. For one thing, Iraq condemned the Soviet invasion of Afghanistan, and for a second, Iraq invaded Iran without informing the Soviets beforehand. This was against the conventional wisdom of the Cold War: if one of the superpowers' Third World vassal states was about to engage in violent conflict it had to inform its own particular superpower in advance and so provide for an eventual political and military cover-up (Bakr, 1991; Mostafa, 1991). For example, this was the case during the Iraqi intrusion on to Kuwaiti territory in 1962 – then the Soviet Union supported the Iraqi claims. Third, during the course of the Iran–Iraq war the Soviet Union was suspicious of the security arrangement in the Gulf area led by the United States, Saudi Arabia, Jordan and Egypt to use the Iraqi military machine to stop the expansion of revolutionary Islam in Iran. This might explain the Soviets' good relations with Iran despite the Khomeini regime's condemnation of communism and the destruction of the pro-Soviet Iranian communist Tudeh Party. Fourth, when Iraq invaded Kuwait, the Soviets, like everybody else, were taken by surprise (Bakr, 1991; Melkumyan, 1992).

32   From April 1990 onward, and from reading the Ba'ath media and Saddam Hussein's speeches, the Iraqi government felt intense pressure and probably genuinely feared that Israel, with US backing and the implicit acceptance of the conservative Arab

regimes, was preparing to carry out a preemptive strike against Iraq's missile plants, just as it had destroyed the Osirak nuclear reactor in 1981. At this point, Richard Herrmann (1991) argues that Iraq might have drawn the conclusion that American pressure was only related to the Iraqi threat to Israel. By shifting attention to the Gulf, the Iraqi leadership might have felt it could act and be exempt from American punishment.

33 Saddam Hussein's meeting with Glaspie and Aziz's interview with Viorst of the *New Yorker* (June 1991). Saddam Hussein seems to have taken into consideration the American experience in Vietnam in 1973 and in Beirut in 1983 after the explosion that killed 250 US marines.

34 Voice of America is a US radio station which broadcasts in Arabic. The editorial on 15 February 1990 entitled 'No more secret police' was 'reflecting the views of the U.S. Government: A successful tyranny requires a strong, ruthless secret police force. A successful democracy requires the abolition of such a force … Secret police are also entrenched in other countries, such as China, North Korea, Iran, Iraq, Syria, Libya, and Albania. The rulers of these countries hold power by force and fear, not by the consent of the governed. But as East Europe demonstrated so dramatically in 1989, the tide of history is against such rulers. The 1990s should belong not to the dictators and secret police, but to the people' (quoted in Stein, 1992: 161–2).

35 Similar to the conflict between China and the US up to the early 1970s, discussed by Zhang (1992). The differences are manifest, as Ken Booth (1979: 13–19, quoted in ibid.: 272) puts it, in 'different modes of thought, implicit and explicit behavioural patterns and social habits, identifiable symbols and signals for acquiring and transmitting knowledge … and particular ways of adapting to the environment and solving problems'.

36 For example, until the invasion of Kuwait on 2 August 1990, and under the banner of the US State Department's policy of constructive engagement, Iraq enjoyed loans and credits guaranteed by the Agriculture Department's Commodity Credit Corporation (CCC) programme (Karabell, 1993). Some scholars blame this very same policy for sending the wrong signals to the Iraqi leadership and, ultimately, for leading to the invasion of Kuwait. For example, Stein (1991, 1992: 148) explains, 'the failure

of the United States to mount an effective strategy of deterrence in the period preceding the invasion of Kuwait, by assuming that if deterrence had been implemented properly, Saddam Hussein might have been deterred'.

37   In this vein, Robert Jervis (1976: 58–67, 94–100) makes a distinction between deterrence and spiral theories of interaction that can be clearly illustrated in the following sense. First, under deterrence theory forceful moves instil fear in the other side to prevent undesired actions. Second, spiral theory maintains that such threats only provoke retaliation and therefore defeat their own purpose. The two theories disagree about the effect of 'negative sanction' or punishment of an actor who is less immune to external pressures of different kinds. However, Jervis concludes that neither deterrence nor spiral theory account for the evidence. Moreover, he rightly argues that no 'well-structured or verified theory' can tell us when force and threat work. One implication of Jervis's argument is that threats of force are appropriate only when the other side is not afraid and needs to be made afraid. Spiral theory predicts that the other side already fears for its security. Israel's reaction to Egypt's threat in 1967 illustrates this approach. For the purpose of achieving accommodation, the threat of force and intimidation is often prompt defiance and accelerates the danger of war. This illustrates the United States' low profile toward Iraq before the invasion of Kuwait.

38   Under the label of deterrence model, Jervis (1976: 79–80) has grouped together a number of additional assumptions characteristic of many works on deterrence: 1) the offender is an outright aggressor and has long-standing objectives; 2) offender and deterrer have no mutual interests to consider; 3) concessions by a deterrer will be taken to strain and shadow any vulnerability that the offender might utilize; 4) the offender usually scrutinizes the pattern of behaviour over time of the deterrer in order to evaluate the validity of its current policies.

39   In the mainstream literature (e.g., Miller and Mylroie, 1990; Karsh and Rautsi, 1991; Simpson, 1991; Freedman and Karsh, 1993; Post, 1993) the Iraqi president was portrayed as 'notoriously cautious', 'naivete is not one of his idiosyncrasies', a *sui generis homo Arabicus,* a great survival tyrant, who usually knows what he does.

40 External guarantees are essential, but do not provide sufficient conditions to ensure deterrence strategy. The United States 'do not have any defence treaties with Kuwait, and there are no special defence or security commitments to Kuwait', said the State Department spokesperson Margaret Tutwiler. To another question relating to whether the US administration considered defending Kuwait from any eventual Iraqi invasion, Tutwiler replied that the United States 'also remain strongly committed to supporting the individual and collective self-defence of our friends in the Gulf with whom we have deep and long-standing ties' (cited in Stein, 1992: 152). This position on the protection of the Gulf states was in line with earlier statements made by senior American officials. On 19 July 1990, the United States secretary of defense, Richard Cheney, declared that the US was committed to defend its allies in the Gulf, and particularly Kuwait, if threatened or attacked. However, Cheney's spokesman, Pete Williams, later modified this and explained that the secretary of defense spoke with 'some degree of liberty' (cited in Bennis and Moushabeck, 1991: 363).

41 Interview with Richard Haass, the White House Middle East adviser, on Swedish Television, 12 June 1996.

42 Preliminary historical and comparative research suggests that strategies of reassurance may at times be effective in reducing some of the obvious risks of deterrence. Restraint, the development of informal norms of competition, and irrevocable commitments can help to reassure a vulnerable adversary, reduce the likelihood of miscalculation, and envisage alternative diplomatic or political openings that defuse the threat of force. See Stein (1991).

43 Examples abound: first, the CIA involvement to overthrow the elected national government in Iran of Prime Minister Mohammad Mossaddeq after the decision to nationalize the oil industry and challenge the Shah's political authority during the disorders in 1953. Second, the Nixon/Kissinger secret plan financing the Kurdish rebellion to overthrow the Ba'athist government, or at a minimum to keep it busy within the borders of Iraq in 1972 (Brown, 1992). And, last but not least, the Iran-Contra scandal in 1986, when it was revealed by a pro-Iranian Beirut-based Arabic newspaper (*al-Shira'a*) that the United States

was selling weapons to Iran during the war with Iraq and was also selling to Iraq, including the provision of satellite information on both countries' troop movements.

44   April Glaspie's testimony before the United States Senate's Foreign Relations Committee, 20 March 1991, cited in Neff (1991: 31).

45   Even though all the forces inside Iraq, the Kurds, the Shi'a, and the other opposition groups, were uniting against Ba'ath. The independent oil policy of the Gulf states, especially Kuwait and the UAE, collided economically with that of Iraq. Additionally, the Rumanian experience of revolution, and the *Voice of America* broadcast of pro-democratic messages to Iraq, unnerved Saddam Hussein with regard to domestic stability and American intentions.

46   The American conservative commentator and politician Patrick Buchanan, who for different reasons was an opponent of any US involvement in the Gulf, and was in implicit agreement with Saddam Hussein, wrote in *The Sunday Times* (24 September 1990) that 'there are only two groups that are beating the drums of war in the Middle East: the Israeli Defence Ministry and its amen corner in the U.S.' (cited in Hiro, 1992: 156). Saddam Hussein told Joseph Wilson, the American chargé d'affaires in Baghdad, on 10 September, that certain Western and US circles had been advising Israel to attack Iraq, and described the sharp tone and the verbal attacks on Israel as an act of peace: 'we believe that helped peace instead of keeping silent and letting Israel attack us and then counter-attacking' (cited in Karsh and Rautsi, 1991: 220).

47   In his speech at the ACC Summit in Amman/Jordan on 24 February 1990, he had declared: 'We all remember, as does the whole world, the circumstances under which the United States deployed and bolstered its fleets in the Gulf. The most important of these circumstances: is the war that was raging between Iraq and Iran. Iranian aggression had extended to other Arabian Gulf countries, most notably the sisterly state of Kuwait.'

48   Despite the fact that the American Ambassador had had 25 years of experience (she had worked in different places within the Arab world since 1966, and speaks Arabic), it was difficult to dispute the Iraqi version, even if it was edited in a way that was deliberately misleading.

49 The role of vowels in the Arabic language is very intricate and makes any political correspondence or discourse a considerable risk indeed. Quite marginal changes in the pronunciation of a word often lead to a literally different context than was intended. These characteristics, to mention only a very few of them, culminate in the richness of nuances that, sometimes, makes it almost impossible for outsiders who speak fairly good Arabic to grasp a dialogue in Arabic (Gibb, 1963: 7–12). Unlike any other language, in order to read any Arabic text one has to have a prior understanding of the entire text. Without this it is virtually impossible to read any Arabic at all, since the vowels are invisible in the written Arabic text. This result depends on the prowess of the reader and rhetorical quality of the text under consideration (Gibb, 1963: 7–12). This reality makes the Arabic language vital in the analysis of political discourse in the Arab world. The lack of linguistic knowledge is a serious obstacle in this context.

50 Cited in Sifry and Cerf (1991: 119–21).

51 United States Department of State, *Current Policy, No. 1273*, 26 April 1990 (cited in Karsh and Rautsi, 1991: 214).

52 Ms Glaspie admitted having told Saddam Hussein that the US had no opinion about Iraq's border disputes with Kuwait, but argued that such aloofness had been the main trait of US policy in the Middle East, where all Arab countries were beset by border disputes of one kind or another (Freedman and Karsh, 1993: 447, n. 30).

53 Kenneth Waltz's (1959: 332) assumption that 'wars occur because there is nothing to prevent them' might be taken as a plausible description, though within a different framework.

54 The Arab League issued a statement on 26 March 1990, condemning Western condemnation of the Bazoft execution and accused the West of interfering in Iraq's internal affairs and assaulting the government's right. A similar statement was issued by the Arab Cooperation Council on 31 March 1990. Moreover, the *Jordan Times* reported on 1 April 1990 that the Islamic Army for the Liberation of Palestine threatened to take action against Great Britain unless the British government ceased its campaign against the people of Iraq.

55 *Economist,* 2 June 1990, p. 44 (quoted in Telhami, 1993: 196).

56 Critics of this approach (e.g. Jervis, 1976; Booth, 1979; Zhang, 1992) point out that decision-makers do not always perceive an adversary's intentions correctly or adequately (Tariq Aziz's interview with Viorst, 1991).

57 Unlike the countries with much more experience of Middle Eastern affairs, such as Britain and France, each of which has had a long colonial history in the area, the United States was virtually a beginner. Moreover, the United States did not have any established academic expertise on the history, society and culture of the Middle East equivalent to that of the two European powers. Interest in the Middle East was necessitated by the Cold War strategy to fight the spread of communism and contain the spread of the influence of the Soviet Union and ultimately to protect the Jewish state. For the Arab the former was of secondary importance and the latter led the United States essentially to favour Israel's interests against those of the Arabs (Brown, 1992; Telhami, 1994; Halliday, 1995; Bill, 1996).

58 The following example might be relevant. King Hussein of Jordan is reported to have said in an interview that 'he was distressed', when he met the Iraqi president on 12 January 1991 to try to persuade him to accept the US-led International Coalition's terms to withdraw unconditionally and accept all the United Nations Security Council Resolutions in order to end the crisis in the Gulf. When the King made it clear to the Iraqi president that the Iraqi military would be no match for the much more modern and very sophisticated armies of American and major European countries, Saddam Hussein angrily replied that '*Allah* is with us, and those who have Him on their side, they would sooner or later prevail' (interview with King Hussein of Jordan, Swedish TV, 12 June 1996).

CHAPTER 3: THE INSTITUTIONAL PERSPECTIVE

1 Foucault (1972: 38) argues that the discursive formation is the '"domain of objectivity", [that is] the conditions to which the elements of this division (objects, modes of statements, concepts, thematic choices) are subjected … the rule of formation. The rules of formations are conditions of existence (but also of

coexistence, maintenance, and disappearance) in a given discursive division.'

2   Keohane (1988: 383, emphasis added) defines the term 'institution' as '*a general pattern or categorisation* of activity or as a *particular* human-constructed arrangement, formally or informally organised'. In a complementary sense, Wendt (1992: 399) defines institution as 'a relatively stable set of identities, roles, and interests'.

3   As Keohane (1988:382) argues, institutions become the embodiment both of individuals' priorities and power networks that facilitate or hinder these priorities, which also affects and regulates people's political objectives and the way they view and exercise political power: 'Institutions are therefore constitutive of actors as well as vice versa ... individuals ... are affected by institutional arrangements, by prevailing norms, and by historically contingent discourse among people seeking to pursue their purposes and solve their self-defined problems.'

4   This is because such approaches only put emphasis on technical-related aspects of the social and political arrangements and the strategic options of states as only being derived from an objectively formulated set of interests. If atomistic and positive assumptions of political behaviour are viewed only in the way social actions are perceived (i.e., as the product of a goal-oriented rational individual, often from an abstract, asocial angle), the contexts in which these goals are pursued become taken for granted, or at best reduced (Kratochwil, 1996).

5   In Weber's analysis of modern bureaucracies there is anxious concern about the impact of cultural constructs upon their performance. For Weber (1968: 4–30), cultural factors have to be considered on equal terms with other structural, demographic and economic forces. The ready availability of massive structural, demographic, and economic empirical data and the easy use of such data through the manipulation of statistical methods and computer technology should not disguise the essential role of culture in sociological analysis. Indeed, as Stephen Kalberg (1994: 204–5) argues, the essence of Weber's sociological enterprise has to be approached in the present juncture as an endeavour 'to keep culture in', on both the analytical and empirical levels (Kratochwil, 1996; Pasic, 1996). Moreover, the social scientist ought to allow culture to mingle with the areas of governance

and the economic system in order to arrive at a clearer comprehension of the intricacies of the international system and the increasing inability of certain polities to act and react with it. As is usually the case, the consequences of great historical transformations and turning points are long-lasting. As the new institutionalists (March and Olsen, 1989: 35ff.) have illustrated, institutions – and the social settings that condition their operation – evolve through history, but they do not reliably reach unique and efficient equilibria, because history is not always efficient in the sense of weeding out social practices that impede progress and encourage collective irrationality (Scaff, 1989: 170). Nor is this inertia attributable to the irrationality of individuals. On the contrary, individuals respond rationally to the social context bequeathed to them by history and reinforce these social pathologies, in contrast with notions of institutionally modelled values or formal symbolic relations.

6   While the Weberian studies of religion and cultural systems are basically derived from the major world religions, they are less tied to specific institutional explanations than earlier elaborations of that same tradition (e.g., Weber, 1947/1964).

7   Here, the state is an institution that provides a blueprint for how governance should be conducted.

8   This can probably be explained by what Lucian Pye (1985: 275) refers to as the sharp line drawn by Islamic creed and tradition 'between good and evil, between purity and pollution, and between virtuous and abominable behaviour'. There are values that make the standards of 'personal conduct so unattainable to the common people that they are driven to compensate for personal failings by expressing righteous indignation toward superiors who appear to them to be violating the spirit of Islam'. See also Barakat (1984: 321–33).

9   At a deeper perspective, for the Arabs, religious and secular alike, the historical, social and cultural substance, the pillars of (the otherwise unmaterialized) *al-umma al-Arabiyya*, the Arab nation, stand on a *raison d'être* emanating from Allah. It follows that any compromise in this regard would, by implication, enfeeble Allah's own social design. As for political leaders, the charge of betraying the Arab nation is the most serious allegation a politician could ever encounter (Noble, 1984; Barnett, 1993, 1996). Examples

abound: the late King Abdallah of Jordan was killed in 1951 for this reason; the Egyptian president Anwar al-Sadat was assassinated in 1981, and so on. Another example, different in character yet based on the same principle, is that of the Lebanese Christian officers Saad Haddad and Anton Lahad who, with a tiny Christian militia that had deserted from the Lebanese army, allied themselves publicly with Israel in southern Lebanon.

10 Like commonly held ideas and mutual symbolic meanings, the sociocultural identities and political attributes of the states, Pasic (1996) argues, are part of a deliberate and conscious game created by their common interactions. As with common symbols and ideas, the 'social' is the derivative and habitual outcome of the interrelationship between states in a given system. It is in this context that a state's sociocultural identity is shaped and reshaped. Over and above this interrelationship, the role of history comes into play through the impact of the evolutionary process of societal and cultural institutions. It is through these that an individual's identity and the definition of his/her interests occurs and derives, and this very same process is even more fundamental when it come to states, 'since states are in their entirety social arrangements. Given the complexity of these processes, static conceptualisation of identity and interests simply from the standpoint of narrowly conceived interactive actors become very problematic indeed' (Pasic, 1996: 90).

11 It must be admitted that there is a paradoxical element in Saddam Hussein's (and, for that matter, many other Arab leaders') political leadership. On the one hand, there is an impressive ability to survive internal plots, wars – such as the critical period of 1981–82 during the Iraq–Iran war, when Iranian forces threatened Iraqi territory and strategic depth and invaded Basra – and defeats, of such magnitude as that of the war over Kuwait. The way Saddam Hussein assesses his immediate surroundings in a shrewd and calculating manner has surprised observers and analysts over and over again. Yet when dealing with the outside world the very same strength and shrewd political calculation turns into a colossal weakness that often manifests itself in an erratic pattern of inter-national behaviour (Korany and Dessouki, 1984: 328ff.; Al-Khalil, 1989: 271ff.). This was evident in the Iraqi president's endless illogical political and military decisions during the Gulf crisis. As

was mentioned earlier, one explanation for this lies in the lack of information necessary for decision-making, the inability to understand the international system, and the rigid and tyrannical nature of the leadership. The conclusion one draws from such a pattern of leadership on the way foreign policy decisions are formulated is unavoidably negative.

12   The exception here is Anwar al-Sadat's decision to make peace with Israel in 1977. Sadat did not need to seek a pan-Arab blessing because the support for his peace initiative was almost overwhelming inside Egypt. More important is the fact that the homogeneous structure of Egyptian society is the opposite to that of Iraq, even though both states in different degrees identify themselves with Arabism.

13   Saddam Hussein was not as successful in attracting the sympathy and support of the grass-roots Arabs during the war with Iran as he was during the Gulf crisis.

14   It is also identified with what Hannah Arendt (1958: 248–85) calls 'worldlessness', world alienation marked by the loss of a solid, stable, common world. Without a stable common world of tangible and visible objectives and steadfast institutions to hold them together, Arendt argues, people are driven back to their own private experience and lose their common sense. They become uprooted peoples who can easily be manipulated and misused for the political ambitions of tyrants.

15   The most active and powerful opposition and even ruling social forces within the Arab world in the last few decades have been the Islamic groups. As such they could have been an enlightening force for democracy and justice against repression and corruption, but the modern literature produced largely by Islamic funda-mentalist movements follows the same path as the old one, namely, the obsession with family-related matters – sex, dress, segregation of the sexes – rather than with matters of social justice, political freedom or disobedience to tyranny (Ayubi, 1991: 44–5). For the Iraqis, this authoritarian political discourse, in which people are denied the means and the possibilities to influence rulers in policy matters, emphasized their inability to resist or even question the aggressive tendencies and the war plans drawn up by their leader. Such passivity and indifference toward the common good of the society allows political leaders to take

decisions with grave consequences for their peoples without being
accountable to them.

16 In recent pan-Arab review of public opinion on matters such as
democracy, economic wellbeing and Arab unity conducted by
the prominent sociologist Saad Eddin Ibrahim (1980) and his
associates at the American University in Cairo, the great majority
thought it was economic wellbeing, Arab wellbeing and unity
that concerned the respondents much more than democracy.

17 The English term 'national interest' is equivalent to the Arabic
Amn qwami 'Arabi, meaning the interest of all the Arab world.
Arab leaders are, so to speak, accountable to all the Arabs in the
same way as they are (theoretically speaking) accountable to their
own immediate subjects.

18 Before 1958, Sati' al-Husari (himself of Kurdish origin), had been
for decades in charge of education and school books under several
governments in Iraq, and as a pioneer of pan-Arabism had had
great influence on leading Ba'athists, especially on the Iraqi branch
of the party. He once defined being an Arab in the following
uncompromising terms: 'Everyone who speaks Arabic is an Arab.
Everyone who is affiliated with these people [e.g., Kurds;
Assyrians; Berber; and other minorities] is an Arab. If he does not
know this or if he does not cherish his Arabism, then we must
study the reasons for his position. It may be a result of ignorance
or deception – then we must awaken him. It may be a result of
selfishness – then we must work to limit his selfishness' (quoted
in Sluglett, 1993a: 445).

19 In the Arab world, there are societies that are distinct in terms of
demographic, tribal, ethnic and religious composition such as the
Sunni, Shi'a, Alawites, Druze, in Islam, or Christians and other
religious minorities. The adherence of the great majority of the
population to Arab/Islamic values and the specific Arab identity
provide the common demotic culture of protest in the face of
perceived external threats. Such threats are usually identified as
Western imperialism and the existence of the Zionist state, or
Arab regimes who are perceived to be working as a fifth column
for the benefit of imperialism and Zionism.

20 In a lecture in the University of Oslo, 31 May 1994, Benedict
Anderson was asked what he meant by 'imagined': whether used
in a negative, illusive sense, or in a positive, innovative one? His

reply was that it is neither; it was only used to refer to the ideational state of mind itself – imagining.

21 In 1933, King Faysal I of Iraq, a man highly regarded by many historians and Iraqis alike for his statesmanship, expressed his misgivings regarding the enigma of state-building when he said that 'In Iraq there is still – and I say this with sorrow – no Iraqi people, but unimaginable masses of human beings, devoid of any patriotic ideal, imbued with religious traditions and absurdities, connected by no common tie, giving ear to evil, prone to anarchy, and perpetually ready to rise against any government whatsoever. Out of these masses we want to train, educate, and refine ... The circumstances being what they are, the immenseness of the efforts needed for this can be imagined' (cited in Batatu, 1978: 25–6).

22 It is of course hazardous to depend on such generalizations, though the renowned Iraqi scholar Ali al-Wardi (1965, cited in Miller and Mylroie, 1990: 84) made these serious observations about the Iraqis in terms similar to those of King Faysal I: 'The personality of the Iraqi individual contains a duality, the Iraqi is enamoured more than others of high ideals which he invokes in his speeches and writing. But he is at the same time, one of those who most deviates from these ideals. He is among those least attached to religion, but deepest in sectarian strife ... There are two value systems in Iraq. One upholds strength, bravery, and arrogance, all qualities of the conquering hero, side by side with another value system which believes in work and patience ... The Iraqis were known to be a people of discord and hypocrisy ... but the Iraqi is not really different from other men. The difference lies in his idealistic thinking. His thought is concerned with principles which he cannot execute and he invokes aims which he cannot reach.'

23 Sunni Arabs constitute one-fifth of the population, Shi'ite Arabs about half and Kurdish tribes one-seventh. Despite the deep modernization process, much of the population find themselves more related to their tribal, ethnic and religious kin. Sunni notables and bureaucrats, installed under Ottoman rule and strengthened by the British, supported the Hashemite monarchy; and tribal sheiks were an important source of support on the provincial level (Bromley, 1994: 138). The Israeli historian Eliezer Be'eri (1970), has observed that the public and social life of Egypt is

peculiarly moderate. Conversely, Syrian public life and politics are characterized by tensions, and those of Iraq by extremism.

24 'Rentier' politics – whereby states used their oil wealth to support allies, purchase the goodwill of rivals and, in effect, bribe sectors of their populations – is a consistent theme of Arab politics (Luciani and Beblawi, 1987).

25 In Anderson's (1991: 9) analysis of South American nationalism he argues that the nation as 'imagined community' can be established by dominant classes (i.e., Creole) against 'the people' (i.e., indigenous Indians).

26 In countries like Egypt, Turkey, Morocco and even Tunisia, the civil society and civic associations, weak and disorganized though they may be, usually have, directly and indirectly, an opinion on public affairs and issues that constitute the formative influence on the polity (Al-Khalil, 1989: 44).

27 To take only one example on how the Iraqi government tried relentlessly to spread its own version of pan-Arab political ideology: in 1980, the Ba'athist government stated that they had distributed through Iraq's embassies, cultural centres and the organizations of the Ba'ath Party on the national level 9,750,000 copies of the two of Iraq's largest daily newspapers, *Al-Thawra* and *Al-Jumhurriyya*. Quite often these were distributed in Arab states where a pro-Iraqi Ba'athist organization exists, such as Jordan, Lebanon, Mauritania and Sudan. Moreover, the government had exported about 4,235,000 periodicals (various titles), and 18,000 copies of every pamphlet or book published by the Iraqi ministry of education, an incredible number for a country the size of Iraq. It is widely believed that Iraq has the largest reading public in the Arab world, and the government may have had this in mind when they announced the annual production of 10,050,000 books and 176,400 magazines dedicated to the social welfare of all the people, including children. Finally, to show that the then vice-president Saddam Hussein was a popular figure, the government claimed that it had distributed three million copies of 19 of his speeches during 1978 alone (Al-Khalil, 1989: 84). See the official pamphlet issued by the Minister of Information Latif Nassif Jassim (1981) *Al-ilm wa al-Ma'rakah* (Science and Warfare). Baghdad: *Dar al-Hurriyya*. As a result of the war with the non-Arab country of Iran, a formidable increase

occurred in the 1980s, with even more emphasis on Iraq's Arab identity.

28   In the Arabic traditions called *Qarun*, the pharaoh's greedy, corrupt and oppressive vizier, who amassed all the world's gold in his caves only to be swallowed up by an earthquake. This is story (or a rather legend) recounted for the purpose of *wa'az* (advice) in the Qur'an.

29   All Saddam Hussein's speeches are quoted from Bengio (1992).

30   Hannah Arendt (1950: 357) argues that when highly unstable and totalitarian political movements (i.e., the Ba'ath) seize political power they are unable to act and behave politically within the given norms common to other states. This is because they adopt ideologies and ideas much larger and wider than they can cope with. Instead, 'they remain movements in motion, more akin to natural processes sweeping across the world than to human constructions. Because they are geared to conquest, they had no respect for boundaries or agreements between states, and because they were in perpetual motion internally they have no respect for laws or established organisations.' The result is inefficiency to the point of chaos, but Arendt claims that considerations as mundane as efficient administration did not concern rulers who think on the grand scale of world-domination and the transformation of humanity. Internally, the dominant organ of government is the secret police, whose task is not so much to watch for people plotting against the regime as to dispose of those who are defined as enemies by the prevailing ideology (Canovan, 1992: 76).

31   All the quotations regarding to this pamphlet are from Simpson (1991: 83–7). I tried with no avail to obtain an original Arabic copy of this pamphlet.

32   The review of the rise and the development of the modern Iraqi state after 1922 stated as follows: 'Britain explained the issue of demarcating Iraq's borders as a bargaining chip to save its interest, particularly exploration for oil. In 1932 the League of Nations admitted Iraq to its membership and ended the British mandate. The pre-independence period was marked with the desire to establish Iraq's borders and complete its institutions' (cited in Simpson, 1991: 86).

33 The booklet was evidently a product of the moment and a piece of Iraqi government propaganda that did not pay attention to historical facts and political credibility. Even though the book was expensively produced it was full of linguistic mistakes, something that is unusual for Iraq's tradition of myths about the 'high' language that is often communicated in public. Above all, the way the book put forward the 'historical claims of Iraq over Kuwait' was unclear, flimsy and irrelevant. Here is an example of such a statement: 'Lorimer ['Gazetteer of the Gulf, Oman and Central Arabia'] admitted in 1775 [sic] that he considered Kuwait as part of Basra. It is known that Lorimer relied on documents of the British East India Company. In 1876, Major Bride and the British Commissioner said that Kuwait, Qatif and Aqir were Turkish ports on the Gulf. In 1911, the Ottoman government honoured Mubarak [al-Sabah] with the Majidi medal of the first class.' Moving from one historical claim to another, the booklet accused Al-Sabah of '[s]ubservience [sic] to Imperialism. In 1914 a charitable institution was set up in India … to raise money to help the wounded in the British army which took part in occupying Iraq. Mubarak [al-Sabah] contributed 50 thousand Rupees' and 'Aggressive attitudes that harm Iraqis and Arabs', Mubarak al-Sabah also 'sent a telegram to the British Government congratulating her [or them] on the advance of British troops on Baghdad in 1917'.

34 *Al-Hawadith*, Lebanon-based Arabic weekly magazine, 31 July 1992; my translation from Arabic.

35 For example, Jervis *et al.* (1985) suggest three factors that one should take into account when explaining why leaders decide to go to war. These are: 1) domestic political and socioeconomic pressures that can motivate leaders in an attempt to divert attention from these internal problems and seek foreign adventures; 2) political pressures and what they perceive as the indifference to their needs and the frustration of achieving their objectives by negotiations, which was the case when the Iraqis portrayed Kuwait's position during the meeting in Jeddah, on the eve of the invasion of Kuwait; 3) decision-makers' assumptions about the geostrategic situation and the potential shifts in the military balance. Iraq (as a target for deterrent strategy) is preoccupied with a domestically driven agenda. This is what might explain

the failed strategy of accommodation (and deterrence?).
Moreover, there are cultural, organizational and circumstantial
factors that constitute barriers whereby the signals of deterrence
or accommodation can be distorted, underestimated, and remain
uncomprehended (Vertzberger, 1989). Jervis *et al.* point out that
leaders who are usually immersed in domestic problems can easily
be drawn into a spiral of escalation-via-miscalculation that
ultimately undermines the deterrence threats, falling prey to a
threat–counterthreat spiral.

36 SIPRI *Yearbook 1991: World Armament and Disarmament*, pp. 175,
177.

37 SIPRI *Yearbook 1990: World Armament and Disarmament,* pp.
228–9; and SIPRI *Yearbook 1991: World Armament and
Disarmament,* pp. 192, 194.

38 * means that the figures on 1990 expenditures for that country
are not included here, as they are not available.

39 What Zhang (1992:8) terms as 'culture-bound', that is, the states'
perceptions and behaviour and how they handle their strategic
interests, is relevant. Being 'culture-bound' is being unable to
put aside one's cultural attitude and imaginatively respond to
perceived challenges from the perspectives of the opponent.

40 Related to this chilling domestic reality within Arab states is the
fact that regimes, through their repressive practices, have only
confirmed what Fouad Ajami in his controversial (and even
indignant) book *The Arab Predicament,* terms as the distance,
aloofness and hostility of the states as political and social organizations toward their own populations. Ajami (1981: 32–3) argues
that the states, through their administrations, treat their citizens
so badly that the latter not only find it futile to even think of
engaging in public life, but also 'wish only to be left alone and
shelter themselves from the capricious will of the state. The state
– as is the case with oriental despotisms – reigns, but does not
rule.' Apart from the conflict between Algeria and Morocco is
also the brief military show of force between Egypt and Libya,
in 1977 and, ironically, the invasion of Kuwait.

41 Here Ajami refers to 'reign', which connotes a tyranny imposed
on the populace, rather than 'rule', which implies a sociopolitical contract between citizens and rulers, who came to power by
virtue of popular consent.

42 Here I agree with Farouk-Sluglett and Sluglett (1991: 1411), and even with Sluglett's (1993b) review in TLS, and the conclusion in regard to Al-Khalil's *Republic of Fear* (1989).

43 The image of the helpless individual in the face of an all-powerful omnipotent modern bureaucracy has been the focus of interest of social thinkers from Max Weber's depiction (or condemnation) of an 'iron cage' and 'the disenchantment with the world', to Hannah Arendt's powerful narrative of modern institutions and their direct connection with the violence, both psychological and physical, inflicted on modern helpless individuals, and has become a common theme. In this vein, Arendt (1970: 81) eloquently depicts the situation as follows: 'The greater the bureaucratisation of public life, the greater will be the attraction of violence. In a fully developed bureaucracy there is nobody left with whom one can argue, to whom one can present grievances, on whom the pressures of power can be exerted. Bureaucracy is the form of government in which everybody is deprived of political freedom, of the power to act; for the rule by nobody is no-rule, and where all are equally powerless we have a tyranny without a tyrant.'

44 However, as Vertzberger (1989: 276) argues, when the political discourse is characterized by excessive authoritarianism and a prominent leadership style, the leader's associates and subordinates are usually prevented from making any assessment of the policy-making process, and are unable to question or to suggest views that contradict the top leader. At the same time, however, such a political discourse provides ample opportunity for leaders to switch the direction of policies, since they take for granted the compliance of their aides and associates.

45 The whole idea of fatherhood, sometimes becoming synonymous with the concept of God as a guarantee of social and material wellbeing, has been one of the most controversial yet appealing in Arabic literature throughout history. Naguib Mahfouz's controversial novel *The Children of Geblawi* (in Arabic *Awlad Haritna*), describes how the Father *Geblawi*, in an unusually outright manner, signifies and alludes to Allah to such an extent that it becomes difficult to distinguish who is who, who is to be blamed for not helping his children from the harsh life of poverty in Cairo's slums (Barakat, 1984: 378ff.).

46   The 'ideal type' of tribe is a stateless, segmentary social group owing allegiances to a myth of common lineage and bound together by linear loyalties. Historically, no such pure tribe has ever existed; there has always been interaction among tribes on all levels (including intermarriage). The Qur'an acknowledges, even praises in some contexts the existence of the tribes in stating, *We have formed you into peoples* [shu'ub] *and tribes* [qaba'il] *that you get to know each other* (49:13). Therefore, in the Arab context the word or the attribute of being 'tribal' does not bear the repugnant allusion that it usually has in other contexts (Zubaida, 1982).

47   To form and organize, out of nothing, a coherent body politic as the basis for the new community, the *umma*, Muhammad 'combined the virtues of religious preacher, military leader, and statesman' (Rodinson, 1971:83). He succeeded in establishing a state among and against the tribes. In Watt's (1974: 142) assessment, Muhammad's accomplishment 'may be regarded as the building on religion's foundations of political, social, and economic system ... His tribal policy was merely an aspect of this.' However, the unity associated with the new state did not eradicate all tribal elements. Rather, the state subordinated these to the new polity. As Watt states, 'the quarrels and rivalries of the tribes had not been removed, but they had been subdued' (1974: 149).

48   The Prophet 'left no clear-cut instructions for the choice of his successor, different groups and individuals were able to claim the right to rule on various grounds of legitimacy. In the last resort, the question of legitimacy was decided by force, but even force had to have an ideological basis' (De Santillana, 1961: 384; Watt, 1974).

49   Those who claim lineage from the Prophet Muhammad *ashraf* of *Qurayshite* and *Hashemite* tribal origins such as the royal families of Jordan, Morocco and the former royal family in Iraq. Saddam Hussein has officially claimed himself a descendent of the Prophet, too.

50   Those who had emigrated with the Prophet from Mecca to Medina in AD 622, fleeing from *Quraysh's* harassment and persecution.

51 The Shi'is, conversely, 'lay the claim to legitimacy primarily on the principle of kinship and nomination by *nass* or designation' (Lambton, 1988: 1–12).

52 Interestingly, these empires housed a mix of tribal formations. In fact, both tribes and chiefdoms were more likely to coexist and coevolve with states and empires than they were to evolve into states and empires (Lapidus, 1990: 25–47).

53 Ibn Khaldun (1967) gave us the concept of *asabiyya*, tribal bonding or the sentiment of group solidarity that results from kinship, blood ties and common descent. This natural sentiment, grounded in the impulse to provide mutual help, leads to the banding together of Bedouins to fight for survival and mutual defence. Their solidarity is reinforced by chiefs who promote internal harmony, fortify the group's will to power and royal authority, and direct it outward to the aggrandisement of its interests.

54 Weber (1968: 3) offered three types whereby the legitimacy of political authority within the framework of the state can, therefore, justify its domination. The first is 'traditional' that call for 'the authority of the mores sanctified through ancient recognition and habitual orientation'. The second is 'charismatic' by virtue of its central attention on divine capacity and the spiritual attraction of the individual's mythical prodigy. Finally, the 'legal rational' that treats the question of governance and sociopolitical control through legal networks and institutions. See also Brint (1991: 88–9).

55 Alawites are ethnically Arabs with beliefs that combine a stream of Muslim, Christian and Pagan dogmas. They are organized in four different tribes: Matawira, Haddadin, Khayatin and Kalbiyya. They distinguish themselves from other Arabs by embracing a myth of common descent and a common belief.

56 See also Patrick Seale's (1989: 8–11) sympathetic and informed insights in to the political situation in Syria since the late 1960s. In particular, the bibliography of President Hafiz al-Assad, who has from the very beginning surrounded himself with close clan and family members from his ethnic group the Alawites.

57 'During the time men live without a common power to keep them all in awe', Hobbes (1967: 82) wrote, 'they are in that condition which is called war; and such a war, as is of every man, against every man.'

58 Along these lines, the great Caliph Umar Ibn al-Khatab (634–44),
    was once quoted as saying: 'Who and how you are?, you will be
    ruled alike.' Since, every return to the tradition constitutes a
    reconstruction of these tradition in line with the desired
    conclusion. The ruling elites in the Arab world attempted to
    reconstitute the people into more than simple objects of rule so
    that they could become knowledgeable and self-disciplined
    subjects in the dual Foucauldian sense – that is, subjects who were
    subjected to 'control and dependence' but who were also subjects
    possessing their own identity by 'conscience or self-knowledge'
    (Foucault, 1980, 208–26, for the quote, p. 212).

59 By the same token, democratic political systems, war-prone
    though they may be, have never fought wars against each other
    since 1789, because democratic systems are more willing to solve
    their conflicts with other similar polities by peaceful means. This
    assumption, based on Kantian premise of 'the republican form of
    rule', is probably due to the cohesion of the domestic environment
    (i.e., civil society), which facilitates open and free debate, that
    makes people aware of the fact that they would bear the cost of
    their leaders' aggressive tendencies and so head-off potential war
    plans (Morgan and Campbell, 1991).

60 Since leaders can hardly create the current or events, they usually
    seek to float and ride with the tide and steer themselves on its
    track. Political actions, it is asserted, are quite often decided on
    the basis of imprecise knowledge and assumptions of a
    hypothetical quality. The actors can never take account of all the
    factors entering into any given situation, nor can they ever know
    all the results after action has been taken. Thus, politics deals with
    both the contingent and the unknown. Thus, political solutions
    are temporary at best, irrelevant at worst (Curtis, 1962: xxvi).

61 As was demonstrated when a group of Shi'ite students attempted
    to assassinate Tariq Aziz (the information minister at the time) in
    downtown Baghdad. This and other incidents inside Iraq made
    Saddam Hussein suspicious of the Mullahs' intentions in regard
    to Iraq.

62 In an interview in the documentary on the Gulf crisis and war
    shown on Swedish TV, Channel 1, on 8 July 1996. Indeed, in
    the Arab world, Ibrahim Abduh (1982) argues, leaders often
    surround themselves by an atmosphere of flattery, adulation and

hypocrisy. This ultimately distorts and destroys a realistic outlook in dealing with outside world. Like many other tyrants who are only told what they want to hear, Saddam Hussein's ability to assess and judge reality, Karsh and Rautsi (1991: 189) argue, 'has been fundamentally distorted by the Byzantine atmosphere of flattery and self-abasement surrounding him.' They mention a bizarre example when, in a cabinet meeting in November 1989, according to the Iraqi National Agency, 12 December 1989, Saddam Hussein boasted that were he to sell pebbles in the streets of Baghdad, 'a thousand Iraqis and foreigners may be there to offer a million dinars for one single pebble, and tell him: Saddam Hussein, you are carrying a gem, not a pebble, without knowing' (quoted in Karsh and Rautsi, 1991: 189).

63 See Sheikh Sabah al-Ahmad the Kuwaiti foreign minister's interview in the Cairo-based weekly newspaper *Al-Musswar* on 18 August 1990; also Tariq Aziz, Letter to the Arab League Secretary General, 16 July 1990.

64 Aristotle, *Politics*, Books II, sections 1266 (cited in Wells, 1967: 202).

65 This is demonstrated by the fact that economic conditions now rarely feature in the terms of peace imposed at the end of wars, as the first and second Gulf wars (among many others) have shown.

66 In the mid-1970s, in addition to the general reserve, a law was issued by the Kuwaiti government to establish a Reserve Fund for Future Generations (RFFG), to which at least 10 per cent of the total revenue must be added annually. It was not intended to be used until the year 2001. Since the beginning of the 1984/85 fiscal year the National Investment Authority has begun to assume the management of all Kuwait's reserves. In 1985, the interest on investments held by the RFFG totalled KD 757 million, which was equivalent to a return of 6.9 per cent. During 1985 Kuwait held 44 per cent of its total reserves in non-Arab countries (about KD 23 billion). In 1987 the RFFG was estimated at KD 14 billion. In 1988/89 budget the Government allocated KD 205.4 million. to the RFFG. In the 1950s Kuwait established the Kuwait Investment Office (KIO) with the aim of providing for its future generations by investing its oil profits. The KIO handles much of Kuwait's investment in Europe, North America and elsewhere.

In 1979 the KIO started to buy small interests in leading Japanese companies as well as in the USA, where Kuwait has some major real estate projects. In 1986 investment income from abroad increased to about $8 billion, overtaking income from petroleum for the first time. In 1987 the KIO acquired further considerable shareholdings in Europe: in particular, it acquired a major stake in BP, and by August 1988 had obtained 21.68 per cent of BP's total shares. Other investments by the KIO include the purchase of a 51 per cent share in the First Capital Corps, a Singapore property developer. In June 1989 the KIO disclosed a 5.2 per cent share in the UK's Midland Bank. From August 1990 until July 1991, Kuwait's sole sources of income were earnings from its international financial investments and profits from Kuwait Petroleum International, which operates Kuwaiti Petroleum companies in Europe and Asia. It was estimated that Kuwait's international investments in August 1990 were worth as much as $100 billion comprising the RFFG and the State General Reserve. The return on these investments was estimated at 5.5 per cent per year. It was estimated that by late 1990 proceeds totalled more than $6 billion, by mid-1992 the total was estimated at $25 billion (Unwin, 1992: 596–7).

67   Sources: *Oil and Gas Journal*, 31 December 1991, *BP Statistical Review of World Energy*, June 1992; UK Department of Trade and Industry, April 1992; *Norges Oljedirektorat*, January 1992, oil figures from Bild (1993: 169), and gas figures from Cragg (1993: 176).

68   Since 1975 no official figures in Iraq have been available for the destination of oil exports.

69   Sources: *Iraq: A Country Study*, Area Handbook Series: Washington DC 1979, p. 265; and the Economic Intelligence Unit Special Report No. 88, *Iraq: A New Market in Region of Turmoil* (London, 1980, p. 31 (cited in Stork, 1989: 33). The United States supplied 5 per cent of Iraq's total import of weapons during the 1980s; Western Europe supplied 22 per cent (against 8 per cent during the 1970s); and the USSR supplied 53 per cent (against 90 per cent during the 1970s), source: SIPRI *Yearbook of World Armament and Disarmament 1990*, p. 233.

70   Source: OECD Statistics 1991 (from Timmerman, 1992, Appendix 1).

71 See also SIPRI *Yearbook 1991: World Armament and Disarmament*, pp. 202–3.

72 Source: SIPRI *Yearbook 1990: World Armament and Disarmament*, p. 187.

73 Source: SIPRI *Yearbook 1990: World Armament and Disarmament*, p. 192.

74 Source: SIPRI *Yearbook 1990: World Armament and Disarmament*, p. 229.

75 As mentioned in the introduction, it has been very difficult to find out exactly what happened at the meeting in Jeddah. However, I favour the version that the Iraqi government was offered financial help and a policy of flexibility on the question of access to the Gulf.

76 In the weekly Cairo-based Arabic newspaper *Al-Musswar* on 18 August 1990).

77 *The Financial Times* of London reported on 18 August 1990.

78 When reading Mohammad Heikal's *Illusions of Triumph,* which is an implicit defence of the Iraqi position, one gets the feeling that Iraqi Intelligence is very active in the Gulf states, and is, indeed, in full control of what is going on: intercepting telephone calls and messages between their heads of state. Heikal (1992: 45, 162, 171, 173, 249) claims that many of the messages and telephone calls that the Iraqi Intelligence intercepted indicated conspiracies by the rulers of the Gulf (Kuwait, United Arab Emirates, and Saudi Arabia), on the one hand, and by the United States and Israel, on the other, against the Ba'athist government in Iraq. The horde of Iraqi intelligence against and informants all over the Gulf states, one might argue, would presumably have informed the Iraq leadership that there were no financial assets within Kuwait's territory at the time. In an area fed by rumour, misinformation, and a political climate cloaked in obscurity and fear of the unknown, this means that any story, however distorted, becomes an accepted fact.

CHAPTER 4: THE REFLECTIVE PERSPECTIVE

1 In the traditional approaches, the nature and the evolution of macro-level social structure (e.g., Waltz's structural realism) are

approached and explained as the implications of their interplay
with other actors in a given system (Keohane, 1986b). Also in
these approaches, the structure of the international system is a by-
product of the (material) power interrelationships and the
interactions between actors. As such, the structure restrains and
inhibits certain actions, but it cannot create or bring about social
actors, nor it can command an autonomous ontological standing
(Finnemore, 1996).

2   See Keohane (1988) and Finnemore (1996), though she terms it
    'sociology's institutionalism'.

3   It was, according to this approach, the rationalism and individ-
    ualism of Western Enlightenment that generated, even invented,
    states, production networks, modern bureaucracies, and indeed,
    capitalism as epiphenomena of this Western rationalism
    (Finnemore, 1996: 333).

4   This approach is situated on the holist side of the agent–structure
    controversy. The structure in sociological institutionalism is similar
    to that of Wallerstein's 'world capitalist system', though they are
    quite different in one essential aspect. Wallerstein's structure is
    filled with economic and other flesh-and-blood productive
    networks, which, by virtue of the powerful capacity of the
    capitalist world system (i.e., the prime ontological variable),
    becomes generative of all the myriad of social actors: states, multi-
    national firms, international regimes, national liberation
    movements, as well as the class struggle (Finnemore, 1996).

5   Initiated primarily by Jamal ad-Din al-Afaghani (1838–1897) and
    his disciple, the influential Egyptian *salafi* scholar Muhammad
    Abduh (1849–1905), and the Tunisian statesman and political
    philosopher Khayr al-Din (1823–1890), who sought to reform
    and modernize Islam, and remedy and rectify the body of dogma
    through reason and adaption to modern science (Hourani, 1983).

6   In this respect, rational calculations 'attributed to *homo sapiens* by
    virtue of the ability to reason and act upon the result of
    deliberation. To say that an individual person processes rationality
    is to say that that person measures up to the minimum standard
    that establishes a presumption of competence', *The Blackwell Ency-
    clopaedia of Political Thought* (1988: 419).

7   Islam and Arabism can be treated as a 'frozen decision', to use
    March's and Olsen's (1989: 35) metaphor, that can be activated

in time of crisis, especially when a non-Arab actor is involved. In this respect, the Gulf crisis was a good example.

8   Durkheim once wrote, 'people work with inherited materials. This social inheritance is all-important, because it signifies an intimate relation between individuals and socio-linguistic communities. Truth is not a ready-made system: it is formed, deformed and reformed in a thousand ways; it varies and evolves like all things human' (1983: 12, quoted in Cladis, 1992).

9   Here politics and political culture become equivalent to the moral order of a society (Topf, 1989: 52–80, n. 53; Street, 1994: 103; Welch, 1993).

10 See also Hourani (1991: 74–89) and Turner (1994: 53–66), for a detailed analysis of Hodgson's *Venture of Islam*.

11 The word 'Allah' in meaning and concept is quite different than the English 'god', and the Islamic concept of god is different in many essential ways from the other two Abrahamic religions, Judaism and Christianity. The close equivalent to the English 'god' in Arabic is 'rabb' and not 'Allah'. However, the word 'Allah' is also used by all Christian Arabs and even other Middle Eastern churches, including Orthodox, Catholic and Protestant.

12 The idea of Islam's association with irrationalism is groundless and, indeed enigmatic. The fact is that at one point Islam as a religion would have to be considered adaptable to the criteria of modernization (Weber, 1965: 85; Holton and Turner, 1989: 85). For example, Allah is portrayed in Islamic scripture as an abstract, rarely metaphorical or representational (with the exception of mysticism, e.g., the writings of Ibn Arabi, al-Jeelani, al-Halaj and others) and definitely without personal or human traits: 'God is one, alone, and eternal', says the Qur'an in a definite and Platonic Arabic form. And, 'He begetteth not neither is He begotten and He hath no peer'. Another, related, question is linked with the evaluation of artistic penmanship in Arabic that came about as a consequence of an exalted rational notion of the god – Allah – which is above and beyond human traits. Under the shadow of this picture the *turath* (tradition) represents human beings as innately righteous, decent, honourable and, by the same token, degenerate and immoral.

13 In the Qur'an and Arabic usage, generally ancient and modern, the term '*al-nas*' is the exact equivalent of the English 'people'.

The term is mentioned frequently in the Qur'an to signify a singular type of people – as in the following verse: 'Our Lord, do not Thou assign us with the people, *qawm*, of the evildoers' (7: 45) – and to a certain people in an organic sense like tribe or ethnic group, and an affiliative sense like religious group – as in 'And we sent Noah to his people, *qawm*' (7: 59). *Al-nas* is mentioned, too, in its English equivalent as in: 'Say O People, *nas*, I am the messenger of God to you all'. And, 'Said He, Moses, I have chosen you above all men, *nas*' (7: 144). There is another, more precise denotation to a human collectivity than *al-nas*: for example the word *qawm* designates a characteristic of organic solidarity and common descent. It is the favourite term of modern pan–Arab nationalists. The term, however, differs from the English 'nationalist' by its attachment to the term *umma,* the moral community of Muslim believers, because the *qawm* are the inhabitants of the *umma.* In this context, by virtue of the Arabic language and culture both denote a coherent and filiative solidarity with a common destiny (Zubaida, 1982; Ghazoul, 1992).

14   As Pasic (1996: 98–102) argues, such human constructions are relevant and even more fitting when approaching the international system, since state systems basically rest on the primordial cultural domains. The efforts to construct a European Union comprised of states merely on the basis of being Europeans is not just an endeavour to achieve the objective of peaceful regional political and economic cooperation. Rather 'it is the institutional realisation of the historically evolving idea of Europe' (p. 102).

15   The mainspring of Islamic *turath* is the prevailing, in a conformist sense, emphasis upon: 1) the authority of the revelations of the Qur'an; 2) the principal place for Prophet Muhammad's *Sunnah* (works and deeds highly regarded mainly by Sunni); 3) the practices attributed to the 'pious forebears', or *as-salaf as-salih,* the Prophet Companions from the first generation of Muslims and other scholars who lived during the heyday of Islam such as al-Bukhari, Abu-Hanifa, Ibn-hanbal, al-Shafi'i and many others (Graham 1993).

16   Here the relationship between dominant (i.e., rulers) and dominated (i.e., ruled) become most obvious, according to Bourdieu (1991: 66) in the market of language, since 'utterances are not only (save in exceptional circumstances) signs to be

understood and deciphered; they are also *signs of wealth* intended to be evaluated and appreciated, and *signs of authority*, intended to be believed and obeyed'.

17 Asserting the significance of history for decision-makers, Jervis (1976) argues that decision-makers usually draw generalizations through a certain perception of history to justify and execute current policy issues. Brecher's (1972) interpretation of the Israeli political elite's obsession with the problem of the security of the Jewish state, reflects what he termed the 'Holocaust Syndrome'. This is the image of history that feeds the Israeli foreign policy-makers' perceptions and the background that constitutes the 'prism' against which current policy decisions are viewed and measured. Vertzberger (1989: 307–21) suggests that history can be most useful in the analysis of foreign policy decision making to 'legitimise policy, rules of behaviour'. Here history serves both as an instrument of legitimacy for the leadership before their people and as an argument that their decision is consistent with national values. In the latter case, foreign policy decisions, as an outcome of the societal values, reflect how 'the analogy between events is replaced by an extrapolation from the abilities or quality of performance of the leadership in the past and into the present' (ibid.: 308).

18 Some might argue that the Ba'ath doctrine is rather a modern product or a secular movement more influenced by modern European, especially German, romanticism than Islam. The intensive use by the Iraqi leadership of Islamic symbolism and sentiments during the Gulf crisis suggests otherwise. As Goldstein and Keohane (1993: 20) put it, 'ideas can have an impact even when no one genuinely believes in them'. The Ba'ath was grounded on – and legitimized its existence with – the aim to rejuvenate and reclaim the early moments of glory in Arab/Islamic history. The pan-Arab movements have tried to convey these sentiments through a number of works, official statements and leaders' speeches deeply permeated by emotions that urge Arabs to unite and repeat the moments of glory.

19 Lecture by Johan P. Olsen at the Department of Political Science, University of Stockholm, 10 October 1991.

20 'Discourse' here is taken to be 'a way of constructing meanings which influences and organizes both our actions and our

conception of ourselves' (*Penguin Dictionary of Sociology*). In this vein, Foucault (1972: 46–8) describe discourse as 'a group of rules that are immanent in a practice, and define it in its specificity ... [the discourse is interpreted] with a view to writing a history of the referent ... without reference to the *ground*, the *foundation of things*, but by relating them to the body of rules that enable them to form as objects of a discourse and thus constitute the conditions for their historical appearance'.

21 The *Areba* Arabs' efforts to spread the Islamic religion through conquest and/or conversion, the seizure of Egypt, North Africa, Mesopotamia and the rest of Middle East after the advent of Islam provide a telling historical example (Hitti, 1970: 32; Hjärpe, 1994: 20ff.). The pre-Islamic Arabs of the Peninsula, called *al-Arab al-Ariba* (the original or true Arabs), and those communities south of Mesopotamia and the Fertile Crescent and others within the modern Arab world became integrated either by intermarriage, socialization or conversion into the abode of Islam – to coin an Arabic neologism for this, *al-Arab al-Musta'aribah* (Arabized or the North Arabs).

22 For some scholars the thesis is a controversial one; see the introduction to *The Protestant Ethic and the Spirit of Capitalism* by Anthony Giddens (1992).

23 The interwovenness of Arabism as a 'superstructure' in connection with the analysis of the term 'culture' implies that it is generally seen not just as a random assembly of specific features, but as having a certain order and coherence (Shweder and Le Vine, 1984). This view is articulated by the anthropologist Marvin Harris (1987: 6) who defines culture as 'the learned, socially acquired life-styles of the members of a society, including their patterned, repetitive ways of thinking, feeling and acting'.

24 For example, Foucault (1978, 1980) examines the way in which social definitions produce divisions between normality and deviance as well as divisions between legitimate knowers and receivers of knowledge. These definitions discredit deviants and alienate most people from a claim to truth and knowledge. Social control results from these divisions in discourse by limiting and structuring people's own understandings of their lives. In this manner, Foucault argues that discourse is an important dimension

of power relations, which links individual understandings of the world to systems of domination.

25 In the same interpretive context, Clifford Geertz's 'hermeneutics of thick descriptions' of culture is a pioneering effort in this context. Defining his own concept of culture, Geertz (1973: 5) writes: 'believing with Max Weber, that man is an animal suspended in webs of significance he himself has spun, I take culture to be those webs, and the analysis of it to be therefore not an experimental science in search of law but an interpretive one in search of meaning'. The interpretive activity of individuals who seek to understand and to make sense of the world in which they live should be comprehended not as an isolated phenomenon, neutralized by a detached pundit, but in terms of their interaction with social practices. The whole idea of meaning is essential to people's social life precisely because it is by virtue of these meanings that members of a human collectivity conceive and understand each other within their common domain of social practice and experience. The essence of Geertz's methodology insists on the appraisal that the symbolic domain is inclusive to politics and not just epiphenomenal to it. In *Negara,* Geertz (1980: 136) asserts such a position by stating that '[t]he real is as imagined as the imaginary … The dramas of the theatre state, mimetic of themselves, were, in the end, neither illusions nor lies, neither sleight of hand nor make-believe. They were what there was.'

26 This actualizes Derek Walcott's notion of language as an all-compassing sphere of life. When people speak a particular language they do not have any choice other than to accept the rules and forms of that language, because they inevitably become immersed in its cultural, political and symbolic frame. Jonsson (1995: 143) here referring to David Montenegro's 'An interview with Walcott', *Partisan Review,* Vol. 57, No. 2 (1990): 208.

27 'Habitus' in Bourdieu's (1977: 42–3, 1990: 53–4, 59) definition is the physical and linguistic dispositions which informs behaviour, drawing on socialization in an unconscious way and varying in relation to social action. 'Habitus', moreover, is 'the dialectical relationship between the objective structures and cognitive and motivating structures which they produce and which tend to reproduce them' (Bourdieu, 1977: 83); habitus also is the 'objectively adjusted to the particular conditions in which it is

constituted' or that '[t]he conditionings associated with a particular class of conditions of existence produce *habitus*' (Bourdieu, 1990: 53).

28   Saddam Hussein's speech on ACC summit in Amman, on 24 February 1990 (cited in Bengio, 1992: 37).

29   *Al-Qabas*, a Kuwaiti Arabic daily newspaper, on 20 July 1990 (cited in Freedman and Karsh, 1993: 49).

30   Leaders are portrayed everywhere, from posters to badges, and are propagated in a way by the state media that makes them appear as superhuman. As in other authoritarian societies, this is essentially an attempt to cover up the weaknesses and contradictions characteristic of these structures of authority.

31   Arabs (and Muslims) hold that Arabic is the most perfect of all languages; it the language of Allah. The place of the Qur'an within the Arabic language and the impact it has had ever since it was revealed to the Prophet around AD 605 is enormous. Muhammad's message was the revealed word of Allah, and absolute transcendental power was in the language as well as in the content of the message. Among orthodox Muslims, Arabic is *Lughat al-Malaeka*, 'the language of the angels', and the language *per excellence* in the world since Allah himself speaks Arabic and has revealed his Holy Book, the Qur'an (that has existed since the advent of Genesis), in the Arabic language. For Muslims the Qur'an is a living masterpiece and powerful expression of oral and formulaic prowess. It was revealed orally to the Prophet, not in written form. The Qur'an's first verse begins with *iqra'a*, or recite, and the entire text encompasses frequent dictates and commandments to the Prophet and his fellow believers always to 'Recite'. In the beginning it was preserved orally, but 15 years after Muhammad's death, and during the reign of the third Caliph Othman (AD 640–56) the Qur'an was compiled in written form. But the beauty of its musical recitation *taratil* is living evidence of its holy attribute (Norton, 1988: 60).

32   A classic in the Arabic tradition (cited in De Santillana, 1961: 291).

33   Power has several synonyms in the Arabic language: *wazi* (Ibn Khaldun), *waz'a* (Jahiz, d. 869), *shawka* (Ghazali, d. 1085), *qahr* (Ibn jama'a), *ghalaba* and *taghalub* (ibn Taimiyya, d. 1327), or

generally *mulk* and *sultan*. Politics is the arena where power is obtained, secured and pursued (Al-Azmeh, 1993: 91).

34 Ibn al-Muqaffaa, *Al-Adab al-kabir wa al-adab al-saghir* ('The Greater and Lesser Disciplines'). Beirut, n.d., p. 11, cited in Al-Azmeh, 1993: 91).

35 A powerful wave of social criticism was initiated by the controversial books *Al-Naqd al-Dháti B'ada al-Hazima* ('Self-criticism after the Defeat', 1968) and *Naqd al-Fikr al-Dini* ('Criticism of the Religious Thinking', 1969), written by the Syrian philosopher Sadiq Jalal al-'Azm. Arab social critics such as Al-'Azm, the Lebanese political scientist Nadim al-Bitar, the Egyptian philosopher Hassan Hanafi, and many others, whom Emmanuel Sivan (1985: 141ff.) calls rational modernists, have come to see social backwardness and political tyranny as a continuation of a most distasteful past that has a powerful 'stranglehold' on Arab peoples and society. Nadim al-Bitar (1982, ch. 6, cited in Sivan, 1985: 141) wrote, 'one used to believe that this cultural change, the liberation from traditional culture, is imminent. It has now become unfortunately evident that this was unwarranted optimism, the forces of the past do not manifest any symptoms of attrition or decline.' In a similar vein, Hanafi (1978: 17–42, cited in Sivan, ibid.: 142) sadly emphasizes, 'As long as such mystifications are prevalent, the Arab will remain devoid of willpower, deficient in perception and reasoning. Whoever wishes can play with our fate. God, fate and the dictator become one in our eyes. He who questions this is accused of atheism. It is as though the era of science and reason has barely touched us.'

36 Reported in the Beirut-based Arabic weekly newspaper *Al-Hawadith* on 31 July 1992.

37 The concept of 'society' denoting a group of people living and collectively in a certain territory, adapted to and organized within a common pattern of socialization, is purely characteristic of modernity. Indeed, there is no accurate equivalent to the word 'society' in classical Arabic (prior to 1850) as distinct from modern Arabic. Rifa'a al-Tahtawi (1801–1873) introduced the term through his translations of classical French social thought. However, in the Islamic *umma*, the idea of communal solidarity was stronger than that of society. The *umma* was essentially a moral community with religion as the prime ground for societal

cohesion (Lapidus, 1988: 28–36). Yet the family, tribe and their extension, in a kinship sense, through which the individual belonged to the community through religious attachment was (and still is) the basis on which individuals relate themselves both in the private and public spheres. In modern Arabic, the words *mugtama'a* and *jamiyya* are equivalent to that of 'society'. The word *jamiyya* is preferred by Arab states to name social movements because it denotes a consensus under harmony. For example, the Muslim fundamentalist groups such as the Society of Muslim Brotherhood are known by the state as and prefer to call themselves *jamiyya* rather than *hizb*, 'party', or *haraka*, 'movement', simply because the word *hizb* originated from divisiveness, etymologized in Islamic traditions from clique or factionalism and not differentiation or plurality as it is the case in English. Also, the word *haraka* denotes belittling, one which is not enjoying a wide support, rather than 'action', or 'instigation'.

38   In this context Michael Walzer (1976: 194) once wrote: 'The state is invisible; it must be personified before it can be seen, symbolized before it can be loved, imagined before it can be conceived.'

39   Richard Schofield (1993: 59, n. 57; see also Draper, 1992: 46, n. 3) argues that Dickson was mistaken when he claimed that Sir Percy Cox had given away two-thirds of Kuwait territory to Najid in compensation for the loss of a large territory entitled to it, which Iraq obtained instead. Further, Schofield maintains that the boundaries marked at Uqair were only a confirmation of the lines that were already considered by the British Colonial Ministry in 1921. It is remarkable, however, that the guidelines of this demarcation at Uqair seemed to suggest that the British government had given Cox full responsibility to decide on such a gravely important issue.

40   Even though it was a brief moment in history, given the fact that the Arab prominence faded away before other ethnic groups like the Turckic elements and the Persians from around the middle of the eighth century AD.

41   Conversely, Ella Shohat (1992: 124ff.), argues that Zionism 'cannot be simplistically equated with colonialism or imperialism. Unlike colonialism, Zionism constituted a response to millennial oppression and, in contradistinction to the classical paradigm, metropolis and colony in this case were located in the self-same

place. The colonial mind-set which regarded non-European continents as "lands without people" here becomes inseparable from the Zionist concept of a Jewish people in need of land. Evertz Israel (the land of Israel), furthermore, had always been the symbolic locus of Jewish cultural identity. Israel does not represent a repetition of the classical colonial case of European expeditions into America, Africa and Asia, since the ideology of Return to the Motherland (a view of the land as belonging to the Jews, with the Palestinians merely a "guests") constitutes a departure from the traditional colonial discourse.'

42 It was reported in the Cairo-based leftist newspaper, *Al-Ahali* (13 November 1996), that the Egyptian government had decided to renounce the citizenship of any Egyptian who married an Israeli. The newspaper estimated that there were more than 10,000 Egyptian citizens who work or travel to Israel. In the same issue there were three pages of advice on how to resist any normalization with Israel.

43 Zur (1991: 350) traces the 'enemy image' to psychological and social-psychological research 'where they are defined, by and large, as the commonly-held, stereotyped, dehumanised images of the "outgroup" also called the "Other", which, by implication, is fundamentally different from "us"' (Harle, 1994: 28).

44 In Lebanon in 1983, a group of men who according to some people were terrorists sponsored by Iran, and according to others were martyrs, drove a truck packed with explosives into an American military barracks, killing 200 marines in one blow. To abandon Lebanon as a result was, for the United States, a pragmatic response comprehensible to an electorate. To others it looks quite different, representing a shaming of the West and Zionism – the enemies of God – and an honour to the anonymous heroes whose bomb proved to be strong enough for supreme arbitration.

45 The words of René Girard (1977: 89–118, quoted in Harle, 1993: 28).

46 The idea that God has enemies is familiar in all the Abrahamic traditions as well as in classical antiquity. As for the Qur'an, *a'adaa-u-Allah* are identified and defined as the unbelievers of his Essence, the Prophet and the Qur'an, and by implication condemned and fated to Hell-fire (2:98; 41:19, 28). Muslim believers are called on to 'strike fear into Allah's enemy and your enemy'. However,

the believers are also enjoined to rethink: 'If the enemy incline towards peace, and trust in Allah' (8: 60–2), since by virtue of His omniscience, He is the ultimate shield and guardian against the deceptions and evasiveness His enemies may contemplate (Lewis, 1993: 32).

47 There are two American universities in the area, the American University in Cairo and the American University in Beirut. Their fields of study are mainly Middle Eastern history, society, culture and politics.

48 A fundamental factor worth mentioning in this context is that the Arabian Peninsula was almost emptied of its population as consequences of the great migration that occurred with the advent of the overstretched expansion of the Islamic empire, immediately after the death of the Prophet in AD 632. The heart of the Islamic empire moved to the urban areas in the Fertile Crescent and North Africa. Arabia, thus stood outside world history almost until after World War II with the discovery of oil (Lapidus, 1990).

49 Abdel-Rahman Munif, 'Ay Aalam Sayakoun?', in *Al-Muthaqafoun al-'Arab wa al-Ndham al-Duwali al-Jadeed* ('Which World Shall It Be? Arab Intellectuals and the New World Order'), published in a booklet comprising work by various Arab authors under the title of *The Return of Colonialism: From Cultural Invasion to the Gulf War*. London: Riadh El-Rayyes Books (cited in Makiya, 1993: 43, 331, n. 14).

50 Marzouki's article, 'L'Occident fourvoye', appeared in *Le Monde*, 6 February 1991 (cited in Makiya, 1993: 42–3).

51 This has also applied to political figures such as Anwar al-Sadat of Egypt during the 1970s when Arabs states boycotted Egypt in protest against the peace with Israel, Sadat was specially harsh against the Gulf states and used the same rhetoric.

52 Published in *an-Naqid*, an Arabic literary magazine in London (No. 10, April 1989). *Abu Jahl* literally means the father of ignorance, and it was the nickname of Prophet Muhammad's uncle who adamantly refused to convert to Islam. Instead, *Abu Jahl* harassed the Muslim community in Mecca and attempted to kill the Prophet (Makiya, 1993: 252, 309, 331, n. 16). After the Arab defeat in the 1967 war Qabbani wrote a poem entitles *Hawamish ala daftar al-naksa* ('Notes in the margins of the notebook of the setback') in which he severely criticized his then beloved

leader Abdul Nassir. In 1991, after the Iraqi defeat in the Gulf war, Qabbani reacted, as he often does, against the Arab hero of the day, Saddam Hussein, who turns out to be a phony. In analogy, he wrote a poem called *Hawamish ala daftar al-Hazima*, ('Notes on the margins of the notebook of defeat') in which in his simple yet deep and outrageous language he mourned 'Every twenty years, a narcissistic self-absorbed man comes to us to claim that he is the Mahdi ... saviour ... the pure, the pious, the strong, the sole one, the all-knowing, the saint and the Imam' (in *Houston Arab Times*, August 1991, cited in Abu Khalil, 1992: 23–4).

53   *The Economist,* 2 June 1990, p. 44 (cited in Telhami, 1993: 196).

54   Steven Holms, *New York Times*, 28 July 1990 (cited in Neff, 1991: 39).

55   It could cost as much as the destruction of an entire city. In March 1982, after the uprising of the Muslim Brotherhood in the city of Hamma, the estimates of those killed vary between 10,000 and 20,000.

56   Ceausescu had warm and close relations with many Arab states and invoked debates and questions about the possibility of democratization in the Arab world as well as Israel. He was instrumental as a secret diplomatic channel whereby the dialogue between Anwar al-Sadat and the Israeli foreign minister Moshe Dayan took place that eventually resulted in the peace accord between the two states. It is reported that Saddam Hussein has time and again played the video tape of Ceausescu's execution to his close aids to warn them against such a destiny.

57   Quoted in Telhami (1993: 187), though Telhami didn't mention the name of Ghorbal, it can be recognized as him. He gave interviews to the Egyptian leftist weekly newspaper *Al-Ahali* during the summer of 1990 on the publication of his memoirs in the newspaper.

58   *Le Figaro*, 4 March 1991 (quoted in Piscatori, 1991: 16).

59   Youssef M. Ibrahim, *New York Times,* 10 April 1990 (cited in Neff, 1991: 36).

60   Caryle Murphy, *Washington Post*, 12 April 1990 (cited in Neff, 1991: 37).

61   The Iraqi News Agency, 4 August 1990.

62   Baghdad Domestic Service, 24 August 1990 (cited in Mattar, 1994: 36).

63 *Financial Times,* 27 February 1991 (cited in Makiya, 1993: 243).
64 *L'Express,* 7 February 1991 (cited in Makiya, 1993: 42–3, 247).
65 *Al-Dustour,* 17 March 1991 (cited in Makiya, 1993: 243).
66 A German writer who played a prominent role in Germany's 1968 student movement. The article appeared first in English in the *Los Angeles Times* on 14 February 1991, and then in several major newspaper all over the world. The reference here is to the version that appeared in *Telos,* No. 68, Winter 1991.
67 Thus, the name Hitler, while evoking agony, anguish or shame for many in Europe, was heard with blessing in the Middle East by the virtue of this background. Some people even called their children Hitler during the first half of the 1940s – the Egyptian Army spokesperson until only two years ago, for example, had the name General Hitler Tantawi.(In a parallel to this within the Marxist movement, the renowned journalist and Marxist Fathi al-Ramli has named his two sons Lenin and Stalin. Lenin al-Ramli is one of modern Egypt's best-known playwrights; Stalin al-Ramli, like his father; works as a journalist.) The issue of the Holocaust and the horror that was inflicted primarily on Jews throughout Europe has a reverse side in Arab historicity, since the Arabs regard themselves as the victim who had to pay the price instead of those who really should have done so – the Europeans. The name 'Hitler' was later invoked against Middle Eastern politicians as a metaphor for evil rule and dictatorship, for example; after nationalizing oil and throwing out the Shah, the prime minister of Iran, Mohammad Mossaddeq, was called Hitler by the West, most notably the United States and Britain; Gamal Abdul Nassir was portrayed as Hitler first by the British prime minister Anthony Eden and later by Israel and the United States. Nassir's book, *Philosophy of the Revolution,* was also described in the Western media as the Arab *Mein Kampf.* During and immediately after the Yom Kippur War, Anwar al-Sadat was described as Hitler until his reconciliation with the West and his famous Jerusalem peace initiative. Finally, Yassir Arafat was called Hitler, and still is depicted as such within some right-wing Israeli circles.
68 The first is a professor of sociology at the American University in Cairo; the second a professor of philosophy at the University of Alexandria, Egypt.

69 In the London-based Arabic daily *al-Quds al-Arabi*, on 11 March 1991.

70 The English quotations of Adonis' article are cited in Makiya (1993: 250).

71 Personal communication, Cairo, 27 December 1994.

72 Alluding to Nero, the fifth Roman emperor (AD 54–68) who become known for his burning of Rome and cheering the destruction of the city afterwards.

73 Elorf writes in the Tunisian journal *al-Cha'ab*, in which he has a weekly column (cited in Makiya, 1993: 243).

74 Quoted in an article from *Ha'artz*, 4 March 1991, by Danny Rubinstein (cited in Makiya, 1993: 244, see also Scott MacLeod's article in Sifry and Cerf, 1991: 415).

75 Scott MacLeod, 'In the wake of "Desert Storm"', *New York Review of Books* (7 March 1991); also reprinted in Sifry and Cerf, 1991: 412–22 (citation from p. 415).

76 I am here drawing on Ann Norton (1988: 106) interesting discussion of the significance of the personality of Salah Eddin to modern Arab politics.

77 Excerpts from Sheikh Asaad al-Tamimi's interview with Radio Baghdad on 7 February 1991 (quoted in Milton-Edwards, 1991: 99).

78 Tony Walker, 'Muslim militant wants Saddam as Caliph', *Financial Times*, 10 January 1991, also Sheikh Asaad al-Tamimi's interview with the Swedish TV reporter Peter Löfgren, 7 January 1991.

79 Milton Viorst, "A reporter at large: the house of Hashem', *New Yorker*, 7 January 1991: 32 (quoted in Milton-Edwards, 1991: 97).

80 Personal communication with Hassan Douh, one of the leaders of the Muslim Brotherhood in Egypt, on 11 January 1992.

81 *The Economist*, 22 September 1990 (cited in Baker, 1994: 446).

82 Eventually such a stand by the party generated division and conflict within the so called Islamic Alliance in Egypt. A peculiar electoral alliance came between the Muslim Brotherhood, the Liberal Party and the Labour Party. The first two were against the act of invading though were supportive of the unity based on consent. Most importantly, they were vehemently against an American or Western intrusion into the area (Brumberg, 1991: 193–5).

83 *The Middle East* (July 1991), see also Baker (1994: 494, 499, n. 21), where the two quotations are cited.

84   The Arabic term '*dukhul*' means entry by way of consent and
     legitimate invitation to someone to enter whatever it can, be it
     a house or a country, while the word '*ghazaw*' denotes warfare
     and a violent action conducted in a manner of a raid aiming at
     gaining plunder, booty being its visible object. It also means a
     resentful/envious incursion designed to employ violence to punish
     someone (e.g., people, society, state, etc.).
85   Hamas communiqué 64, 26 September 1990 (cited in Legrain,
     1991: 75–6).
86   Tariq Aziz had said in an interview with Milton Viorst in the *New
     Yorker* (June 1991), and again with Peter Arnett of CNN on 20
     January 1996, that the invasion and annexation of Kuwait as a
     defensive measure against Zionism and imperialism was a necessity
     for the common good of the Arab nation.

EPILOGUE

1   Tariq Aziz in an interview with Milton Viorst in the *New Yorker*
    (June 1991), and again with Peter Arnett of CNN on 20 January
    1996.
2   Literature found within social and cultural studies (e.g., Bourdieu,
    1977; Geertz, 1973; Foucault, 1978, 1980; Shweder and Le Vine,
    1984), maintains that individual interests are historically and
    culturally contingent.
3   Also, why does dissatisfaction accelerate protests against the West
    and Israel rather than political passivity, as in the case of the great
    majority of Arabs who abstain from demanding their political
    rights from their mainly authoritarian government?
4   Hedley Bull (1977: 316–17) make use of this distinction in finding
    in all historical international societies some element of a common
    intellectual culture – language, philosophical outlook, artistic
    tradition – some element of common values (Gibbins, 1989).

APPENDIX: WRITING TO UNDERSTAND OR MAPPING
TO CONQUER

1   There are countless biographies on Saddam Hussein's personality
    and leadership written by Western journalists and area specialists.

Few of them are helpful. There are at least seven known authorized biographies, two of them are translated into English: Fouad Matar (1981) *Saddam Hussein: The Man, the Cause and the Future*. London: Third World Centre; and Amir Iskander (1981) *Saddam Hussein: Munadhilan, wa Mufakiran wa Insanan. A Fighter, a Thinker and a Man*. Paris: Hachette.

2 Classical Arabists and students of Middle Eastern history, like Albert Hourani, Marshal Hodgson, Maxime Rodinson, and W. Montgomery Watt, to mention only a few, have linguistic skills, among many other things, as the most important tools for their research (Bill, 1996).

3 Unlike the two more experienced colonial powers Britain and France, until the end of World War II the United States did not possess an elite academic tradition of expertise in the histories and cultures of the Middle East. It was the pressures of the Cold War and the pursuit of the policy of Soviet containment together with the emergence of the newly independent states of the Third World, and the ideological and political division between East and West that necessitated the establishment of institutions of research and knowledge about the Middle East, one of many non-Western regions (Bill, 1996).

4 Lord Palmerston once remarked that those who wished to be misled and get a superficial picture of a country's history, culture and society are recommended to ask somebody who has lived there for 15 years (Brown, 1993: 19).

5 The examples here are those supplied by Freedman and Karsh (1993); Jentelson (1994); Karsh and Rautsi (1991); Miller and Mylroie (1990); Post (1993); Simpson (1991).

6 Previously known as Samir Al-Khalil, also nicknamed by his opponents the Arab world's V.S. Naipaul.

7 This category of books written on the Gulf crisis, Iraq and Saddam Hussein takes at face value the material and analysis in Al-Khalil's book, *Republic of Fear: The Politics of Modern Iraq*. Despite his in-depth and learned analysis of modern Iraq, and of the pan-Arab movement inside both Iraq and the Arab world, he undermines his own analysis by the anguished and inflamed tone so evident in the text. Even though the book might be taken as 'an account of a distorted vision' (Sluglett, 1993), it is definitely not to be seen as a serious analysis whereby the Ba'ath rule and modern Iraq can

be understood and objectively viewed, as they can in Hanna Batatu's seminal *The Old Social Classes*; Farouk-Sluglett's and Sluglett's several works on Iraq, in particular their lucid analysis (1990) *Iraq Since 1958: From Revolution to Dictatorship*, and 'The historiography of Modern Iraq' (1991); or in E. Kedourie's short but insightful works. We should also mention here Ali al-Wardi's (1965) *magnum opus*, *Tabi'at al-Mujtam'a al-Iraqi* ('The Nature of Iraqi Society'), published in 6 volumes.

8   For example, Freedman's and Karsh's (1993) analysis of the causes and motivation of the invasion of Kuwait has been drawn largely from Karsh and Rautsi (1991), and from writers such as Miller and Mylroie (1990); Simpson (1991) and Jentelson (1994), to mention only a few.

9   Bruce Jentelson, as stated in the book, was on the staff of the then Governor Clinton's presidential campaign and worked later as a policy analyst at the US State Department.

10   The same type of argument – in the way they begin, reason and conclude – applies to the following works: Pierre Salinger and Eric Laurent, *Secret Dossier: The Hidden Agenda Behind the Gulf War*. New York: Penguin, 1991; John Bulloch and Harvey Morris, *Saddam's War: The Origins of Kuwait Conflict and the International Response*. London: Faber and Faber, 1991; Adel Darwish and Gregory Alexander, *Unholy Babylon: the Secret History of Saddam's War*. New York: St. Martin's Press, 1991; Elaine Sciolino, *The Outlaw State: Saddam Hussein's Quest for Power and the Gulf Crisis*. New York: John Wiley and Sons, 1991; and Simon Henderson, *Instant Empire: Saddam Hussein's Ambition for Iraq*. San Francisco, CA: Mercury House, 1991.

11   For example, Jentelson (1994: 31–67); Karsh and Rautsi (1991: 1–84); Miller and Mylroie (1991: 3–84); Simpson (1991: 17–36, 87–8); Post (1993).

12   Under the heading 'Manifest and latent Orientalism', Edward Said (1978: 206) argues that the whole issue is about minimizing the significance of 'the various stated views about Oriental society ... Whatever change occurs in knowledge of the Orient is found almost exclusively in manifest Orientalism; the unanimity, stability, and durability of latent Orientalism are more or less constant.'

BIBLIOGRAPHY

NEWSPAPERS

Al-Ahram (Cairo)
Al-Ahali (Cairo)
Al-Musswar (Cairo)
Al-Hawadith (Beirut)
Al-Qabas (Kuwait)
Al-Thawra (Baghdad)
Al-Jumhurriyya (Baghdad)

BOOKS AND ARTICLES

Abdel-Mallek, Anouar (1963), 'L'Orientalism en crise' ('The crisis of Orientalism'), *Diogenes: The UNESCO Journal*, Vol. 63, Paris.

Abduh, Ibrahim (1982), *Khetabat al-Nifaq* (Letters of Hypocrisy). Cairo: unknown publisher.

Abu-Hakima, Ahmed M. (1983), *The Modern History of Kuwait. Kuwait: 1750–1965*. London: Luzac and Company.

Abu Khalil, Asaad (1992), 'A new Arab ideology? The rejuvenation of Arab nationalism', *Middle East Journal*, Vol. 46, No. 1, Winter: 22–36.

—— (1994), 'The incoherence of Islamic fundamentalism: Arab Islamic thought at the end of the 20th century', *Middle East Journal*, Vol. 48, No. 4, Autumn: 677–94.

Adams, William (1986), 'Politics and the archeology of meaning', *Western Political Quarterly*, Vol. 39, No. 3, September: 548–63.

Aflaq, Michel (1958), *Fí Sábil al-Ba'ath* (In the path of the Ba'ath). Beirut: Dar al–Tali'ah.

Ahmad, Ahmad Yossef (1991), 'Al-Nizam al-Arabi Wa Azmat al-Khaleej' (The Arab order and the Gulf crisis), in A. Al-Rasheedi (ed.), *Al-In'akasat al-Duwliyya Wa al-Iqleemiyya Li-Azmat al-Khaleej* (The International and Regional Dimension to the Gulf Crisis). Cairo: Cairo University Centre for Political Research and Studies.

Ahmad, Mumtaz (1991), 'The politics of war: Islamic fundamentalisms in Pakistan', in J. Piscatori (ed.), *Islamic Fundamentalism and the Gulf Crisis*. The Fundamentalism Project, American Academy of Arts and Sciences.

Ahmed, Akbar (1992), *Postmodernism and Islam*. London: Routledge.

Aho, James (1981), *Religious Mythologies and the Art of War*. London: Aldwych Press.

Ajami, Fouad (1981), *The Arab Predicament: Arab Political Thought and Practice Since 1967*. Cambridge: Cambridge University Press.

al-'Azm, Sadiq Jalal (1984), 'Orientalism and Orientalism in reverse', in *Forbidden Agendas: Intolerance and Defiance in the Middle East*, selected and introduced by Jon Rothschild. London: Al-Saqi Books.

Al-Azmeh, Aziz (1993), *Islams and Modernities*. London: Verso.

al-Bitar, Nadim (1974), 'Asbab takhaluf al-Arab al-ssiyasi' ('Major causes of Arab political backwardness'), *Dirását Arabiyya*, August: 17–42.

—— (1982), 'Mina al-Isteshraq al-Gharbi ila al-Isteshraq al-Arabi' ('From Western Orientalism to Arab Orientalism'), in N. al-Bitar, *Hudud al-Huwiyya al-Qawmiyya* (The Boundaries of National Identity). Beirut: Dar al-Tali'ah.

Al-Gosaibi, Ghazi A. (1992), *Azmat al-Khaleej: Mohawalh Li-lfahm* (The Gulf Crisis: An Attempt to Understand). London: Al-Saqi Books.

Ali, Omar (1993), *Crisis in the Arabian Gulf: An Independent Iraqi View*. London: Praeger.

Al-Khalil, Samir (1989), *Republic Of Fear: The Politics of Modern Iraq*. Berkeley, CA: University of California Press.

Allison, Graham T. (1971), *Essence of Decision: Explaining the Cuban Missiles Crisis*. Boston, MA: Little, Brown.

al-Naqeeb, Hassan Khaldoun (1987), *State and Society in the Gulf and Arabian Peninsula*. Beirut: Markaz Dirását al-wahda al-Arabiyya.

al-Wardi, Ali (1994), *Ausstorat al-Adab al-Rafie* (The Myth of Fine Literature), 2nd edn. London: Dar Kofan.

—— (1965), *Tabiat al-Mujetama al-Iraqi* (The Nature of Iraqi Society), 6 Vols. Baghdad: al-Aani.

Anderson, Benedict (1991), *Imagined Communities: Reflections on the Spread of Nationalism*. London: Verso.

Anderson, Berry (1974), *Lineages of the Absolutist State*. London: New Left Books.

Anderson, Lisa (1987), 'The state in the Middle East and North Africa', *Comparative Politics*, Vol. 20, No. 1, October: 1–18.

Arendt, Hannah (1950), *The Origin of Totalitarianism*. London: Harvest/HBJ.

—— (1958), *The Human Condition*. Chicago, IL: University of Chicago Press.

—— (1970), *On Violence*. London: Penguin.

Ashley, Richard K. (1986), 'The poverty of neorealism', in R. O. Keohane (ed.) *Neorealism and its Critics*. New York: Columbia University Press.

Assiri, Abdul-Reda (1990), *Kuwait's Foreign Policy: City-State in World Politics*. Boulder, CO: Westview Press.

Ayoob, Mohammad (1995), *The Third World Security Predicament: State Making, Regional Conflict, and the International System*. Boulder, CO: Lynne Reinner Publishers.

Ayubi, Nazih (1991), *Political Islam: Religion and Politics in the Arab World*. London: Routledge.

Baker, Raymond W. (1994), 'Islam, democracy, and Arab future: contested Islam in the Gulf crisis', in T. Y. Ismael and J. S. Ismael (eds), *The Gulf War and the New World Order: International Relations of the Middle East*. Miami, FL: University of Florida Press.

Bakr, Hassan (1991), 'The role of the two superpowers in the Gulf crisis', in N. M. Ahmed (ed.), *The Arab World in a Changing World: The Second Gulf Crisis*. Cairo University: Centre for Political Research and Studies.

Ball, Nicole (1988), *Security and Economy in Third World*. Princeton, NJ: Princeton University Press.

Barakat, Halim (1984), *Al-Mujetama al-Arabi al-Muasir* (Contemporary Arab Society). Beirut: Markaz Dirását al wahda al-Arabiyya.

—— (1993), *The Arab World: Society, Culture, and State*. Berkeley, CA: University of California Press.

Baram, Amatzia (1991), 'From radicalism to radical pragmatism: the Shi'ite fundamentalist opposition movements of Iraq', in J. Piscatori (ed.), *Islamic Fundamentalism and the Gulf Crisis*. Chicago, IL: The Fundamentalism Project, American Academy of Arts and Sciences.

Barnett, Michael (1993), 'Institutions, roles, and disorder: the case of the Arab state system', *International Studies Quarterly*, Vol. 37: 271–96.

—— (1996), 'Identity and alliances in the Middle East' in Peter Katzenstein (ed.) *The Culture of National Security Norms and Identity in World Politics*. New York: Columbia University Press.

Batatu, Hanna (1978), *Old Social Classes and the Revolutionary Movements of Iraq*, 3 Vols. Princeton, NJ: Princeton University Press.

—— (1981), 'Some observations on the social roots of Syria's ruling military group and the causes of its dominance', *Middle East Journal*, Vol. 35, No. 3: 578–94.

—— (1985), 'Class analysis and Iraqi society', in Saad Eddin Ibrahim and Nicholas Hopkins (eds), *Arab Society: Social Science Perspectives*. Cairo: The American University in Cairo Press.

Bayomi, Khalid (1995), 'Egyopten och den regionala maktbalansen i Arabösten – Ett annorlunda perspektiv', unpublished paper presented at the Nordic Middle East Conference in Joensuu, Finland, 19–22 June.

Bayyumi, Zakariyya S. (1979), *Al-Ikhwan al-Muslimun wa al-Jamiat al-Islamiyya* (The Muslim Brothers and the Islamic Groupings). Cairo: Wahba.

Be'eri, Eliezer (1970), *Army Officers in Arab Politics and Society*, trans. Dov Ben-Abba. London: Praeger.

Bengio, Ofra (1992), *Saddam Speaks on the Gulf Crisis: A Collection of Documents*. Tel-Aviv: The Moshe Dayan Centre for Middle Eastern and African Studies, The Shiloah Institute, Tel-Aviv University.

Bennis, Phyllis and Michel Moushabeck (eds) (1991), *Beyond the Storm: A Gulf Crisis Reader*. New York: Olive Branch Press.

Bild, Peter (1993), 'Oil in the Middle East and North Africa' in *The Middle East and North Africa 1993*, updated by John Cranefield. London: Europa Publications.

Bill, James A. (1996), 'The study of Middle East politics, 1946–1996: a stocktaking', *Middle East Journal*, Vol. 50, No. 40: 501–12.

Bloom, William (1990), *Personal Identity, National Identity and International Relations*. Cambridge: Cambridge University Press.

Booth, Ken (1979) *Strategy and Ethnocentrism*. London: Croom Helm.

Bourdieu, Pierre (1977), *Outline of a Theory of Practice*. Cambridge: Cambridge University Press.

—— (1990), *The Logic of Practice*. Cambridge: Polity Press.

—— (1991), *Language and Symbolic Power*, ed. J. B. Thompson. Cambridge: Polity Press.

Brecher, Michael (1972), *The Foreign Policy System of Israel: Setting, Images, and Process*. Oxford: Oxford University Press.

Brecher, Michael, B. Steinberg and J. G. Stein (1969), 'A framework for research on foreign policy behaviour', *Journal of Conflict Resolution*, Vol. XIII, No. 1, March: 75–94.

Brint, Michael (1991), *A Genealogy of Political Culture*. Oxford: Westview Press.

Bromley, Simon (1994) *Rethinking the Middle East Politics: State Formation and Development*. London: Polity Press.

Brown, L. Carl (1992), 'Built on sand? America's Middle Eastern policy, 1945–1991', in I. Ibrahim (ed.), *The Gulf Crisis: Background and Consequences*. Washington, DC: Center for Contemporary Arab Studies, Georgetown University.

—— (1993), 'Pattern forged in times: Middle Eastern mind-sets and the Gulf War', in S. A. Renshon (ed.), *The Political Psychology of the Gulf War: Leaders, Publics, and the Process of Conflict*. Pittsburgh, PA: University of Pittsburgh Press.

Brumberg, Daniel (1991), 'Islamic fundamentalism, democracy, and the Gulf War', in J. Piscatori (ed.), *Islamic Fundamentalism and the Gulf Crisis*. Chicago, IL: The Fundamentalism Project, American Academy of Arts and Sciences.

Bull, Hedley (1977), *The Anarchical Society: A Study of Order in World Politics*. London: Macmillan.

Buzan, Barry (1987) *An Introduction to Strategic Studies*. London: Macmillan/IISS.

Canovan, Margaret (1992), 'Hannah Arendt and the human condition', in Leonard Tivey and Anthony Wright (eds), *Political Thought Since 1945: Philosophy, Science, Ideology*. London: Edward Elgar.

Cladis, Mark S. (1992) 'Durkheim's individual in society: a sacred marriage?', *Journal of the History of Ideas*, Vol. 53, No. 1, January–March: 71–90.

Coleman, James (1990), *Foundations of Social Theory*. Cambridge, MA: Harvard University Press.

Connolly, William (1983), *The Terms of Political Discourse*, 2nd edn. Princeton, NJ: Princeton University Press.

Corm, Georges (1992), 'Political and economic development in Iraq and the Arabian Peninsula from 1919 to 1980', *THESIS ELEVEN*, Vol. 33: 131–47.

Cox, Robert (1986), 'Social forces, states and world orders: beyond international relation theory', in R. O. Keohane (ed.), *Neorealism and its Critics*. New York: Columbia University Press.

Cragg, Chris (1993), 'Natural gas in the Middle East and North Africa', in *The Middle East and North Africa 1993*, updated by John Cranefield. London: Europa Publications.

Curtis, Michael (1962), *The Nature of Politics*. New York: Avon Book Division.

Dawisha, Adeed (1977), 'The Middle East', in Christopher Clapham (ed.), *Foreign Policy Making in Developing States: A Comparative Approach*. London: Saxon House.

—— (1983), 'Islam in foreign policy: some methodological issues', in A. Dawisha (ed.), *Islam in Foreign Policy*. Cambridge: Cambridge University Press.

—— (1990), 'Arab regimes: legitimacy and foreign policy', in G. Luciani (ed.), *The Arab State*. Berkeley, CA: University of California Press.

De Santillana, David (1961), 'Law and society', in Thomas Arnold and Alfred Guillaume (eds), *The Legacy of Islam*. London: Oxford University Press.

Dickson, Harold R. P. (1956), *Kuwait and her Neighbours*. London: Allen and Unwin.

Djäit, Hichem (1985), *Europe and Islam: Culture and Modernity*, trans. Peter Heinegg. Los Angeles, CA: University of California Press.

Draper, Theodore (1992), 'The Gulf War reconsidered', *The New York Review of Books*, 16 January.

Dunn, Michael C. (1992), 'Gulf security: past and future', in I. Ibrahim (ed.), *The Gulf Crisis: Background and Consequences*. Washington, DC: Center for Contemporary Arab Studies, Georgetown University.

Durkheim, Emile (1983), *Pragmatism and Sociology*, trans. J. C. Whitehouse, Cambridge. Cambridge University Press.

Bibliography   255

Eisenstadt, S. N. (1973), 'Post-traditional societies and continuity and reconstruction of tradition', *Daedalus*, Vol. 102, No. 1, winter: 1–28.

Eisenstadt, S. N. and L. Roniger (1984), *Patrons, Clients, and Friends: Interpersonal Relations and the Structure of Trust in Society*. Cambridge: Cambridge University Press.

Enzensberger, Hans Magnus (1990/1991), 'Hitler's successor: Saddam Hussein in the context of German History', *Telos: A Quarterly Journal of Critical Thought*, No. 68, winter: 153–7.

Eppel, Michael (1994), *The Palestine Conflict in the History of Modern Iraq: The Dynamics of Involvement, 1928–1948*. London: Frank Cass.

Farouk-Sluglett, Marion and Peter Sluglett (1990), *Iraq Since 1958: From Revolution to Dictatorship*. London: I. B. Tauris.

—— (1991), 'The historiography of modern Iraq', *The American Historical Review*, Vol. 96, No. 5, December: 1408–21.

Finnie, David H. (1992), *Shifting Lines in the Sand: Kuwait's Elusive Frontier with Iraq*. Cambridge, MA: Harvard University Press.

Finnemore, Marie (1996), 'Norms, culture, and world politics: insights from sociology's institutionalism', *International Organization*, Vol. 50, No. 2, spring: 325–47.

Fisher, W. B. (1993), 'Iraq: economy and statistical survey', in *The Middle East and North Africa 1993*, updated by Alan J. Day. London: Europa Publications.

Foucault, Michel (1970), *The Order of Things: An Archaeology of the Human Sciences*. New York: Random House.

—— (1972), *The Archeology of Knowledge*, trans. A.M. Sheridan Smith. New York: Pantheon.

—— (1978), *The History of Sexuality, Vol. 1: An Introduction*, trans. Robert Hurley. New York: Random House.

—— (1980), *Power and Knowledge: Selected Interviews and Other Writings, 1972–1977*, ed. Colin Gordon. New York: Pantheon.

—— (1982), 'The subject and power,' published as an Afterward to H. L. Dreyfus and P. Rabinow (eds), *Michel Foucault: Beyond Structuralism and Hermeneutics*. Chicago, IL: University of Chicago Press.

Freedman, Laurence and Ephraim Karsh (1993), *The Gulf Conflict 1990–1991: Diplomacy and War in the New World Order*. London: Faber and Faber.

Friedman, Robert (1991), 'War and peace in Israel', in M. L. Sifry and C. Cerf (eds), *The Gulf War Reader: History, Documents and Opinions*. New York: Random House.

Garnett, John (1991), 'The role of military power', in Michael Smith *et al.* (eds) *Perspectives on World Politics*. London: Croom Helm.

Geertz, Clifford (1973), *The Interpretation of Culture*. New York: Basic Books.

—— (1980), *Negara*. Princeton, NJ: Princeton University Press.

Gellner, Ernest (1983), *Nations and Nationalism*. Cambridge: Cambridge University Press.

—— (1990), 'Tribalism and the state in the Middle East', in P. S. Khoury and J. Kostiner (eds), *Tribes and States Formation in the Middle East*. Berkeley, CA: University of California Press.

Ghazoul, Ferial J. (1992), 'The resonance of the Arab–Islamic heritage in the work of Edward Said', in M. Sprinker (ed.), *Edward Said: A Critical Reader*. Oxford: Blackwell.

Gibb, Hamilton, A. R. (1963), *Arabic Literature: An Introduction*. Oxford: Oxford University Press.

Gibbins, John R. (1989), 'Introduction' to J. R. Gibbins (ed.), *Contemporary Political Culture: Politics in a Post Modern Age*. London: Sage.

Giddens, Anthony (1985), *The Nation-State and Violence* , Vol, II of *The Contemporary Critique of Historical Materialism*. Cambridge: Polity Press.

—— (1992), 'Introduction' to Max Weber's *The Protestant Ethic and the Spirit of Capitalism*. London: Routledge.

Gilsenan, Michael (1982), *Recognising Islam: Religion and Society in the Modern Arab World*. London: Croom Helm.

Gilpin, Robert (1981) *War and Change in World Politics*. Cambridge: Cambridge University Press.

—— (1986) 'The richness of the traditions of political realism', in R. O. Keohane (ed.) *Neorealism and its Critics*. New York: Columbia University Press.

Girard, René (1977), *Violence and the Sacred*. London: Johns Hopkins University Press.

Goldstein, Judith and Robert O. Keohane (1993), ' Introduction' to J. Goldstein and R. O. Keohane (eds), *Ideas and Foreign Policy*. Ithaca, NY: Cornell University Press.

Gould, S. J. (1987), 'Institution', in *The Blackwell Encyclopaedia of Political Institutions*. Oxford: Blackwell.

Gown, Peter (1991), 'The Gulf War, Iraq and Western liberalism', *New Left Review* No. 187, May/June: 29–70.

Graham, William (1993), 'Traditionalism in Islam: an essay in interpretation', *Journal of Interdisciplinary History*, Vol. XXIII, No. 3, winter: 495–522.

Granovetter, Mark (1973), 'The strength of weak ties', *American Journal of Sociology*, Vol. 78: 1360–80.

Gray, Colin (1986), *Nuclear Strategy and National Style*. Lanham, MD: Hamilton.

Greenfeld, Liah and Chirot, Daniel (1994), 'Nationalism and aggression', *Theory and Society*, Vol. 32, No. 1, February: 79–130.

Grunebaum, Gustave von (1955), *Islam: Essays in the Nature and Growth of a Cultural Tradition* . London: Routledge & Kegan Paul.

Gusdorf, Georges (1965), *Speaking (La Parole)*, trans. Paul T. Brockelman. Evanston: Northwestern University Press.

Hall, Stuart, David Held and Tony McGraw (1992), *Modernity and its Futures*. London: Polity Press.

Halliday, Fred (1995) *Islam and the Myth of Confrontation: Religion and Politics in the Middle East*. London: I.B. Tauris.

Hanafi, Hassan (1978), 'Intibaat ala al-taakhour al-Arabi' (Reflection on Arab backwardness), in *Qadaya Arabiyya*, Vol. 2: 17–42. Beirut.

Harle, Vilho (1994), 'On the concept of the "Other" and the "enemy"', *History of European Ideas*, Vol. 19, Nos 1–3: 27–34.

Harik, Iliya (1990), 'The origins of the Arab state system', in G. Luciani (ed.) *The Arab State*. Berkeley, CA: University of California Press.

Harris, Marvin (1987), *Cultural Anthropology*, 2nd edn. New York: Harper and Row.

Hashem, Hazem (1986), *Al-Muaamara al-Israeeliyya ala al-Aql al-Misri* (The Israeli Conspiracy on the Egyptian Mind). Cairo: Dar al-Mustaqbal al-Arabi.

Hassan, Hamdi A. (1995) 'Orientalism reconsidered', *TFMS* (Tidskrift för mellanösternstudier), Vol. 2, spring, Lund. (in Swedish): 28–49.

Heikal, Mohammed H. (1992) *Awham al-Qowa wa al-Nassr* (Illusion of Power and Triumph). Cairo: al-Ahram.

Hermassi, M. Abd al-Baki (1987) 'State-building and regime performance in the Greater Maghreb', in G. Salamé (ed.) *The Foundations of the Arab State*. London: Croom Helm.

Herrmann, Richard K. (1991), 'The Middle East and the new world order: rethinking US political strategy after the Gulf War', *International Security*, Vol. 16, No. 2, fall: 42–75.

Hetata, Sherif (1991), 'What choice did Egypt have?', in P. Bennis and M. Maushabeck (eds), *Beyond the Storm: A Gulf Crisis Reader*. New York: Olive Branch Press.

Hijazi, Mustapha (1980), *Al-Takhaluf al-Ijtima: Psychologiyat al-Insan al-Maqhoor* (Social Backwardness: The Psychology of the Subjugated Man). Beirut: The Arab Development Institute.

Hiro, Dilip (1991), 'A few of our favourite kings', in M. L. Sifry and C. Cerf (eds), *The Gulf War Reader: History, Documents and Opinions*. New York: Random House.

—— (1992), *Desert Shield to Desert Storm: The Second Gulf War*. Glasgow: Paladin.

Hitti, Philip (1970), *History of the Arabs*. London: Macmillan.

Hjärpe, Jan (1985), *Islam: Lära och Livsmönster*. AWE/Geber. Stockholm.

—— (1994), *Araber och Arabism*. Stockholm: Rabén Prisma.

Hobbes, Thomas (1651/1967), *Leviathan*, ed. and intr. C. B. McPherson. Harmondsworth: Penguin.

Hodgson, Marshal G. S. (1974), *The Venture of Islam: Conscience and History in a World Civilization*, 3 Vols: I. *The Classical Age of Islam*; II. *The Expansion of Islam in the Middle Period*; III. *The Gunpowder Empires and Modern Times*. Chicago, IL: University of Chicago Press.

Hoffmann, Stanley (1965), *The State of War*. New York: Praeger.

Hollis, Martin and Steven Lukes (1982) 'Introduction' in M. Hollis and S. Lukes (eds), *Rationality and Relativism*. Cambridge, MA: The MIT Press.

Holsti, Kaj J. (1970), 'National role conception in the study of foreign policy'. *International Studies Quarterly*, Vol. 14: 233–309.

—— (1972), *An Introduction to International Relations*. Englewood Cliffs, NJ: Prentice Hall.

Holton Robert and Bryan S. Turner (1989), *Max Weber on Economy and Society*. London: Routledge.

Hourani, Albert (1983), *Arabic Thought in the Liberal Age*. Cambridge: Cambridge University Press.

—— (1991), *A History of the Arab Peoples*. London: Faber and Faber.

—— (1992), *Islam in European Thought*. Cambridge: Cambridge University Press.

Hurewitz, Jacob C. (1972), *Diplomacy in the Near and Middle East: A Documentary History.* New York: Van Nostrand.

Husayn, Taha (1967), 'Al–Fitna–l–Kubra' (The great civil war), in his *Islamiyyat* (On Islam). Beirut: Dar al–Adab.

Huth, Paul and Bruce Russet (1990), 'Testing deterrence theory: rigour makes a difference', *World Politics*, Vol. 36, No. 4, July: 496–526.

Ibn Abdul-Aziz, Khalid S. (1995), *A Fighter From The Desert: The Memoir of The Arab Forces' Commander in the Gulf War.* London: Al-Saqi Books.

Ibn Khaldun (1967), *The Muqaddimah: Introduction to History,* trans. Frantz Rosenthal. New York: Bollingen.

Ibrahim, Ibrahim (1992), 'Sovereign states and borders in the Gulf region: a historical perspective', in I. Ibrahim (ed.), *The Gulf Crisis: Background and Consequences.* Washington, DC: Center for Contemporary Arab Studies, Georgetown University.

Ibrahim, Saad Eddin (1980), *Itigahat al-Raei al-Aam al-Arabi fi Massalat al-wahda.* (Trends of Arab Public Opinion Toward the Question of Unity). Beirut: Markaz Dirását al–Wahda al–Arabiyya.

Jentelson, Bruce W. (1994), *With Friends Like These: Reagan, Bush, and Saddam 1982–1990.* New York: W. W. Norton.

Jervis, Robert (1976), *Perception and Misperception in International Politics.* Princeton, NJ: Princeton University Press.

—— (1987), 'Strategic theory: what's new and what's true,' in R. Kolkowicz (ed.), *The Logic of Nuclear Terror.* Boston, MA: Allen and Unwin.

—— (1990) *The Meaning of the Nuclear Revolution.* Ithaca, NY: Cornell University Press.

Jervis, Robert, R. Lebow and J. G. Stein (1985), *Psychology and Deterrence.* Baltimore, MD: Johns Hopkins University Press.

Joffé, George (1993), 'Prelude to the 1991 Gulf War', in *The Middle East and North Africa 1993.* London: Europa Publications.

Jonsson, Stefan (1995), *Andra platser. en essä om kulturell identitet.* Stockholm: Nordstedts.

Kalberg, Stephen (1994), *Max Weber's Comparative-Historical Sociology.* Cambridge: Polity Press.

Karabell, Zakary (1993), 'Backfire: US policy towards Iraq, 1988 – 2 August 1990', *Middle East Journal*, Vol. 49, No. 1, winter: 28–47.

Karawan, Ibrahim (1992) 'Monarchs, mullahs and marshals: Islamic regimes?', *The Annals of the American Academy of Political and Social Science*, November: 103–119.

Karsh, Ephraim and Rautsi, Inari (1991), *Saddam Hussein: A Political Biography*. London: Brassey's.

Kedourie, Elie (1961) *Nationalism*. London: Hutchinson.

—— (1970), *The Chatham House Version and Other Middle Eastern Studies*. London: Weidenfeld.

—— (1980), *Islam in the Modern World*. London: Mansell.

Kelly, John B. (1964), *Eastern Arabian Frontiers*. London: Frederick A. Praeger.

—— (1980), *Arabia, The Gulf and The West*. New York: Basic Books.

Keohane, Robert O. (1986a), 'Realism, neorealism and the study of world politics', in R. O. Keohane (ed.), *Neorealism and its Critics*. New York: Columbia University Press.

—— (1986b), 'Theory of world politics: structural realism and beyond', in R. O. Keohane (ed.), *Neorealism and its Critics*. New York: Columbia University Press.

—— (1988), 'International institutions: two approaches', *International Studies Quarterly*, Vol. 32: 379–96.

Khalidi, Walid (1991), *The Gulf Crisis: Origin and Consequences*, Washington, DC: Institute for Palestine Studies.

Khouri, Rami G. (1991) 'The bitter fruits of war', in M. L. Sifry and C. Cerf (eds), *The Gulf War Reader: History, Documents and Opinions*. New York: Random House.

Kim, Samuel (1983), *The Quest for a Just World Order*. Boulder, CO: Westview Press.

Koelble, Thomas A. (1995), 'The new institutionalism in political science and sociology', *Comparative Politics*, Vol. 27, No. 2, January: 231–44.

Korany, Bahgat (1983), 'The take-off of Third World studies? The case of foreign policy', *World Politics* , Vol. 35, No. 3: 465–87.

Korany, Bahgat and Ali E. H. Dessouki (1984), *The Foreign Policy of Arab States*. Cairo: The American University in Cairo Press.

Khouri, Rami G. (1991), 'The bitter fruits of war,' in M. L. Sifry and C. Cerf (eds), *The Gulf War Reader: History, Documents and Opinions*. New York: Random House.

Kratochwil, Friedrich (1986), 'Of systems, boundaries, and territoriality: an inquiry into the formation of the state system', *World Politics*, Vol. XXXIX, No. 1, October: 27–52.

—— (1996), 'Is the ship of culture at sea or returning?', in Y. Lapid and F. Kratochwil (eds), *The Return of Culture and Identity in IR*. Boulder, CO: Lynne Reinner Publishers.

Lambton, Ann K. S (1988), 'Introduction' to F. Klaus and M. Mozaffari (eds), *Islam: State and Society*. Kobenhagen: Scandinavian Institute of Asian Studies.

Lapidus, Ira (1988) *A History of Islamic Societies*. Cambridge: Cambridge University Press.

—— (1990), 'Tribes and state formation in Islamic history', in P. S. Khoury, and J. Kostiner (eds), *Tribes and States Formation in the Middle East*. Berkeley, CA: University of California Press.

Lawrence, Phillip K. (1987), 'Strategy, the state and the Weberian legacy', *Review of International Studies*, October: 295–310.

Lebow, Richard Ned and Janice G. Stein (1989), 'Rational deterrence theory: I think, therefore I deter', *World Politics*, Vol. 40, No. 2, January: 208–24.

—— (1990) 'Deterrence: the elusive dependent variable', *World Politics*, Vol. 42, No. 3, April: 336–69.

Legrain, Jean-Francois (1991), 'A defining moment: Palestinian Islamic fundamentalism', in J. Piscatori (ed.), *Islamic Fundamentalism and the Gulf Crisis*. Chicago: IL: The Fundamentalism Project, American Academy of Arts and Sciences.

Lewis, Bernard (1973) *Islam in History: Ideas, Men and Events in the Middle East*. London: Alcove Press.

—— (1975), *History – Remembered, Recovered, Invented*. Princeton, NJ: Princeton University Press.

—— (1984) 'Preface' to Gilles Kepel, *The Prophet and Pharaoh: Muslim Extremism in Egypt*. London: Al Saqi Books.

—— (1986), *Smites and Anti-Smites: An inquiry into Conflict and Prejudice*. London: Weidenfeld and Nicolson.

—— (1988), *The Political Language of Islam*. Chicago, IL: University of Chicago Press.

—— (1993a), *Islam and the West*. Oxford: Oxford University Press.

—— (1993b), 'The enemies of God', *The New York Review of Books*, March.

Luciani, Giacomo (1990) 'Introduction', in G. Luciani (ed.) *The Arab State*. Berkeley, CA: University of California Press.

Luciani, Giacomo and Beblawi, Hazem (1987), *The Rentier State*. London: Croom Helm.

MacLeod, Scott (1991), 'In the wake of "Desert Storm"', in M. L. Sifry and C. Cerf (eds), *The Gulf War Reader: History, Documents and Opinions*. New York: Random House.

Makiya, Kanan (1993), *Cruelty and Silence: War and Tyranny in the Arab World*. London: W. W. Norton.

Maksoud, Clovis (1991), 'The Arab world in the "new world order"', in P. Bennis and M. Maushabeck (eds), *Beyond the Storm: A Gulf Crisis Reader*. New York: Olive Branch Press.

Malley, Robert (1996), *The Call From Algeria: Third Worldism Revolution and the Turn to Islam*. Berkeley, CA: University of California Press.

March, James and Olsen, Johan P. (1989) *Rediscovering the Institutions: The Organizational Basis of Politics*. New York: Free Press.

Mathews, Ken (1993), *The Gulf Conflict and International Relations*. London: Routledge.

Mattar, Philip (1994), 'The PLO and the Gulf Crisis,' *Middle East Journal*, Vol. 48, No. 1, winter: 31–46.

Melkumyan, Yellena (1992), 'Soviet policy and the Gulf crisis', in I. Ibrahim (ed.), *The Gulf Crisis: Background and Consequences*. Washington, DC: Center for Contemporary Arab Studies, Georgetown University.

Merelman, Richard M. (1991), *Partial Vision: Culture and Politics in Britain, Canada, and United States*. Madison, WI: University of Wisconsin Press.

Miller, Judith and Mylroie, Laurie (1990), *Saddam Hussein and the Crisis in the Gulf*. New York: Random House.

Milton-Edwards, Beverly (1991), 'A temporary alliance with the Crown: Islamic response in Jordan', in J. Piscatori (ed.), *Islamic Fundamentalism and the Gulf Crisis*. Chicago, IL: The Fundamentalism Project, American Academy of Arts and Sciences.

Moore, Barrington, Jr (1967) *Social Origins of Dictatorship and Democracy*. London: Penguin.

Morgan, Patrick (1977), *Deterrence: A Conceptual Analysis*. Beverly Hills, CA: Sage.

Morgan, T. Clifton and Sally Howard Campbell (1991) 'Domestic structure, decisional constraints, and war: so why Kant democracies fight?', *Journal of Conflict Resolution*, Vol. 35, No. 2, June: 187–211.

Morgenthau, Hans J. (1940), 'Positivism, functionalism and international law', *American Journal of International Law*, Vol. 34: 260–84.

—— (1978), *Politics Among Nations: The Struggle for Power and Peace*, 5th edn. New York: Knopf.

Mostafa, Nadia M. (1991), 'Azmat al-Khaleej Wa al-Nizam al-Duwali' (The Gulf crisis and the international system), in A. Al-Rasheedi (ed.), *Al-In'akasat al-Duwliyya Wa al-Iqleemiyya Li-Azmat al-Khaleej* (The International and Regional Dimension to the Gulf Crisis). Cairo University: Centre for Political Research and Studies.

Munif, Abdel-Rahman (1991) 'Ay Aalam Sayakoun?', in *Al-Muthaqafoun al-'Arab wa al-Ndham al-Duwali al-Jaheed* (Which World Shall it Be? Arab Intellectuals and the New World Order). London: Riadh El-Rayyes Books.

Muslih, Muhammad (1992), 'The shift in Palestinian thinking', *Current History*, Vol. 91, No. 561, January: 22–8.

Mylroie, Laurie (1991) 'Why Saddam Hussein invaded Kuwait', *Orbis: A Journal of World Affairs*, Vol. 37, No. 1, winter: 123–34.

Nardin, Terry (1983), *Law, Morality and the Relations of States*. Princeton, NJ: Princeton University Press.

Ned Lebow, Richard and Janice G. Stein (1989), 'Rational deterrence theory: I think, therefore I deter', *World Politics*, Vol. 40, No. 2, January: 208–24.

—— (1990), 'Deterrence: the elusive dependent variable', *World Politics*, Vol. 42, No. 3, April: 336–69.

Neff, Donald (1991), 'The US, Iraq, Israel, and Iran: backdrop to war', *Journal of Palestine Studies*, Vol. XX, No. 4, summer: 23–41.

Nicholson, Michael (1992), *Rationality and the Analysis of International Conflict*. Cambridge: Cambridge University Press.

Noble, Paul (1984), 'The Arab system: opportunities, constraints, and pressures', in B. Korany and A. E. H. Dessouki (eds), *The Foreign Policy of Arab States*. Cairo: The American University in Cairo Press.

Norton, Ann (1988), *Reflections on Political Identities*. Baltimore, MD: Johns Hopkins University Press.

Ong, Walter, J. (1982), *Orality and Literacy*. London: Routledge.

Pasic, Sujata Chakrabarti (1996), 'Culturing international relations theory: a call for extension', in Y. Lapid and F. Kratochwil (eds),

The Return of Culture and Identity in IR. Boulder, CO: Lynne Reinner Publishers.

Pasquino, Pasqule (1993), 'Michel Foucault: the will to knowledge', in Mike Gane and Terry Johnson (eds), *Foucault's New Domains*. London: Routledge.

Piscatori, James (1991), 'Religion and *realpolitik*: Islamic responses to the Gulf War', in J. Piscatori (ed.), *Islamic Fundamentalism and the Gulf Crisis*. Chicago, IL: The Fundamentalism Project, American Academy of Arts and Sciences.

Pocock, John (1975), *The Machiavellian Moment: Florentine Political Thought and the Atlantic Republican Tradition*. Princeton, NJ: Princeton University Press.

Post, Jerrold M. (1993), 'The defining moment of Saddam's life: a political psychology perspective on the leadership and decision making of Saddam Hussein during the Gulf crisis', in S.A. Renshon (ed.), *The Political Psychology of the Gulf War: Leaders, Publics, and the Process of Conflict*. Pittsburgh, PA: University of Pittsburgh Press.

Putnam, Robert D. with Robert Leonardo and Raffaella Y. Nanetti (1993), *Making Democracy Works: Civic Traditions in Modern Italy*. Princeton, NJ: Princeton University Press.

Pye, Lucian W. (1985), *Asian Power and Politics: The Culture Dimensions of Authority*. Cambridge, MA: Belknap Press.

Ramsay, Gail (1996), *The Novels of an Egyptian Romanticist: Yusuf al-Siba'i*. Stockholm: Institute of Oriental Languages, University of Stockholm.

Rapoport, Anatol (1982), 'Introduction' to Clausewitz, *On War*. Harmondsworth: Penguin.

Regan, Patrick M. (1994), *Organizing Societies for War: The Process and Consequences of Societal Militarization*. Westport, CT: Praeger.

Robertson, David (1985), *The Penguin Dictionary of Politics*. Harmondsworth: Penguin.

Robinson, P. Stuart (1994), 'Reason, meaning, and the institutional context of foreign policy decision-making', *International Journal: Canadian Institute of International Affairs*, Vol. XLIX, No. 2, spring: 408–33.

Rodinson, Maxim (1971), *Mohammed*, trans. Ann Carter. Harmondsworth: Penguin.

—— (1979), *The Arabs*. Chicago, IL: University of Chicago Press.

—— (1980), *The Fascination with Islam*. Paris: Maspiro.

Rose, Richard (1980), *Politics in England: An Interpretation for the 1980s.* London: Faber and Faber.

Rosenau, James N. (1967) *Domestic Sources of Foreign Policy.* New York: Free Press for Princeton Center of International Studies.

Rosenau, James (1981), 'Pre-theories and theories of foreign policy', in J. Rosenau, *The Scientific Study of Foreign Policy.* London: Frances Pinter.

Rothstein, Robert (1977), *The Weak in the World of Strong: The Developing Countries in the International System.* New York: Colombia University Press.

Ruggie, John Gerard (1986), 'Continuity and transformation in the world polity: toward a neorealist synthesis', in R. O. Keohane (ed.), *Neorealism and its Critics.* New York: Columbia University Press.

Ruggie, John Gerard (1993), 'Territoriality and beyond: problematizing modernity in international relations', *International Organisation,* Vol. 47, No. 1, winter: 139–74.

Said, Edward W. (1978), *Orientalism.* London: Routledge.

—— (1980), *The Question of Palestine.* London: Routledge.

—— (1981), *Covering Islam: How the Media and the Experts Determine How We See the Rest of the World.* London: Routledge.

—— (1983), *The World, the Text, and the Critic.* London: Faber and Faber.

—— (1991a), 'On linkage, language, and identity', in M. L. Sifry and C. Cerf, (eds), *The Gulf War Reader: History, Documents and Opinions.* New York: Random House.

—— (1991b), 'Thoughts on a war: ignorant armies clash by night', Foreword to Phyllis Bennis and M. Maushabeck (eds), *Beyond the Storm: A Gulf Crisis Reader.* New York: Olive Branch Press.

—— (1993), *Culture and Imperialism.* New York: Alfred Knopf.

—— (1998) 'Clinton's rampage', *Al-Ahram Weekly,* 24 December, Cairo.

Salamé, Ghasán and Giacomo Luciani (1990), 'The politics of Arab integration', in G. Luciani (ed.), *The Arab State.* Berkeley, CA: University of California Press.

—— (1988), *The Politics of Arab Integration.* London: Croom Helm.

Salem, Latifa M. (1989), *Farooq wa soqout al-Malakiyya fi Misr 1936-1952* (Farooq and the Downfall of the Monarchy in Egypt). Cairo: Madbouli.

Salinger, Pierre and Eric Laurent (1991), *Secret Dossier: The Hidden Agenda Behind The Gulf War*. New York: Penguin.

Sayigh, Yazid (1991), 'The Gulf crisis: why the Arab regional order failed', *International Affairs*, Vol. 67, No. 3: 485–97.

Scaff, Lawrence (1989), *Fleeing the Iron Cage: Culture, Politics, and Modernity in the Thought of Max Weber*. Berkeley, CA: University of California Press.

Schofield, Richard (1993), *Kuwait and Iraq: Historical Claims and Territorial Disputes*. London: Royal Institute of International Affairs.

Schroeder, Rolf (1992), *Max Weber and the Sociology of Culture*. London: Sage.

Seale, Patrick (1986), *The Struggle for Syria*. New Haven, CT: Yale University Press.

—— (1989), *Assad: The Struggle for the Middle East*. Berkeley, CA: University of California Press.

Shachar, Nathan (1996), *Vilsenhetens förklädnader: Essäer om myter, modernitet och tradition i Mellanöstern*. Stockholm: Atlantis.

Shalabi, Ali (1982), *Misr al-fataah wa dwaraha fi al-siyasa al-miseriyya* ('Young Egypt' Movement and its role in Egyptian Politics). Cairo: Dar al-kitab al-gamei.

Sharabi, Hisham (1971), *Arab Intellectuals and the West: The Formative Years, 1875–1914*. Baltimore, MD: Johns Hopkins University Press.

—— (1987), *Al-Binya al-batrakiyya* (The Patriarchal Structure: A Study in Contemporary Arab Society). Beirut: Dar a-Talia.

—— (1988), *Neopatriarchy: A Theory of Distorted Change in Arab Society*. New York: Oxford University Press.

Sheth, D. L. (1989), 'Nation-building in multi-ethnic societies', *Alternatives*, Vol. XIV, No. 4, October: 379–90.

Shildo, Gideon (1993), 'Third World arms exports to Iraq before and after the Gulf War', in A. Klieman and G. Shildo (eds), *The Gulf Crisis and its Global Aftermath*. London: Routledge.

Shohat, Ella (1992), 'Antinomies of exile: Said at the frontiers of national narrations', in M. Sprinker (ed.) *Edward Said: A Critical Reader*. Oxford: Blackwell.

Shouby, E. (1951), 'The influence of the Arabic language on the psychology of the Arabs', *Middle East Journal*, Vol. 5, No. 3: 284–302.

Shweder, Richard (1986), 'Divergent rationalities', in Donald W. Fiske and R. Shweder (eds), *Metatheory in Social Science*. Chicago, IL: University of Chicago Press.

Shweder, Richard A. and Robert A. LeVine, (1984) *Culture Theory*. Cambridge: Cambridge University Press.

Sid-Ahmed, Mohammad (1984), 'Armament culture: trends in the Middle East', *Alternatives*, Vol. X, No. 1: 139–59.

Sifry. M. L. and C. Cerf (eds), *The Gulf War Reader: History, Documents and Opinions*. New York: Random House.

Simon, Herbert (1983), *Reason in Human Affairs*. Stanford: Stanford University Press.

Simpson, John (1991), *From the House of War*. London: Arrow Books.

SIPRI *Yearbook 1990: World Armament and Disarmament*. Oxford: Oxford University Press.

SIPRI *Yearbook 1991: World Armament and Disarmament*. Oxford: Oxford University Press.

Sivan, Emmanuel (1985), *Interpretations of Islam: Past and Present*. Princeton, NJ: Darwin Press.

Sluglett, Peter (1993a), 'Pan-Arabism', in *The Blackwell Dictionary of Twentieth-Century Social Thought*. Oxford: Blackwell.

Sluglett, Peter (1993b), 'An account of a distorted vision', *The Times Literary Supplement*, 15 March.

Smith, Anthony (1986), *The Ethnic Origins of Nations*. Oxford: Blackwell.

Smith, Steve (1995), 'The self-image of a discipline: a genealogy of international relations theory', in Booth and Smith (eds), *International Relations Theory Today*. London: Polity Press.

Snyder, Glenn (1983), 'Deterrence and defence', in R. Art and K. Waltz (eds), *The Use of Force*. Lanham, MD: University Press of America.

Somjee, A. (1984), *Political Society in Developing Countries*. London: Macmillan Press.

Stake, Robert E. (1995), *The Art of Case Study Research*. London: Sage.

Stein, Janice G. (1991), 'Reassurance in international conflict management', *Political Science Quarterly*, Vol. 106, no. 3, fall: 431–52.

—— (1992), 'Deterrence and compellence in the Gulf, 1990–91: a failed or impossible task?', *International Security*, Vol. 71, No. 2, fall: 147–79.

Steiner, Miriam (1977), 'The elusive essence of decision', *International Studies Quarterly*, Vol. 21, June: 398–422.

—— (1983), 'The search for order in a disorderly world: world views and prescriptive decision paradigms', *International Organisation*, Vol. 37, summer: 373–413.

Stork, Joe (1989), 'Class, state and politics in Iraq', in Berch Berberoglu (ed.), *Power and Stability in the Middle East*. London: Zed Books.

Street, John (1994), 'Political culture – from civic culture to mass culture', *British Journal of Political Science*, Vol. 24: 95–114.

Telhami, Shibley (1993), 'Arab public opinion and the Gulf War', in S.A. Renshon (ed.), *The Political Psychology of the Gulf War: Leaders, Publics, and the Process of Conflict*. Pittsburgh, PA: University of Pittsburgh Press.

Telhami, Shibley (1994), 'Between theory and facts: explaining US behaviour in the Gulf crisis', in T. Y. Ismael and J. S. Ismael (eds), *The Gulf War and the New World Order: International Relations of the Middle East*. Miami, FL: University of Florida Press.

Terzian, Pierre, (1991), interviewed in the *Journal of Palestine Studies*, Vol. XX, No. 2, winter: 102–3.

Thompson, John P. (1980), *Ideology and Modern Culture*. Cambridge: Polity Press.

Tibi, Bassam (1987), 'Islam and Arab nationalism', in Barbara Stowasser (ed.), *The Islamic Impulse*. London: Croom Helm.

—— (1990a), *Arab Nationalism: A Critical Study*, ed. and trans. Marion Farouk-Sluglett and Peter Sluglett. New York: St. Martin Press.

—— (1990b), 'The simultaneity of the unsimultaneous: old tribes and imposed nation-states in the modern Middle East', in P. S. Khoury and J. Kostiner (eds), *Tribes and States Formation in the Middle East*. Berkeley, CA: University of California Press.

—— (1991), 'The Gulf crisis and the fragmentation of the Arab world: the policies of Egypt, Syria and Jordan', *Cairo Papers in Social Science*, Vol. 14, No. 1, spring. Cairo: The American University in Cairo Press.

Timmerman, Kenneth R. (1992), *The Death Lobby: How the West Armed Iraq*. London: Fourth Estate.

Topf, Richard (1989), 'Political change and political culture in Britain, 1959–87', in John R. Gibbins (ed.), *Contemporary Political Culture*. London: Sage.

Tschirgi, Dan (1991), 'The United States, the Arab world and the Gulf crisis', *Cairo Papers in Social Science*, Vol. 14, No. 1, spring. Cairo: The American University in Cairo Press.

Turner, Bryan S. (1974), *Weber and Islam: A Critical Study*. London: Routledge.

—— (1994), *Orientalism, Postmodernism and Globalism*. London: Routledge.

Tylor, Alan R. (1988), *The Islamic Question in the Middle Eastern Politics*. Boulder, CO: Westview Press.

—— (1993), 'Political currents in the Arab world before the Iraqi invasion of Kuwait', in Robert F. Helms and Robert H. Dorff (eds), *The Gulf Crisis: Power in The Post-Cold War World*. London: Praeger.

Unwin, P. T. H. (1993), 'Kuwait economy', in *The Middle East and North Africa 1993 Survey*. London: Europa Publications.

Van Evera, Stephen (1984), 'The cult of the offensive and the origin of the First World War', *International Security*, Vol. 9, summer: 58–107.

Vasquez, John (1983), *The Power of Power Politics: A Critique*. London: Frances Pinter.

—— (1992), *The War Puzzle*. Cambridge: Cambridge University Press.

Vertzberger, Yaccov (1986), 'Foreign policy decisionmakers as practical-intuitive historians: applied history and its shortcomings', *International Studies Quarterly*, Vol. 3, No. 2: 223–74.

—— (1989), *The World in Their Minds*. Stanford, CA: Stanford University Press.

Viorst, Milton (1991), 'Report from Baghdad', *The New Yorker*, 24 June: 55–73.

Walker, Stephen G. (1991), 'Role theory and managing foreign policy change: lessons from Iraq's Gulf initiative', unpublished paper.

Waltz, Kenneth (1959), *Man, The State and War: A Theoretical Analysis*. New York: Columbia University Press.

—— (1979), *Theory of International Politics*. New York: Random House.

—— (1986), 'Reflections on *Theory of International Politics*: a response to my critics', in R. O. Keohane (ed.), *Neorealism and its Critics*. New York: Columbia University Press.

Walzer, Michael (1976), 'On the role of symbolism in political thought', *Political Science Quarterly*, Vol. 82, June: 191–204.

Watt, W. Montgomery (1968), *Islamic Political Thought*. Edinburgh: The Basic Concepts.

—— (1974), *Muhammad: Prophet and Statesman*. New York: Oxford University Press.

Weber, Max (1930/1992), *The Protestant Ethic and the Spirit of Capitalism*, trans. Talcott Parsons, intr. Anthony Giddens. London: Routledge.

—— (1947/1964), *The Theory of Social and Economic Organization*, trans. A. M. Henderson and Talcott Parsons. New York: Free Press.

—— (1965), *The Sociology of Religion*, trans. Ephraim Fischoff, intr. Talcott Parsons. London: Methuen.

—— (1968), *Economy and Society: An Outline of Interpretive Sociology*, 3 vols, ed. Guenther Roth and Claus Wittich. New York: Bedminster Press.

Welch, Stephen (1993), *The Concept of Political Culture*. Basingstoke: Macmillan Press.

Wells, Donald A. (1967), *The War Myth*. New York: Pegasus.

Welsh, Jennifer M. (1993), 'The role of the inner enemy in European self-definition: identity, culture and international relations theory', *History of European Ideas*, Vol. 19, No. 1–3: 53–61.

Wendt, Alexander (1992), 'Anarchy is what states make of it: anarchy and the social construction of power politics', *International Organization*, Vol. 46, spring: 391–426.

Wight, Martin (1966), 'Why is there no international theory?', in H. Butterfield and M. Wight (eds), *Diplomatic Investigations: Essays in the Theory of International Politics*. London: Allen and Unwin.

—— (1977), *System of States*, ed. and intr. H. Bull. Leicester: Leicester University Press.

Williams, Michael C. (1992), 'Rethinking the "logic" of deterrence', *Alternatives*, Vol. 17: 67–93.

Williams, Howard (1992) *International Relations in Political Theory*. London: Open University Press.

Wittfogel, Karl (1963), *Oriental Despotism: A Comparative Study of Total Power*. New Haven, CT: Yale University Press.

Workman, W. Thom (1994), *The Social Origins of the Iran–Iraq War*. Boulder, CO: Lynne Reinner Publishers.

Wright, Quincy (1986), 'War: the study of war', in *International Encyclopaedia of the Social Sciences*. London: Macmillan.

Yassin, El-Sayed (1981a), *al-Shakhssiyyah al-Arabiyya Bayna Sourat al-Zat wa Mafhoum al-Waqi'a* (Arab Personality Between Self-Image and the Concept of the Other). Beirut: Al-Tanweer.

—— (1981b), *Tahlil Madmoun al-Fikr al-Qawmi al-Arabi* (Analysis of the Concept of Arab Nationalism). Beirut: Markaz Dirását al-wahda al-Arabiyya.

Zhang, Shu Guan (1992), *Deterrence and Strategic Culture: Chinese–American Confrontations, 1949–1958*. Ithaca, NY: Cornell University Press.

Zubaida, Sami (1982), 'Ideological condition for Khomeini's doctrine of government', *Economy and Society*, Vol. 11, No. 2: 138–72.

—— (1989), *Islam, the People and the State: Essays on Political Ideas and Movements*. London: Routledge.

—— (1991), 'Community, class and minorities in Iraqi politics', in Robert Fernea and Roger Louis (eds), *The Iraqi Revolution of 1958: The Old Social Classes Revisited*. London: I. B. Tauris.

Zur, Ofra (1991), 'The love of hating', *History of European Ideas*, Vol. 13, No. 4.

INDEX

Compiled by Sue Carlton